Constructing Measures:
An Item Response Modeling Approach

Constructing Measures:
An Item Response Modeling Approach

Mark Wilson
University of California, Berkeley

LAWRENCE ERLBAUM ASSOCIATES, PUBLISHERS
2005   Mahwah, New Jersey   London

Senior Editor:	Debra Riegert
Editorial Assistant:	Kerry Breen
Cover Design:	Sean Trane Sciarrone
Textbook Production Manager:	Paul Smolenski
Composition:	LEA Book Production
Text and Cover Printer:	Hamilton Printing Company

Lawrence Erlbaum Associates, Inc., Publishers
10 Industrial Avenue
Mahwah, New Jersey 07430
www.erlbaum.com

Library of Congress Cataloging-in-Publication Data

Wilson, Mark, 1954–
  Constructing measures : an item response modeling approach / Mark Wilson.
    p. cm.
Includes bibliographical references and index.
ISBN 0-8058-4785-5 (casebound : alk. paper)
1. Psychometrics. 2. Psychology—Research—Methodology. I. Title.
BF39.W56   2004
150'.28'7—dc22

                                                          200404971
                                                                CIP

Books published by Lawrence Erlbaum Associates are printed on acid-free paper, and their bindings are chosen for strength and durability.

Printed in the United States of America
10 9 8 7 6 5 4 3

To Penelope Jayne Wilson:

This book has been brewing all your life.

Contents

Part III: Quality Control Methods

Part IV: A beginning rather than a conclusion

Preface

It is often said that the best way to learn something is to do it. Because the purpose of this book is to introduce principles and practices of sound measurement, it is organized so that the reader can learn measurement by doing it. Although full participation in the construction of an instrument is not a requirement for readers of the book, that is the way to the best learning experience.

AIMS OF THE BOOK

After reading this book, preferably while applying what is learned to the construction of an instrument, the reader should be in a position to (a) appreciate the advantages and disadvantages of specific instruments, (b) responsibly use such instruments, and (c) apply the methods described in the book to develop new instruments and/or adapt old ones. It is important for the reader to appreciate that the point of learning about how to develop an instrument is not just so that the reader can then go on and develop others (although this is indeed partly the aim). The main reason is that this is the best way to learn about good measurement, whether as an instrument developer, a person who must choose from among instruments to use, a critic of instruments, or a consumer of the results of using instruments. At the point of finishing, the reader can by no means claim to be an experienced instrument developer—that can only come with more experience, including more iterations on the initial instrument. By understanding the process of measurement, the reader will indeed have learned the basics of measurement and will have had an opportunity to see how they integrate into a whole argument.

Although the book is written as a description of these steps and can be read independently without any co-construction of an instrument, it is best read concurrently with the actual construction of an instrument. Reading through the chapters should be instructive, but developing an instrument at the same time will make the concepts concrete and give the reader the opportunity to explore both the basics and complexities of the concepts of measurement.

This book is designed to be used as either (a) the core reference for a first course in measurement, or (b) the reference for the practical and conceptual aspect of a course that uses another reference for the other, more technical, aspects of the course. In approach (a), the course would normally be followed by a second course that would concentrate on the mathematical and technical expression of the ideas introduced here.[1] Thus, this book attempts to convey to readers the measurement ideas that are behind the technical realizations of measurement models, but does not attempt to explore those technical matters in any depth—a second course is needed for that. For example, although the final chapters do introduce the reader to the use of output from an item-response model, the Rasch model, and does give a motivation for using that particular formulation, the book does not attempt to place it within the larger panoply of measurement models that are available. Similar remarks could also be made about topics such as DIF and item and person fit. This seems a natural pedagogic order—find out what the scientific ideas are, then learn about the technical way to express them. It may be that some will prefer to teach both the concepts and technical expression at the same time—for such, the best option is to read a more traditional technical introduction in parallel with this book.

---

[1] A book based on this second course is currently in preparation—please look out for it.

AUDIENCE FOR THE BOOK

To be well prepared to read this book, the reader should have (a) an interest in understanding the conceptual basis for measurement through the discipline of developing a measure, (b) an interest in developing a specific instrument, and (c) a certain minimal background in quantitative methods, including knowledge of basic descriptive statistics, an understanding of what standard errors mean and how confidence intervals are used, a familiarity with correlation, *t* tests, and elementary regression topics, and a readiness to learn about how to use a computer program for quantitative analysis. This would include first- and/or second-year graduate students, but also would include undergraduates with sufficient maturity of interests.

ORGANIZATION

This book is organized to follow the steps of a particular approach to constructing an instrument. So that readers can see where they are headed, the account starts off in the first chapter with a summary of the constructive steps involved, which is expanded on in chapters 2 through 5. Each of these chapters develops one of the four building blocks that make up the instrument. Chapter 2 describes the construct map—that is the idea that the measurer has of what is being measured. The construct is the conceptual heart of this approach— along with its visual metaphor, the construct map. Chapter 3 describes the design plan for the items—the ways that prompts such as questions, tasks, statements, and problems are used to encourage responses that are informative of the construct. Chapter 4 describes the outcome space—the way these responses are categorized and then scored as indicators of the construct. Chapter 5 describes the measurement model—the statistical model that is used to organize the item scores into measures. This statistical model is used to associate numbers with the construct map—to calibrate the map.

This initial set of chapters constitutes the constructive part of measuring. The next three describe the quality control part of the process. Chapter 6 describes how to check that the scores are operating consistently in the way that the measurement model assumes they do. Chapter 7 describes how to check that the instrument has demonstrated sufficient consistency to be useful—termed the *reliability* evidence. Chapter 8 describes how to check whether the instrument does indeed measure what it is intended to measure—termed the *validity* evidence. Both of these latter two chapters capitalize on the calibrated construct map as a way to organize the arguments for the instrument. The final chapter, chapter 9, is quite different in its plan. It is designed as a beginning to the reader's future as a measurer, rather than a conclusion.

LEARNING TOOLS

Each chapter includes several features to help the reader follow the arguments. There is an overview of the chapter with a list of the key concepts—these are typically single words or phrases that are the main ones introduced and used in the chapter. After the main body of the chapter, there is Resources section that the reader can consult to investigate these topics further. There is also a set of Exercises and Activities for the reader at the end of most chapters. These serve a dual purpose: (a) giving the reader an opportunity to try out some of the strategies for themselves and extend some of the discussions beyond where they go in the text, and (b) encouraging the reader to carry out some of the steps needed to apply the content of the chapter to developing an instrument. Several chapters also include appendixes. These serve several different purposes. Some describe parts of the instrument development process in more detail than is provided in the text, some describe in detail numerical manipulations that are described in the text, and some record the details of results of computer analyses of data, parts of which are used in the text.

There are several other parts of the book that are designed to support the reader; these are available on the compact disk that accompanies the book. First, there is a Cases Archive. In the text, several examples are used in various places to provide concrete contexts for the concepts being discussed. To supplement these, the Cases Archive includes several examples of instrument development using the approach of this book; the examples are recorded in considerable detail as they work through the steps to completion. In particular, this is useful to illustrate the ways that the approach can vary under differing circumstances. Second, all the computations are carried out with a particular program—*GradeMap* (Wilson, Kennedy, & Draney,

2004)—which is included on the disk, along with the control files used to run the program, the output from the runs, and the data used in the analysis. This allows the reader to emulate all the computations carried out in the text, and explore other analyses that are suggested as exercises and ones that the reader devises for him or herself.

In teaching this course, I most often supplement this text with a series of readings that provide background and enliven particular parts of the subject matter. A list of such readings, and a guide as to where I have found them useful, is also provided in the appendix to chapter 9.

USING THE BOOK TO TEACH A COURSE

This book is the core reference for the first of a series of instruction courses taught by the author at the University of California, Berkeley, since 1986. It evolved into its current form over several years, finding a fairly stable structure about 1990. Thus, the book has a natural relationship to a course that is based on it. The chapters form a sequence that can be used as a core for a 14- to 15-week semester-length course where the students create their own instruments, or for an 8-week quarter-length course where the students create an instrument as a group exercise.

As mentioned earlier, the ideas of the book are best taught while the students are actually creating their own instruments (which is how it is taught by the author). This makes it more than just a "concepts and discussion" course—it becomes an entry point into one of the core areas of the professional world of measurement. At the same time, this does not make it into a mere "instrument development" course—the purpose of having the students take the practical steps to create an instrument is to help them integrate the many ideas and practices of measurement into a coherent whole. This process of conceptual integration is more important than the successful development of a specific instrument—indeed a flawed instrument development can be more efficacious in this way than a successful instrument development. (Students sometimes think that when their plans go awry, as they often do, I am just trying to make them feel good by saying this, but it really is true.)

The commitment needed to follow an instrument through the development process from chapters 2 to 8 is really quite considerable.

To do it individually, most students need to have a genuine and specific interest in the construction of a successful instrument to carry them through these steps in good spirit. This is not too hard to achieve with the many students in a master's or doctoral program who need to develop or adapt an instrument for their thesis or dissertation. If, however, students are too early in their program, where they have, say, not yet decided on a dissertation or thesis topic, then it can be somewhat artificial for them to engage in the sustained effort that is required. For such students, it is more practicable to treat the instrument design as a group project (or perhaps several group projects), where many of the practical steps are streamlined by the planning and organization of the instructor.

Students benefit greatly from the interactions and examples that they supply for one another. If the instructor follows the advice in the Exercises and Activities sections of the chapters, then each major stage of instrument development is shared with the whole class by each student. This is particularly important for the item panel (chap. 3) and the instrument calibration (chap. 5) steps.

The nature of the array of examples and the range of measurement procedures included reflect strongly the range of types of instruments that students typically bring to the course. For example, students bring polytomous instruments (such as surveys, attitude scales, etc.) more often than dichotomous ones (such as multiple-choice tests)—that is why, for example, there is little fuss made over the distinction between dichotomous and polytomous items, often a considerable stumbling block in measurement courses. Many students bring achievement or cognitive testing as their topics, but this is usually only a plurality rather than a majority—students also commonly bring attitude and behavioral topics to the class, as well as a variety of more exotic topics such as measures of organizations and even nonhuman subjects.

ACKNOWLEDGMENTS

The four building blocks used in this volume have been developed from joint work with Geoff Masters and Ray Adams (Masters, Adams, & Wilson, 1990; Masters & Wilson, 1997). This work was inspired by the foundational contributions of Benjamin Wright of the University of Chicago. There are also important parallels with the "evidentiary reasoning" approach to assessment described in Mislevy, Steinberg, and Almond (2003) and Mislevy, Wilson, Ercikan, and Chudowsky (2003). I would like to acknowledge the intellectual contributions made by these authors to my thinking and hence to this work.

The students of EDUC 274A (initially 207A) at the University of California, Berkeley, have, through their hard work and valuable insights, been instrumental in making this work possible. In particular, I would like to thank the members of my research group "Models of Assessment," many no longer students, who provided close and critical readings of the text: Derek Briggs, Nathaniel Brown, Brent Duckor, John Gargani, Laura Goe, Cathleen Kennedy, Jeff Kunz, Lydia Liu, Qiang Liu, Insu Paek, Deborah Peres, Mariella Ruiz, Juan Sanchez, Kathleen Scalise, Cheryl Schwab, Laik Teh, Mike Timms, Marie Wiberg, and Yiyu Xie.

Many colleagues have contributed their thoughts and experiences to this volume. I cannot list them all, but must acknowledge the important contributions of the following: Ray Adams, Alicia Alonzo, Paul De Boeck, Karen Draney, George Engelhard, Jr., William Fisher, Tom Gumpel, P. J. Hallam, June Hartley, Machteld Hoskens, Florian Kaiser, Geoff Masters, Bob Mislevy, Stephen Moore, Pamela Moss, Ed Wolfe, Benjamin Wright, and Margaret Wu.

The team that worked on *GradeMap* also made important contributions: Cathleen Kennedy, Karen Draney, Sevan Tutunciyan, and Richard Vorp.

I would also like to acknowledge the assistance provided by several institutions during the writing of this book: primarily the Graduate School of Education at the University of California, Berkeley, which allowed the intellectual freedom to pursue a different way of teaching this subject, but also the K. U. Leuven in Belgium, the University of Newcastle in NSW, Australia, and the Australian Council for Educational Research, all of which supported the writing of sections of the manuscript while I was visiting.

I would also like to thank the manuscript reviewers who provided valuable comments: George Engelhard, Jr., from Emory University, and Steve Reise, from UCLA.

—*Mark Wilson*
Berkeley, California, USA

Part I

A Constructive Approach to Measurement

Chapter 1

Construct Modeling: The "Four Building Blocks" Approach

1.0 CHAPTER OVERVIEW AND KEY CONCEPTS

construct modeling
the "four building blocks"
construct map
items design
outcome space
measurement model

This chapter begins with a description of what is meant by *measurement* in this book. The remainder of the chapter then outlines a framework, which I call *construct modeling*, for understanding how an instrument works by understanding how it is constructed. Construct modeling is a framework for developing an instrument by using each of four "building blocks" in turn. This chapter summarizes all four building blocks, and the following chapters describe each in detail. In this volume, the word *instrument* is defined as a technique of relating something we observe in the real world (sometimes called *manifest* or *observed*) to something we are measuring that only exists as part of a theory (sometimes called *latent* or *unobserved*). This is somewhat broader than the typical usage, which focuses on the most concrete manifestation of the instrument—the items or questions. Because part of the purpose of the book is to expose the less obvious aspects of measurement, this broader definition has been chosen. Examples of types and formats of instruments that can be seen as coming under the "construct mapping" framework are shown in this and the next few chapters. Generally, it is assumed that there is a *respondent* who is the object of measurement, and there is a *measurer* who seeks to measure something about the respondent. While reading the text, the reader should mainly see him or herself as the measurer, but it is always useful to assume the role of the respondent as well. The next four chapters explain each of the four building blocks in turn, giving much greater detail, many examples, and discussion of how to apply the ideas to instrument development.

1.1 WHAT IS MEASUREMENT?

In some accounts, *measurement* is defined as the assignment of numbers to categories of observations. The properties of the numbers become the properties of the measurement—nominal, ordinal, interval, ratio, and so on. (Stevens, 1946).[1] Assigning numbers to categories is indeed one feature of the account in this book; correspondingly, those numbers have certain properties. Yet that is only one aspect of the process of measurement—there are steps preceding the assignment of numbers that prepare the ground for measuring, and there are also steps after the assignment of numbers that (a) check that the assignment was successful, and (b) make use of the measurements.

---

[1] In Stevens' (1946) classic account, measures are classified into successively more number-like categories as follows: (a) when the objects of measurement can be placed into (unordered) categories, the measurement is *nominal*; (b) when the objects can be placed into ordered categories, the measurement is *ordinal*; (c) when the objects of measurement can be labeled with numbers that can be added and subtracted, the measurement is *interval*; and (d) when the objects of measurement can be labeled with numbers that can be used as divisors, the measurement is *ratio*.

The central purpose of measurement, as interpreted here, is to provide a reasonable and consistent way to summarize the responses that people make to express their achievements, attitudes, or personal points of view through instruments such as attitude scales, achievement tests, questionnaires, surveys, and psychological scales. That purpose invariably arises in a practical setting where the results are used to make some sort of decision. These instruments typically have a complex structure, with a string of questions or tasks related to the aims of the instrument. This particular structure is one reason that there is a need to establish measurement procedures. A simpler structure—say just a single question—would allow simpler procedures. However, there are good reasons that these instruments have this more complex structure, and those reasons are discussed in the following chapters.

The approach adopted here is predicated on the idea that there is a single underlying characteristic that an instrument is designed to measure. Many surveys, tests, and questionnaires are designed to measure multiple characteristics—here it is assumed that we can consider those characteristics one at a time so that the real survey or test is seen as being composed of several instruments, each measuring a single characteristic (although the instruments may overlap in terms of the items). This intention, which is later termed the *construct*, is established by the person who designs and develops the instrument. This person is called the *measurer* throughout this book. The instrument, then, is seen as a logical *argument* that the results can be interpreted to help make a decision as the measurer intended them to be. The chapters that follow describe a series of steps that can be used as the basis for such an argument. First, the argument is constructive—that is, it proceeds by constructing the instrument following a certain logic (this occupies the contents of chaps. 2–5). Then the argument is reflective, proceeding by gathering information on whether the instrument did indeed function as planned (this occupies the contents of chaps. 6–8). The book concludes with a discussion of next steps that a measurer might take. This lays the groundwork for later books.

In this book, the concept being explored is more like a verb, *measuring*, than a noun, *measurement*. There is no claim that the procedures explored here are the only way to measure—there are other approaches that one can adopt (several are discussed in chaps. 6 and 9). The aim is not to survey all such ways to measure, but to lay out one particular approach that the author has found successful over the last two decades in teaching measurement to students at the University of California, Berkeley, and consulting with people who want to develop instruments in a wide variety of areas.

1.2 THE CONSTRUCT MAP

An instrument is always something secondary: There is always a purpose for which an instrument is needed and a context in which it is going to be used (i.e., involving some sort of decision). This precipitates an idea or a concept that is the theoretical object of our interest in the respondent. Consistent with current usage, I call this the *construct* (see Messick, 1989, for an exhaustive analysis). A construct could be part of a theoretical model of a person's cognition—such as their understanding of a certain set of concepts or their attitude toward something—or it could be some other psychological variable such as "need for achievement" or a personality variable such as a bipolar diagnosis. It could be from the domain of educational achievement, or it could be a health-related construct such as "Quality of Life" or a sociological construct such as "rurality" or migrants' degree of assimilation. It could relate to a group rather than an individual person, such as a work group or sports team, or an institution such as a workplace, or it could be biological phenomena such as a forest's ability to spread in a new environment. It could even be a complex inanimate object such as a volcano's proclivity to erupt or the weathering of paint samples. There is a multitude of theories—the important thing here is to have one that provides motivation and structure for the construct to be measured.

The idea of a *construct map* is a more precise concept than *construct*. We assume that the construct we wish to measure has a particularly simple form—it extends from one extreme to another, from high to low, small to large, positive to negative, or strong to weak. There may be some complexity in what happens in between these extremes, but we are primarily interested in where a respondent stands on this range from one extreme to the other. In particular, there may be distinguishable qualitative levels between the extremes—these are important and useful in interpretation. At this point, it is still an idea, latent rather than manifest. Although qualitative levels are definable, we assume that the respondents can be at any point in between—that is, the underlying construct is continuous. In summary, a construct map can be said to be a unidimensional latent variable. Many constructs are more complex than this. For example, they may be multidimensional. This is not a barrier to the use of the methods described in this book—the most straightforward thing to do is tackle each dimension one at a time—that way they can each be seen as a construct map. There are also constructs that are quite different from those that can be well described by a construct map. For example, suppose the construct consists of two different groups, say those who are likely to immigrate and those who are not. This construct is not much like that of a construct map and, hence, is not likely to be well represented by one.

In this chapter, the four building blocks are illustrated with a recent example from educational assessment—an assessment system built for a high school chemistry curriculum, "Living by Chemistry: Inquiry-Based Modules for High School" (Claesgens, Scalise, Draney, Wilson, & Stacey, 2002). The Living by Chemistry (LBC) project at the Lawrence Hall of Science was awarded a grant from the National Science Foundation in 1999 to create a year-long course based on real-world contexts that would be familiar and interesting to students. The goal is to make chemistry accessible to a larger and more diverse pool of students while improving preparation of students who traditionally take chemistry as a prerequisite for scientific study. The focus is on the domain knowledge they have acquired during instructional interactions in terms of how the students are able to think and reason with chemistry concepts.

The set of constructs on which both the LBC curriculum and its assessment system (an application of the *BEAR Assessment System*; Wilson & Sloane, 2000) are built is called "Perspectives of Chemists." Three variables or strands have been designed to describe chemistry views regarding three "big ideas" in the discipline: matter, change, and stability. *Matter* is concerned with describing atomic and molecular views of matter. *Change* involves kinetic views of change and the conservation of matter during chemical change. *Stability* considers the network of relationships in conservation of energy. The matter progress variable is shown in Fig. 1.1. It describes how a student's view of matter progresses from a continuous, real-world view to a particulate view accounting for existence of atoms and molecule, and then builds in sophistication. This progression is conceptualized as being reflected in two substrands within matter: visualizing and measuring.

Levels of success	ATOMIC AND MOLECULAR VIEWS	MEASUREMENT AND MODEL REFINEMENT
5 Integrating	bonding and relative reactivity	models and evidence
4 Predicting	phase and composition	limitations of models
3 Relating	properties and atomic views	measured amounts of matter
2 Representing	matter with chemical symbols	mass with a particulate view
1 Describing	properties of matter	amounts of matter
	A Visualizing matter	B Measuring matter

Fig. 1.1   A construct map for the Matter strand from LBC.

Assessments carried out in pilot studies of this variable show that a student's atomic views of matter begin with having no atomic view at all, but simply the ability to describe some characteristics of matter, such as differentiating between a gas and solid on the basis of real-world knowledge of boiling solutions such as might be encountered in food preparation, for instance, or bringing logic and patterning skills to bear on a question of why a salt dissolves. This then became the lowest level of the matter variable. At this most novice level of sophistication, students employ no accurate molecular models of chemistry, but a progression in sophistication can be seen from those unable or unwilling to make any relevant observation at all during an assessment task on matter, to those who can make an observation and then follow it with logical reasoning, to those who can extend this reasoning in an attempt to employ actual chemistry knowledge, although they are typically done incorrectly at first attempts. All these behaviors fall into Level 1, called the "Describing" level, and are assigned incremental 1– and 1+ scores, which for simplicity of presentation are not shown in this version of the framework.

When students begin to make the transition to accurately using simple molecular chemistry concepts, Level 2 begins, which is called the "Representing" level. At Level 2 of the matter progress variable, we see students using one-dimensional models of chemistry: A simple representation or a single definition is used broadly to account for and interpret chemical phenomena. Students show little ability to combine ideas. Here students begin extending experience and logical reasoning to include accurate chemistry-specific domain knowledge. In the conceptual framework, this is when students begin to employ definitions, terms, and principles with which they later reason and negotiate meaning. At this level, students are concerned with learning the language and representations of the domain of chemistry and are introduced to the ontological categories and epistemological beliefs that fall within the domain of chemistry. Students may focus on a single aspect of correct information in their explanations, but may not have developed more complete explanatory models to relate to the terms and language.

When students can begin to combine and relate patterns to account for (e.g., the contribution of valence electrons and molecular geometry to dissolving), they are considered to have moved to Level 3, "Relating." Coordinating and relating developing knowledge in chemistry becomes critical to move to this level. Niaz and Lawson (1985) argued that without generalizable models of understanding, students choose to memorize rules instead, limiting their understanding to the Representing level of the perspectives. Students need a base of domain knowledge before integration and coordination of the knowledge develops into understanding (Metz, 1995). As they move toward the Relating level, students should be developing a foundation of domain knowledge so that they can begin to reason like chemists by relating terms to conceptual models of understanding in chemistry, rather than simply memorizing algorithms and terms. Students need to examine and connect ideas to derive meaning in order to move to the Relating level.

The LBC matter strand is an example of a relatively complete construct map, although as yet untested at the upper end: These cover college and graduate levels—those interested in the upper levels should contact the LBC project at Lawrence Hall of Science. When a construct map is first postulated, it is often much less well formed than this. The construct map is refined through several processes as the instrument is developed. These processes include: (a) explaining the construct to others with the help of the construct map, (b) creating items that you believe will lead respondents to give responses that inform levels of the construct map, (c) trying out those items with a sample of respondents, and (d) analyzing the resulting data to check whether the results are consistent with your intentions as expressed through the construct map.

1.3 THE ITEMS DESIGN

Next the measurer must think of some way that this theoretical construct could be manifested in a real-world situation. At first this will be not much more than a hunch, a context that one believes the construct must be involved in—indeed that the construct must play some determining role in that situation. Later this hunch will become more crystallized and will settle into a certain pattern. The relationship between the items and the construct is not necessarily one way as it has just been described. Often the items will be thought of first and the construct will be elucidated only later—this is simply an example of how complex a creative act such as instrument construction can be. The important thing is that the construct and items should be distinguished, and that *eventually* the items are seen as realizations of the construct.

For example, the LBC items often began as everyday events that have a special significance to a chemist. Typically, there will be more than one real-world manifestation used in the instrument; these parts of the instrument are generically called *items*, and the format in which they are presented to the respondent is called the *items design*. An item can also take on many forms. The most common ones are probably the multiple-choice item from achievement testing and the Likert-type item (e.g., with responses ranging from *strongly agree* to *strongly disagree*) from surveys and attitude scales. Both are examples of the forced-choice type of item, where the respondent is given only a limited range of possible responses. There are many variants on this, ranging from questions on questionnaires to consumer rankings of products. The respondent may also produce a free response within a certain mode, such as an essay, interview, or performance (such as a competitive dive, piano recital, or scientific experiment). In all of these examples so far, the respondent is aware that they are being observed, but there are also situations where the respondent is being observed without such awareness. The items may be varied in their content and mode: Interview questions typically range over many aspects of a topic; questions in a cognitive performance task may be presented depending on the responses to earlier items; items in a survey may use different sets of options; and some may be forced-choice and some free-response.

In the case of LBC, the items are embedded in the instructional curriculum, so much so that the students would not necessarily know that they were being assessed unless the teacher tells them. An example LBC item is shown in Fig. 1.2. This task was designed to prompt student responses that relate to the lower portions of the matter construct described in Fig. 1.1. (An example of student response to this task is shown later in Fig. 1.6.)

The initial situation between the first two building blocks can be depicted as in Fig. 1.3. Here the construct and items are both only vaguely known, and there is some intuitive relationship between

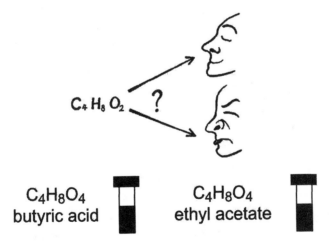

Both of the solutions have the same molecular formulas, but butyric acid smells bad and putrid while ethyl acetate smells good and sweet. Explain why these two solutions smell differently.

FIG. 1.2   An example LBC item.

FIG. 1.3   A picture of an initial idea of the relationship between construct and item responses.

them (as indicated by the dotted line). Causality is often unclear at this point, perhaps the construct "causes" the responses that are made to the items, perhaps the items existed first in the developer's plans and hence could be said to "cause" the construct to be developed. It is important to see this as an important and natural step in instrument development—a step that always occurs at the beginning of instrument development and can need to recur many times as the instrument is tested and revised.

Unfortunately, in some instrument development efforts, the conceptual approach does not go beyond the state depicted in Fig. 1.3, even when there are sophisticated statistical methods used in the data analysis. This unfortunate abbreviation of the instrument development typically results in several shortcomings: (a) arbitrariness in choice of items and item formats, (b) no clear way to relate empirical results to instrument improvement, and (c) an inability to use empirical findings to improve the idea of the construct. To avoid these problems, the measurer needs to build a structure that links the construct closely to the items—that brings the inferences as close as possible to the observations.

One way to do that is to see causality as going from the construct to the items—the measurer assumes that the respondent "has" some amount of the construct, and that amount of the construct is a *cause* of the responses to the items in the instrument that the measurer observes. That is the situation shown in Fig. 1.4—the causal arrow points from left to right. However, this causal agent is latent—the measurer cannot observe the construct directly. Instead the measurer observes the responses to the items and must then *infer* the underlying construct from those observations. That is, in Fig. 1.4, the direction of the *inference* made by the measurer is from right to left. The remaining two building blocks embody two different steps in

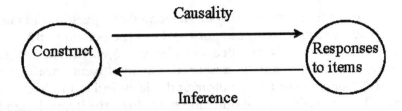

FIG. 1.4   A picture of the construct modeling idea of the relationship between degree of construct possessed and item responses.

that inference. Note that the idea of causality here is an assumption; the analysis does not prove that causality is in the direction shown, it merely assumes it goes that way. In fact the actual mechanism, like the construct, is unobserved or latent. It may be a more complex relationship than the simple one shown in Fig. 1.4. Until research reveals the nature of that complex relationship, the measurer is forced to act as if the relationship is the simple one depicted.

1.4 THE OUTCOME SPACE

The first step in the inference is to make a decision about which aspects of the response to the item will be used as the basis for the inference, and how those aspects of the response are categorized and then scored. This I call the *outcome space*. Examples of outcome spaces include: The categorization of question responses into "true" and "false" on a survey (with subsequent scoring as, say, "1" and "0"); the question and prompt protocols in a standardized open-ended interview (Patton 1980) and the subsequent categorization of the responses; and the translation of an educational performance into ordered levels using a so-called *rubric*, more plainly called a *scoring guide*. Sometimes the categories are the final product of the outcome space, sometimes the categories are scored so that the scores can (a) serve as convenient labels for the outcomes categories, and (b) be manipulated in various ways. To emphasize this distinction, the outcome space may be called a *scored* outcome space. The resulting scores play an important role in the construct mapping approach. They are the embodiment of the direction of the construct map (e.g., positive scores go upwards in the construct map).

The outcome space is usually implemented by a person who rates the responses into certain categories—I call the person in this role the *rater* (sometimes also called a *reader* or *judge*). The rater might also be a piece of software as is needed in an intelligent tutoring system (ITS), or it can be a fully automated rule, as in a multiple-choice item. The distinction of the outcome space from the items design is not always obvious mainly due to the special status of the two most common item formats—the multiple-choice item and the Likert-style item. In both of these item formats, the item design and outcome space have been collapsed—there is no need to categorize the responses because that is done by the respondents. In most cases, the scores to be applied to these categories are also fixed beforehand. However, these common formats should really be seen as "special cases"—the more generic situation is that of free-responses—this becomes clear when one sees that the development of these fixed-choice item formats (properly) includes an iteration that is in the free-response format (this point is returned to in Section 3.3).

The outcome space for the LBC matter constructs is summarized in Fig. 1.5—it is divided into ordered categories because the LBC curriculum developers see the underlying latent construct as a dimension—that is, as they see the students as progressing from little of it at the beginning of the year, and (if the curriculum developers and teachers have been successful) to having more at the end. This scoring guide allows a teacher to score student responses to the questions related to the matter constructs into the six different levels. Level 1, "Describing," has been further differentiated into three ordered sublevels—similar differentiation is planned for the other levels where it is found to be appropriate. Note how the scores (even the + and –) relate the categories to the desired direction of student progress. As well as the scoring guide in Fig. 1.5, teachers have available to them examples of student work (called *exemplars* in LBC), complete with adjudicated scores and explanations of the scores. An example is shown in Fig. 1.6. A training method called *moderation* is also used to help teachers be accurate raters and interpret the results in the classroom (see Wilson & Sloane, 2000, for a discussion of this). Really, it is the sum of all these elements that is the true outcome space, Fig. 1.5 is just a summary of one part of it. What we get out of the outcome space is a score, and for a set of tasks it gives a set of scores.

X. No opportunity.

There was no opportunity to respond to the item.

0. Irrelevant or blank response.

Response contains no information relevant to item.

1. *Describe the properties of matter*

The student relies on macroscopic observation and logic skills rather than employing an atomic model. Students use common sense and experience to express their initial ideas without employing correct chemistry concepts.

    1 –   Makes one or more macroscopic observation and/or lists chemical terms without meaning.

    1   Uses macroscopic observations/descriptions and restatement AND comparative/logic skills to generate classification, BUT shows no indication of employing chemistry concepts.

    1+   Makes accurate simple macroscopic observations (often employing chemical jargon) and presents supporting examples and/or perceived rules of chemistry to logically explain observations, BUT chemical principles/definitions/rules cited incorrectly.

2. *Represent changes in matter with chemical symbols*

The students are "learning" the definitions of chemistry to begin to describe, label, and represent matter in terms of its chemical composition. The students are beginning to use the correct chemical symbols (i.e. chemical formulas, atomic model) and terminology (i.e. dissolving, chemical change vs. physical change, solid liquid gas).

    2-   Cites definitions/rules/principles pertaining to matter somewhat correctly.

    2   Correctly cites definitions/rules/principles pertaining to chemical composition.

    2+   Cites and appropriately uses definitions/rules/principles pertaining to the chemical composition of matter and its transformations.

3. *Relate*

Students are relating one concept to another and developing behavioral models of explanation.

4. *Predicts how the properties of matter can be changed.*

Students apply behavioral models of chemistry to predict transformation of matter.

5. *Explains the interactions between atoms and molecules*

Integrates models of chemistry to understand empirical observations of matter/energy.

FIG. 1.5   The LBC outcome space, represented as a scoring guide.

1.5 THE MEASUREMENT MODEL

The second step in the inference is to relate the scores to the construct. This is done through the fourth building block, which is traditionally termed a *measurement model*—sometimes it is also called a *psychometric model*, sometimes a *statistical model*, although the

A response at the Representing Level:

"They smell differently b/c even though they have the same molecular formula, they have different structural formulas with different arrangements and patterns."

Analysis: Appropriately cites principle that molecules with the same formula can have different arrangements of atoms. But the answer stops short of examining structure-property relationships (a relational, level 3 characteristic).

FIG. 1.6   Student respose to the item in Fig. 1.2.

conceptualization used in this chapter does not require that a statistical model be used, hence it might also be termed an *interpretational model* (National Research Council, 2001). The measurement model must help us understand and evaluate the scores that come from the item responses and hence tell us about the construct, and it must also guide the use of the results in practical applications. Simply put, the measurement model must translate scored responses to locations on the construct map. Some examples of measurement models are the "true-score" model of classical test theory, the "domain score" model, factor analysis models, item response models, and latent class models. These are all formal models. Many users of instruments (and also many instrument developers) also use informal measurement models when they think about their instruments.

The interpretation of the results is aided by graphical summaries that are generated by a computer program (*GradeMap*; Wilson, Kennedy, & Draney, 2004). For example, a student's profile across the four constructs is shown in Fig. 1.7—this has been found useful by teachers for student and parent conferences. Other displays are also available: time charts, whole-class displays, subgroup displays, and individual "fit" displays (which are displayed and described in later chapters).

Note that the direction of inference in Fig. 1.8—going from the items to the construct—should be clearly distinguished from the direction of causality, which is assumed to go in the opposite direction. In this figure, the arrow of causality does not go through the outcome space or measurement model because (presumably) the construct would have caused the responses regardless of whether the measurer had constructed a scoring guide and measurement model.

This sometimes puzzles people, but indeed it amply displays the distinction between the *latent* causal link and the *manifest* inferential link. The initial, vague link (as in Fig. 1.3) has been replaced in Fig. 1.8 by a causal link and several inferential links.

GradeMap				
Name: Mary Rodgers				
	Visualizing Matter	Measuring Matter	Characterizing Change	Quantifying Change
2+				
2		*		
2-	*			
1+			*	
1				
1-				*
0				
To improve your performance you can:	Review periodic table trends, octet rule and phase changes. Be careful to answer questions completely and do not leave out key details.	You will often need to consider two or more aspects of the atomic model when you solve problems. Don't rely on just 1 idea.	Review phase changes and the kinetic view of gases. You need to know more about motions of atoms and molecules.	Keeping track of mass as it reacts or changes form is challenging. Consider the info you are given and be willing to take a best guess.

FIG. 1.7   A student's profile on the LBC constructs.

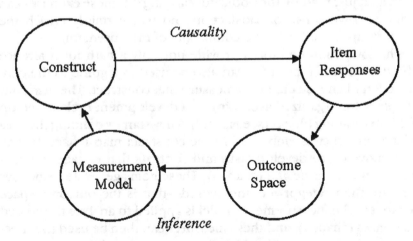

FIG. 1.8   The "four building blocks" showing the directions of causality and inference.

1.6 USING THE FOUR BUILDING BLOCKS TO DEVELOP AN INSTRUMENT

The account so far, apart from the LBC example, has been at quite an abstract level. The reader should not be alarmed by this because the next four chapters are devoted, in turn, to each of the four building blocks and provide many examples of each across a broad range of contexts and subject matters. One purpose of this introductory chapter has been to orient the reader to what is to come.

Another purpose of this chapter is to start the reader thinking and learning about the practical process of instrument development. If the reader wants to learn to develop instruments, it is obvious that he or she should be happy to read through this section and carry out the exercises and class projects that are described in the chapters that follow. However, even if practical experience about how to develop instruments is not the aim of the reader, then this section, and later sections like it, should still be studied carefully and the exercises carried out fully. The reason for this is that learning about measurement without actually developing an instrument leaves the reader in an incomplete state of knowledge—it is a bit like learning how to ride a bike, cook a soufflé, or juggle by reading about it in a book without actually trying it. A great deal of the knowledge is only appreciated when you experience how it all works together. It can be difficult to actually carry out the exercises, and certainly it takes more time than just reading the book, but carrying out these exercises can bring its own sense of satisfaction and will certainly enrich the reader's appreciation of the complexity of measurement.

The four building blocks provide not only a path for inference about a construct, but they can also be used as a guide to the construction of an instrument to measure that construct. The next four chapters are organized according to a development cycle based on the four building blocks (see Fig. 1.9). They start by defining the idea of the construct as embodied in the construct map (chap. 2), and then move on to develop tasks and contexts that engage the construct—the items design (chap. 3). These items generate responses that are then categorized and scored—that is the outcome space (chap. 4). The measurement model is applied to analyze the scored responses (chap. 5), and these measures can then be used to reflect back on the success with which one has measured the construct— which brings one back to the construct map (chap. 2), so this se-

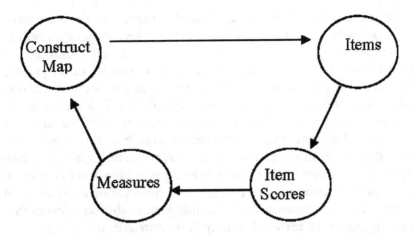

FIG. 1.9   The instrument development cycle through the four building blocks.

quence through the building blocks is actually a cycle—a cycle that may be repeated several times. The following three chapters (6, 7, and 8) help with this appraisal process by gathering evidence about how the instrument works: on model fit, reliability evidence, and validity evidence, respectively.

Every new instrument (or even the redevelopment or adaptation of an old instrument) must start with an idea—the kernel of the instrument, the "what" of the "what does it measure?", and the "how" of "how will the measure be used?" When this is first being considered, it makes a great deal of sense to look broadly to establish a dense background of knowledge about the content and uses of the instrument. As with any new development, one important step is to investigate (a) the theories behind the construct, and (b) what has been done in the past to measure this content—in particular, the characteristics of the instrumentation that was used. Thus, a *literature review* is necessary and should be completed before going too far with other steps (say, before commencing the activities discussed in chap. 3). However, a literature review is necessarily limited to the insights of those who previously worked in this area, so other steps also have to be taken.

At the beginning, the measurer needs to develop a small set of informants to help with instrument design. They should be chosen to span as well as go slightly outside the usual range of respondents.

Those outside the usual range would include (a) professionals, teachers/academics, and researchers in the relevant areas; as well as (b) people knowledgeable about measurement in general and/or measurement in the specific area of interest; and (c) other people who are knowledgeable and reflective about the area of interest and/or measurement in that area, such as policymakers, and so on. At this point, this group (which may change somewhat in nature over the course of the instrument development) can help the measurer by discussing experiences in the relevant area, criticizing and expanding on the measurer's initial ideas, serving as guinea pigs in responding to older instruments in the area, and responding to initial item formats. The information from the informants should overlap that from the literature review, but may also contradict it in parts.

1.7 RESOURCES

For an influential perspective on the idea of a construct, see the seminal article by Messick (1989) referenced earlier. A contemporary view that builds on that perspective, and one that is similar in a number of ways to the current account, is given in Mislevy, Wilson, Ercikan, and Chudowsky (2003), and a similar one is found in Mislevy, Steinberg, and Almond (2003).

The link between the construct map and measurement model was made explicit in two books by Wright (Wright & Stone, 1979; Wright & Masters, 1981), which are also seminal for the approach taken in this book.

The BEAR Assessment System (Wilson & Sloane, 2000), which is based on the four building blocks, has been used in other contexts besides the LBC example given earlier (Claesgens, Scalise, Draney, Wilson, & Stacey, 2002). Some are: (a) SEPUP's IEY curriculum (see Wilson & Sloane, 2000), and (b) the Golden State Exams (see Wilson & Draney, 2000).

A closely related approach is termed *Developmental Assessment* by Geoffery Masters and his colleagues at the Australian Council for Educational Research—examples are given in Department of Employment, Education and Youth Affairs (1997) and Masters and Forster (1996). This is also the basis of the approach taken by the Organization for Economic Co-operation and Development's (1999) PISA project.

Many examples of construct maps across both achievement and attitude domains are given in the series of edited books called "Objective Measurement: Theory into Practice" (see Engelhard & Wilson, 1996; Wilson, 1992a, 1992b, 1994a, 1994b; Wilson & Engelhard, 2000; Wilson, Engelhard, & Draney, 1997). Further examples can be found among the reference lists in those volumes.

1.8 EXERCISES AND ACTIVITIES

1. Explain what your instrument will be used for and why existing instruments will not suffice.
2. Read about the theoretical background to your construct. Write a summary of the relevant theory (keep it brief—no more than five pages).
3. Research previous efforts to develop and use instruments with a similar purpose and ones with related, but different, purposes. In many areas, there are compendia of such efforts—for example, in the areas of psychological and educational testing, there are series like the Mental Measurements Yearbook (Plake, Impara, & Spies, 2003)—similar publications exist in many other areas. Write a summary of the alternatives that are found, summarizing the main points perhaps in a table (keep it brief—no more than five pages).
4. Brainstorm possible informants for your instrument construction. Contact several and discuss your plans with them—secure the agreement of some of them to help you out as you make progress.
5. Try to think through the steps outlined earlier in the context of developing your instrument, and write down notes about your plans, including a draft timetable. Try to predict problems that you might encounter as you carry out these steps.
6. Share your plans and progress with others—discuss what you and they are succeeding on and what problems have arisen.

Part II

The Four Building Blocks

Chapter 2

Construct Maps

2.0 CHAPTER OVERVIEW AND KEY CONCEPTS

construct
construct maps

This chapter concentrates on the concept of the *construct map* introduced in the previous chapter. The aim is to introduce the reader to this particular approach to conceptualizing a construct—an approach found to be useful as a basis for measuring. There is no claim being made here that this approach will satisfy every possible measurement need (this point is expanded on at the end of the chapter). However, both for didactic purposes and because it will prove a useful tool in many applications, this chapter concentrates on just this one type of construct, as does the rest of the book. It consists of a series of construct maps, illustrating the main different types: respondent maps, item-response maps, and construct maps. All of the examples are derived from published applications. The reader can also find examples of construct maps within each of the cases in the cases archive in the compact disk included with this book. These contain both instances where the measurer has shared both the initial ideas and images of the construct map, as well as construct maps that have been through several iterations.

2.1 THE CONSTRUCT MAP

The type of construct described in this chapter is one that is particularly suitable for a visual representation—it is called a *construct map*. Its most important features are that there is (a) a coherent and substantive definition for the content of the construct; and (b) an idea that the construct is composed of an underlying continuum— this can be manifested in two ways—an ordering of the respondents and/or an ordering of item responses. The two different aspects of the construct—the respondents and their responses—lead to two different sorts of construct maps: (a) a respondent construct map, where the respondents are ordered from greater to less, and qualitatively may be grouped into an ordered series of levels; and (b) an item-response construct map, where the item responses are ordered from greater to less, and qualitatively may also be grouped into an ordered series of levels.

A generic construct map is shown in Fig. 2.1. The variable being measured is called "X." The depiction shown here is used throughout this book, so a few lines are used to describe its parts before moving on to examine some examples. The arrow running up and down the middle of the map indicates the continuum of the construct, running from "low" to "high." The left-hand side indicates qualitatively distinct groups of respondents, ranging from those with high "X" to those with low "X." A respondent construct map would include only the left side. The right-hand side indicates qualitative differences in item responses, ranging from responses that indicate high "X" to those that indicate low "X." An item-response construct map would include only the right side. A full construct map has both sides represented.

Note that this depicts an idea rather than being a technical representation. Indeed, later this idea is related to a specific technical representation, but for now just concentrate on the idea. Certain features of the construct map are worth highlighting.

1. There is no limit on the number of locations on the continuum that could be filled by a student (or item-response label). Of course one might expect that there will be limitations of accu-

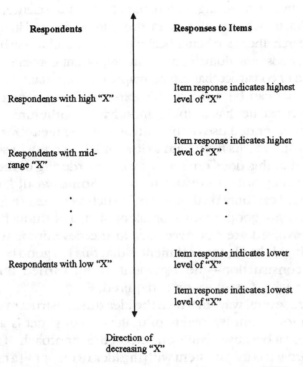

FIG. 2.1   A generic construct map in construct "X."

racy, caused by limitations of data, but that is another matter (see chaps. 5 and 6).

2. The item labels are actually summaries of responses. Although one might tend to reify the items as phenomena in their own right, it is important to keep in mind that the locations of the labels are not the locations of items per se, but are really the locations of certain types of responses to the items. The items' locations are represented via the respondents' reactions to them.

Of course words like *construct* and *map* have many other usages in other contexts, but in this book they are reserved for just this purpose. Examples of constructs that can be mapped abound: In attitude surveys, for example, there is always something that the respondent is agreeing to or liking or some other action denoting an ordering; in educational testing, there is inevitably an underlying idea of increasing correctness, of sophistication or excellence; in marketing, there are some products that are more attractive or satisfying than others; in political science, there are some candidates who are more attractive than others; and in health outcomes research, there are better health outcomes and worse health outcomes. In almost any domain, there are important contexts where the special type of construct that can be mapped is important.

A construct can be most readily expressed as a construct map, where the construct has a single underlying continuum—implying that, for the intended use of the instrument, the measurer wants to array the respondents from high to low, or left to right, in some context. Note that this does not imply that this ordering of the respondents is their only relevant feature. Some would see that measurement can only be thought of in such a context (e.g., Wright, 1977). There are good reasons for taking such a position, but the arguments involved are not necessary to the development in these chapters. In this book, the argument is that this is a good basis for instrument construction—the argument is not carried through to show that such an assumption is required.

There are several ways in which the idea of a construct map can exist in the more complex reality of usage—a construct is always an ideal; we use it because it suits our theoretical approach. If the theoretical approach is inconsistent with the idea of mapping a construct, it is hardly sensible to use a construct map as the fundamental approach—an example would be where the theory was based on an unordered set of latent classes. There are also constructs that are more complex than construct map, yet contain construct maps as a component. Probably the most common would be a multidimensional construct (e.g., the three LBC strands). In this sort of situation, to use the construct mapping approach, it is necessary merely to focus on one dimension at a time. Another common case is that where the construct can be seen as a partially ordered set of categories, such as where learners use different solution strategies to solve a problem. In this situation, the partial ordering can be used to simplify the problem so that it is collapsed into a construct map. In this case, there will be a loss of information, but this simplified construct may prove useful, and the extra complications can be added back in later. For other examples of more complex structures, see the Resources section at the end of this chapter.

Consider the LBC example introduced in the previous chapter. Here the construct described in Fig. 1.1 can be re-expressed as a construct map as in Fig. 2.2. The levels given in Fig. 1.1 are essentially different levels of student thinking, so consequently they are given on the left-hand side of the construct map.

2.2 EXAMPLES OF CONSTRUCT MAPS

The idea of a construct map is natural in the context of educational testing. It is also just as amenable to use in other domains where it is less common. For example, in attitude measurement one often finds that the underlying idea is one of increasing or decreasing amounts

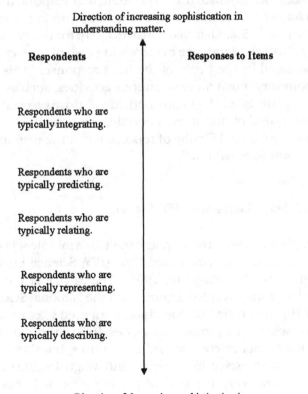

FIG. 2.2   A sketch of the construct map for the matter construct of the LBC instrument.

of something, and that something might be satisfaction, liking, agreement, and so on. The construct map is also applicable in a wide variety of circumstances as illustrated next.

2.2.1 The Health Assessment (PF-10) Example

An example of a self-report attitude-like construct that can be mapped in this way is the Physical Functioning subscale (PF-10; Raczek et al., 1998) of the SF-36 health survey (Ware & Gandek, 1998). This instrument is used to assess generic health status, and the PF-10 subscale assesses the physical functioning aspect of that. The items of the PF-10 consist of descriptions of various types of physical activities to which the respondent may respond that they are *imited a lot*, *a little*, or *not at all*. The actual items in this instrument are given in Table 5.2. An initial construct map for the PF-10 is shown in Fig. 2.3. Note the sequence of increasing ease of physical functioning as indicated by the order of the item responses. This sequence ranges from very much more strenuous activities, such as those represented by the label "Vigorous Activities," down to activities that take little physical effort for most people. Note that the order shown indicates the relative difficulty of reporting that the respondents' activities are *not limited at all*.

2.2.2 The Science Assessment (IEY) Example

This example is an assessment system built for a middle school science curriculum, "Issues, Evidence and You" (IEY; Science Education for Public Understanding Program, 1995). The SEPUP at the Lawrence Hall of Science was awarded a grant from the National Science Foundation in 1993 to create year-long issues-oriented science courses for the middle school and junior high grades. In issues-oriented science, students learn science content and procedures, but they are also required to recognize scientific evidence and weigh it against other community concerns, with the goal of making informed choices about relevant contemporary issues or problems. The goal of this approach is the development of an understanding of the science and problem-solving approaches related to social issues without promoting an advocacy position. The course developers were interested in trying

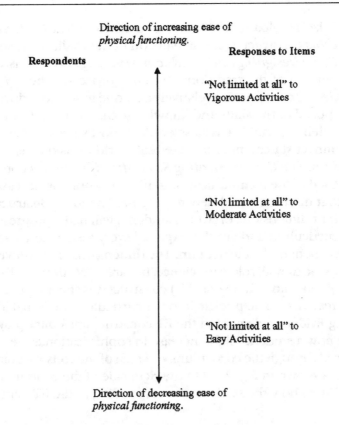

Direction of increasing ease of
physical functioning.

Respondents

Responses to Items

"Not limited at all" to
Vigorous Activities

"Not limited at all" to
Moderate Activities

"Not limited at all" to
Easy Activities

Direction of decreasing ease of
physical functioning.

FIG. 2.3   A sketch of the construct map for the Physical Functioning subscale (PF-10) of the SF-36 Health Survey.

new approaches to assessment in the *Issues, Evidence, and You* course materials for at least two reasons. First, they wanted to reinforce the problem-solving and decision-making aspects of the course—to teachers and to students. Traditional fact-based chapter tests would not reinforce these aspects and, if included as the only form of assessment, could direct the primary focus of instruction away from the course objectives the developers thought were most important. Second, the developers knew that, to market their end product, they would need to address questions about student achievement in this new course, and traditional assessment techniques were not likely to demonstrate student performance in the key objectives (problem solving and decision making).

Both the IEY curriculum and its assessment system is built (which, like the LBC example, uses the *BEAR Assessment System* as its foundation; Wilson & Sloane, 2000) on four constructs. The *Understanding Concepts* construct is the IEY version of the traditional "science content." The *Designing and Conducting Investigations* construct is the IEY version of the traditional "science process." The *Evidence and Trade-offs* construct is a relatively new one in science education. It is composed of the skills and knowledge that would allow one to evaluate, debate, and discuss a scientific report such as an environmental impact statement and make real-world decisions using that information. The *Communicating Scientific Information* construct is composed of the communication skills that would be necessary as part of that discussion and debate process. The four constructs are seen as four dimensions on which students will make progress during the curriculum and are the target of every instructional activity and assessment in the curriculum. The dimensions are positively related because they all relate to science, but are educationally distinct.

The Evidence and Trade-offs (ET) construct was split into two parts (called *elements*) to help relate it to the curriculum. An initial idea of the Using Evidence element of the ET construct was built up by considering how a student might increase in sophistication as he or she progressed through the curriculum. A sketch of the construct map for this case is shown in Fig. 2.4. On the right side of the continuum is a description of how the students are responding to the ET items.

2.2.3 The Study Activities Questionnaire (SAQ) Example

An example of a construct map in a somewhat different domain can be found in the Study Activities Questionnaire (SAQ; Warkentin, Bol, & Wilson, 1997). This instrument is designed to survey students' activities while studying; it is based on a review of the literature in the area (Thomas & Rohwer, 1993) and the authors' interpretation of the study context. There are several dimensions mapped out in the instrument; but the focus here is on the "Learning Effectiveness" dimension of the "Effort Management" hierarchy. The authors referred to it as a *hierarchy* because they saw that each successive level could be built on the previous one—note that the hierarchy in this case is not necessarily seen as one that is inevitable—students could engage in planning without self-monitoring—but the authors saw this ordering as being the most efficacious. For the purposes of this instrument, *effort management* is the set of metacognitive and self-

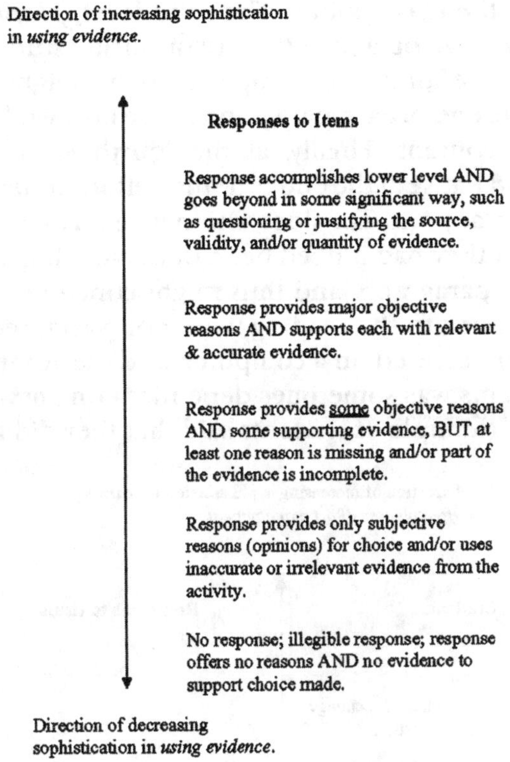

Direction of increasing sophistication
in *using evidence*.

Responses to Items

Response accomplishes lower level AND
goes beyond in some significant way, such
as questioning or justifying the source,
validity, and/or quantity of evidence.

Response provides major objective
reasons AND supports each with relevant
& accurate evidence.

Response provides some objective reasons
AND some supporting evidence, BUT at
least one reason is missing and/or part of
the evidence is incomplete.

Response provides only subjective
reasons (opinions) for choice and/or uses
inaccurate or irrelevant evidence from the
activity.

No response; illegible response; response
offers no reasons AND no evidence to
support choice made.

Direction of decreasing
sophistication in *using evidence*.

FIG. 2.4   A sketch of the construct map for the Using Evidence construct of the
IEY ET constructs.

regulatory processes involved in planning and evaluating one's concentration, time, and learning effectiveness. The instrument posits
four levels of increasing proficiency in effort management that form
a continuum of proficiency, with each higher level subsuming lower
level activities (see Fig. 2.5).

The first level is *monitoring*—being aware of one's learning effectiveness. For example, students might note how well they are
learning the ideas in a paragraph by stopping at the end of the paragraph and recalling the main points. The second level, *self-regulation*, involves using the self-knowledge gained from monitoring
to redirect or adjust one's behaviors. For example, if students
noted that there seemed to be something missing in recalling the
main points of the paragraph, they might re-read the paragraph or

make a list of the main points. The third level, *planning*, occurs when students develop a plan (before or during study) to manage or enhance their efforts. For example, students might decide to always stop at the end of each paragraph to see how well they had understood the content. Finally, at the fourth level, *evaluation*, students would pause at the end of a study effort, reflect on the success of their plan, and consider alternatives. For example, they might find that they had indeed been understanding all the major points of each paragraph, and thus might conclude that the constant interruptions to the reading were not warranted. The questions were administered on a computer, and the administration of subsequent items was sometimes dependent on answers to previous ones—for example, if students said that they did not monitor,

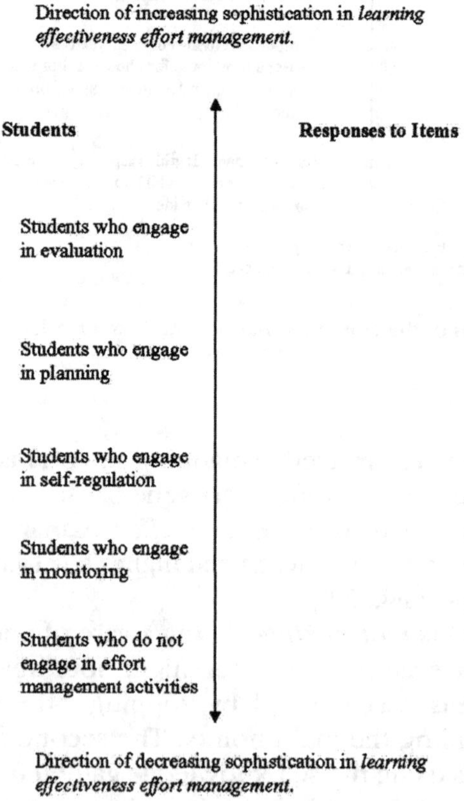

Direction of increasing sophistication in *learning effectiveness effort management.*

Students	Responses to Items
Students who engage in evaluation	
Students who engage in planning	
Students who engage in self-regulation	
Students who engage in monitoring	
Students who do not engage in effort management activities	

Direction of decreasing sophistication in *learning effectiveness effort management.*

FIG. 2.5 A sketch of the construct map for the "Learning Effectiveness" construct in the "Effort Management" part of the SAQ.

then they were not asked about self-regulation (although they were still asked about planning and evaluation; see Fig. 2.5).

2.2.4 The Interview (Good Education) Example

Interviews can also be used as the basis for developing construct maps. Dawson (1998) used the Good Education Interview in a clinical interview format developed by Armon (1984) to investigate the complexity of arguments used by adults discussing issues about quality of education. She used questions such as, "What is a good education?" and "What are the aims (goals, purposes) of a good education?," along with probes such as "Why is that good?," to explore the interviewees' thinking. Interviewees' responses were divided into scorable arguments (Stinson, Milbrath, & Reidbord, 1993), and these were then scored with Commons' Hierarchical Complexity Scoring System (HCSS; Commons et al., 1983, 1995). The resulting construct map is shown in Fig. 2.6. The respondent levels on the left-hand side are stages in the HCSS scheme. The responses on the right-hand side show typical statements made by people at the corresponding levels. Note that this is the first example shown where both sides of the construct map are populated.

2.2.5 A Historical Example: Binet and Simon's Intelligence Scale

The earliest example I have found of a construct map was in Binet and Simon's (1905) description of their Measuring Scale of Intelligence. Binet and Simon identified tasks that they considered to be examples of differing levels of "intelligent behavior" and that could be easily administered and judged. By grouping these into sets that could typically be successfully performed by children of varying ages (and adults), they could set up a set of expectations for what a "normal" child should be able to do as she progressed toward adulthood. An example of such an item is "Arrangement of weights." They described it thus (Note that they have included a scored outcome space for this item in their description.):

Five little boxes of the same color and volume are placed in a group on a table. They weigh respectively 2, 6, 9, 12, and 15 grams. They are

Direction of increasing *Argument Complexity*.

Respondents	Responses: *A good education ...*
Metasystematic: The notion that good learning takes place in social interactions is coordinated with the idea that learning is discursive. Learning is viewed as a dialectical process in which teacher and student (or student and student) get caught up in the playful activity of learning. Testing—as a continuous spiral of feedback—is one way of conceptualizing this playful back-and-forth. This dialectic defines the learning process.	is one in which teaching involves constant testing requires a dialectical engagement with the learning process
Systematic: The notion of active participation in learning is coordinated with the idea that intellectual engagement can be increased through social interaction to produce the idea that good learning takes place in a discursive, participatory context. This is not the defining context for learning, but is the most enjoyable.	includes conversation/discussion includes group activities
Formal: Active engagement in learning is central to the learning process. The concept, interest, is differentiated into concepts like involvement, engagement, and inspiration, all of which point both to the absorption of the learner. Inspiration, stimulation, involvement, and engagement are generated by others (teachers). Social interaction is important insofar as it enhances engagement.	is one in which students are encouraged to ask questions is stimulating/involving/engaging includes social interaction includes active/experiential learning
Abstract: Knowledge acquisition is enhanced when students have fun. Interest motivates learning because it makes learning fun. Fun learning is interesting learning. Certain fun or playful activities are explicitly seen as educational. It is the teacher's job to make learning interesting	includes playing games/doing fun things includes learning through play is one in which subjects/teachers are interesting is one in which learning is fun
Concrete: A good school (for concrete children, education equals school) is one in which you get to play and have fun. The child does not connect concepts of fun and play to learning.	includes play is one in which students have fun

Direction of decreasing *Argument Complexity*.

FIG. 2.6   A sketch of the construct map for the items in the Good Education Interview.

shown to the subject while saying to him: "look at these little boxes. They have not the same weight; you are going to arrange them here in their right order. Here to the left first the heaviest weight; next, the one a little less heavy; here one a little less heavy; here one a little less heavy; and here the lightest one."

There are three classes to distinguish. First the subject who goes at random without comparing, often committing a serious error, four degrees for example. Second the subject who compares, but makes a slight error of one or two degrees. Third the one who has the order exact. WE propose to estimate the errors in this test by taking account of the displacement that must be made to re-establish the correct order. Thus in the following example: 12, 9, 6, 3, 15,—15 is not in its place and the error is of 4 degrees because it must make 4 moves to find the place where it belongs. All the others must be changed one degree. The sum of the changes indicates the total error which is of eight degrees. (pp. 62–63)

The corresponding construct map is shown in Fig. 2.7. Sets of tasks that children tended to perform successfully at approximately the same age are shown on the right, and the corresponding ages (being descriptions of the respondents) are shown on the left. Binet and Simon used this construct to describe children with developmental

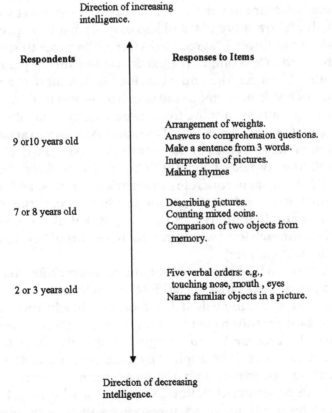

FIG. 2.7   A sketch of the construct map for Binet and Simon's (1905) Measuring Scale of Intelligence.

problems in French asylums: Those who could not succeed at the 2- to 3-year-old tasks were classified as "idiots," those who could succeed at that level but could not succeed at the 7-to 8-year-old tasks were classified as "imbeciles," and those who could succeed at that level but could not succeed at the next level were classified as "debile." Interestingly enough, they found children in French asylums who had been diagnosed into these classifications, but were actually succeeding at a level above that typical of their age.

2.3 USING CONSTRUCT MAPPING TO HELP DEVELOP AN INSTRUMENT

The central idea in using the construct mapping concept at the initial stage of instrument development is for the measurer to focus on the essential feature of what is to be measured—in what way does an individual show more of it and less of it—it may be expressed as from "higher to lower," "agree to disagree," "weaker to stronger," or "more often to less often," the particular wording dependent on the context. However, the important idea is that there is a qualitative order of levels inherent in the construct—and underlying that there is a continuum running from more to less—that allows it to be thought of as a construct map. One successful way to approach it is to think of the extremes of that continuum (say "novice" to "expert," or in the context of an attitude toward something, "loathes" to "loves"), make them concrete through descriptions, and then develop some intermediate stages or levels between the two extremes. It is also helpful to start thinking of typical responses that respondents at each level would give to first drafts of items (more of this in the next chapter).

Before this can be done, however, the measurer often has to engage in a process of "variable clarification," where the construct to be measured is distinguished from other, closely related, constructs. Reasonably often the measurer finds that there were several constructs lurking under the original idea—the four building blocks method can still be applied by taking them one at a time.

In creating a construct map, the measurer must be clear about whether the construct is defined in terms of who is to be measured, the respondents, or what responses they might give—the item responses. Eventually both will be needed, but often it makes sense in a specific context to start with one rather than the other. For instance, on the one hand, when there is a developmental theory of how individuals increase on the construct or a theory of how people array themselves between the extremes of an attitude, the respondent side is probably developed first. On the other hand, if the construct is mainly defined by a set of items and the responses to those items, it is probably easier to start by ordering the item responses.

2.4 RESOURCES

Examples of construct maps are given in the series of references cited in the Resources section of chapter 1. However, few of them incorporate both the respondent and item response sides of the continuum.

One important issue is that one needs to distinguish constructs that are amenable to the use of construct mapping and constructs that are not. Clearly any construct that is measured using a single score for each person can be a candidate for mapping. If a construct is a series of such, then each in turn can be seen as a construct map. Also exemplified earlier were constructs that are partially ordered—these too can be simplified so that they can be treated as construct maps.

The major type of construct that is not straightforwardly seen as a candidate for mapping is one where there is no underlying continuum—where, for example, there is assumed to be just a set of discrete, unordered categories. This is seen in areas such as cognitive psychology, where one might assume that there are only a few strategies available for solving a particular problem. Latent class analysis (e.g., Collins & Wugalter, 1992) is an approach that posits such a construct; it should be used when the measurer is seriously wanting to use that as the basis for reporting.

When there is an order (perhaps partial) between the latent classes, such as an increasing complexity in the nature of the strategies, then other possibilities arise. For example, one could have the strategies treated as observed categories with an underlying latent continuum of increasing sophistication (e.g., Wilson, 1992a, 1992b).

One could also try and combine the two types of constructs, adding a construct map within classes (e.g., Wilson, 1989; Mislevy & Wilson, 1996) or adding a dimension as a special class (e.g., Yamamoto & Gitomer, 1993). Increasingly complex combinations of all of these are also possible, leading to some complicated possibilities (see Junker, 2001; National Research Council, 2001).

2.5 EXERCISES AND ACTIVITIES

(following on from the exercises and activities in chap. 1)

1. Lay out the different constructs involved in the area in which you have chosen to work. Clarify the relationships among them and concentrate on one.
2. For your chosen construct, write down a brief (1–2 sentences) definition of the construct. If necessary, write similar definitions of related constructs to help distinguish among them.
3. Describe different levels of the construct—start with the extremes and then develop qualitatively distinguishable levels in between. Distinguish between levels among the respondents and levels in potential item responses. Write down the successive levels in terms of both aspects, if possible at this point.
4. Take your description of the construct (and any other clarifying statements) to a selected subset of your informants and ask them to critique it.
5. Try to think through the steps outlined earlier in the context of developing your instrument, and write down notes about your plans.
6. Share your plans and progress with others—discuss what you and they are succeeding on and what problems have arisen.

Chapter 3

The Items Design

3.0 CHAPTER OVERVIEW AND KEY CONCEPTS

    item formats
    participant observation
    topic guide
    standardized open-ended
    standardized fixed-response
    components of the items design
    construct component
    distributional components

This chapter concentrates on ways to stimulate responses that can constitute observations about the construct that the measurer wishes to measure. *Observation* means more than just seeing something and recording it, remembering it, or jotting down notes about it. What is being referred to is a special sort of observation that is generically called an *item*. This means that there exists (a) a procedure, or *design*, that allows the observations to be made under a set of standard conditions that span the intended range of the item contexts; and (b) a procedure for classifying those observations into a set of standard categories. The first part is the topic of this chapter, and the second is the topic of the next chapter. The instrument is then a set of these procedures (i.e., items). First, the following section develops the idea of an item and discusses some typical types of items. Then a typology of items is introduced that is designed to show connections among many different sorts of items. This leads to the definition of the items design and its components in the next section. Finally, the last section discusses ways to develop items. In the following chapter, this standardization is extended to include the way that the observations are recorded into a standardized categorization system.

3.1 THE IDEA OF AN ITEM

Often the first inkling of an item comes in the form of an idea about how to reveal a respondent's particular characteristic (construct). The inkling can be quite informal—a remark in a conversation, the way a student describes what he or she understands about something, a question that prompts an argument, a particularly pleasing piece of art, or a newspaper article. The specific way that the measurer prompts an informative response from a respondent is crucial to the value of the measures that finally result. In fact in many, if not most, cases, the construct is not clearly defined until a large set of items has been developed and tried out with respondents. Each new context brings about the possibility of developing new and different sorts of items or adapting existing ones.

A rich variety of types of items has been developed to deal with many different constructs and contexts. We have already seen two different formats. In chapter 1, much was said about the LBC chemistry example, which uses an open-ended short-answer type of item, as in Fig. 1.2. In chapter 2, the PF-10 health survey asked the question, "Does your health now limit you in these activities?" with respect to a range of physical activities, but restricted the responses to a forced choice among:*Yes, limited a lot*, *Yes, limited a little*, and *No, not limited at all*. These are examples of two ends of a range of item formats that stretch from the very open to the very closed. In chapter 2, the SAQ was another example of the closed-response type, as is the familiar multiple-choice item from educational testing. The IEY science achievement test and the Good Education Interview were examples of the open-response type. In the following section, a typology that spans this range is described. Many other types of items exist (e.g., see Nitko, 1983, for a large assortment from educational assessment), and the measurer should be aware of both the specific types of items that have been used in the past in the specific area in which an instrument is being developed, and also of item types that have been used in other contexts.

Probably the most common type of item in the experience of most people is the general *open-ended item format* that was used (and continues to be used) every day in school classrooms and many other settings around the world. The format can be expressed orally or in writing, and the response can also be in either form, or indeed in other forms, such as concrete products or active performances. The length of the response can vary from a single number or word, to a simple product or performance, to extremely lengthy essays, complex proofs, interviews, extended performances, or multipart products. The item can be produced extemporaneously by the teacher or be the result of an extensive development process. This format is also used outside of educational settings in workplaces, other social settings, and in the everyday interchanges we all enjoy. Typical subforms are the essay, the brief demonstration, the product, and the short-answer format.

In counterpoint, probably the most common type of item in published instruments is the *fixed-response format*. Some may think that this is the most common item format, but that is because they are discounting the numerous everyday situations involving open-ended item formats. The multiple-choice item is familiar to almost every educated person; it has had an important role in the educational trajectories of many. The fixed-response or Likert-type response format is also common in surveys and questionnaires used in many situations—in health, applied psychology, and public policy settings; in business settings such as employee and consumer ratings; and in governmental settings. The responses are most commonly *Strongly Disagree* to *Strongly Agree*, but many other response options are also found (as in the PF-10 example). It is somewhat paradoxical that the most commonly experienced format is not the most commonly published format. As becomes clear to readers as they pass through the next several chapters, the view developed here is that the open-ended format is the more basic format, and the fixed-response format can be seen as a specialized version of the open-ended format.

The relationship of the item to the construct is an important one. Typically the item is but one of many (often one from an infinite set) that could be used to measure the construct. Ramsden et al. (1993), writing about the assessment of achievement in physics, noted:

> Educators are interested in how well students understand speed, distance and time, not in what they know about runners or powerboats or people walking along corridors. Paradoxically, however, there is no other way of describing and testing understanding than through such specific examples. (Ramsden et al., 1993, p. 312)

Similarly, consider the health measurement (PF-10) example described previously. The specific questions used are neither necessary for defining the construct nor sufficient to encompass all the possible meanings of the concept of physical functioning. Thus, the task of the measurer is to choose a finite set of items that represent the construct in some reasonable way. As Ramsden hinted, this is not the straightforward task one might, on initial consideration, think it to be. Often one feels the temptation to seek the "one true task," the "authentic item," or the single observation that will supply the mother lode of evidence about the construct.

Unfortunately, this misunderstanding, common among beginning measurers, is founded on a failure to fully consider the need to establish sufficient levels of validity and reliability for the instrument. Where one wishes to represent a wide range of contexts in an instrument, it is better to have more items rather than less—this is because (a) the instrument can then sample more of the content of a construct (see chap. 8 for more on this), and (b) it can then generate more bits of information about how a respondent stands with respect to the construct, which gives greater accuracy (see chap. 7 for more on this). This requirement has to be balanced against the requirement to use item formats that are sufficiently complex to prompt responses that are rich enough to stand the sorts of interpretations that the measurer wishes to make with the measures. Both requirements need to be satisfied within the time and cost limitations imposed on the measuring context.

3.2 THE COMPONENTS OF THE ITEMS DESIGN

One way to understand the *items design* is to see it as a description of the population of items, or "item pool," from which the specific items in the instrument are to be sampled. As such the instrument is the result of a series of decisions that the measurer has made regarding how to represent the construct or, equivalently, how to stratify the "space" of items (sometimes called the *universe* of items) and then sample from those strata. Some of those decisions are principled ones relating to the fundamental definition of the construct and the research background of the construct. Some are practical, relating to the constraints of administration and usage. Some are rather arbitrary, being made to keep the item-generation task within reasonable limits. Generically, one can distinguish between two types of components of items that are useful in describing the item pool: (a) construct, and (b) descriptive.

3.2.1 The Construct Component

One essential component that is common to all items designs intended to relate to a construct is that used to provide criterion-referenced interpretations along the construct, from high to low. It provides interpretational levels within the construct, and hence it is called the *construct* component. For example, the construct component in the LBC matter construct is provided in Fig. 1.1. Thus, the construct component is essentially the content of the construct map—where an instrument is developed using a construct map, the construct component has already been established by that process.

However, one important issue still needs to be investigated and a policy decided. Each item can be designed to generate responses that span a certain number of qualitative levels—two is the minimum (otherwise the item would not be useful)—but beyond that any number is possible up to the maximum number of levels in the construct. For example, the item shown in Fig. 1.2 has been found to generate student responses at three levels: below describing, describing, and representing. Thus, it is essentially trichotomous (i.e., gives three levels of response). Yet another item may not be complex enough to generate a representing response, hence that item would only be dichotomous. With fixed response items, this range is limited by the options that are offered. In attitude scales, this distinction is also common: For some instruments one might only ask for *agree* versus *disagree*, but for others a polytomous choice is offered, such as *strongly agree*, *agree*, *disagree*, and *strongly disagree*. Although this choice can seem innocuous at the item design stage, it is in fact quite important and needs special attention when we get to the fourth building block (in chap. 5).

3.2.2 The Descriptive Components

Having specified the construct component, all that is left to do is decide on all the *other* characteristics that the set of items needs to have: Here I use the term *descriptive component* because each of these components is used to describe some aspect of the items. These are the components, other than the construct components, that are used to establish classes of items to populate the instrument—they are an essential part of the basis for item generation and classification. For example, in the health assessment (PF-10) example, the items are all self-report measures—this represents a decision to use self-report as a component of the instrument (and hence to find items that people in the target population can easily respond to) and not to use other potential components, such as giving the respondents actual physical tasks to complete.

There are many other components for a construct, and typically decisions are made by the measurer to include some and not others. Sometimes these decisions are made on the basis of practical constraints on the instrument usage (partly responsible for the PF-10 design—it was deemed too time-consuming to set up physical functioning tasks), sometimes on the basis of historical precedents (also partly responsible for the PF-10 design—it is based on research on an earlier, larger instrument), and sometimes on a somewhat arbitrary basis because the realized item pool must have a finite set of components, whereas the potential pool has an infinite set of components. Note how these decisions are not entirely neutral to the idea of the construct. Although the underlying PF-10 construct might be thought of as encompassing many different manifestations of physical functioning, the decision to use a self-report component alone restricts its actual interpretation of the instrument (a) away from items that could look beyond self-report, such as performance tasks; and (b) to items that are easy to self-report.

The science achievement (IEY) item shown in Fig. 3.1 demonstrates several of the distributional features of IEY tasks designed with the ET construct as the target. A portion of the test blueprint is shown in Table 3.1. In this case, the item is shown by two of its properties: (a) the

You are a public health official who works in the Water
Department. Your supervisor has asked you to respond to the public's
concern about water chlorination at the next City Council meeting.
Prepare a written response explaining the issues raised in the
newspaper articles. Be sure to discuss the advantages and
disadvantages of chlorinating drinking water in your response, and
then explain your recommendation about whether the water should be
chlorinated.

FIG. 3.1   An example IEY task.

construct it relates to (columns), and (b) the unit ("activity") of the
curriculum in which it is embedded. Note that a third characteristic is
also indicated: (c) Whether it is a major assessment (denoted by "A") or
a minor assessment (denoted by "✓" for "quick-check"). Some of the
characteristics of the IEY items are: (d) they are embedded in, and
hence to a certain extent determined by, the materials of the curriculum—thus, they are not completely specified by their literal content;
(e) they feature a brief description of a "real-world" situation, where
the students need to take on a specific role (sometimes one that they
might well take on themselves in their own everyday lives, sometimes
one that they could not take on, such as the role in this task); (f) they
usually ask the students to carry out some sort of procedure and then
write about it (in this case, the task of reading the newspaper articles is
implicit, more often it is explicit); (g) they often include references to
terms and actions featured in the relevant scoring guide (e.g., "advantages and disadvantages"); (h) they are *always* designed to produce
responses that can be scored by the generic scoring guide for each
construct; and (i) they very often have a two-part structure—they ask
for a decision regarding the real-world situation, and then an explanation of that decision.

The decision to deploy these nine descriptive components was
made by the assessment designers in consultation with the curriculum developers. As is the case for many instruments, these descriptive
components do not fully specify the set of items that were used in the
full instrument—each item represents a further realization beyond
these nine features. Also most of the components are somewhat
fuzzily described—again a common feature of many instruments.
Other designs would have been possible, and some were in fact tried
out. For example, an initial item type used a unique scoring guide for

TABLE 3.1
Portion of the IEY Instrument Blueprint

			Variable • *Elements*		
Activity	Designing and Conducting Investigations • Designing Investigation • Selecting & Performing Procedures • Organizing Data • Analyzing and Interpreting Data	Evidence and Tradeoffs • Using Evidence • Using Evidence to Make Tradeoffs	Understanding Concepts • Recognizing Relevant Content • Applying Relevant Content	Communicating Scientific Information • Organization • Technical Aspects
1 Water Quality				
2 Exploring Sensory Thresholds				
3 Concentration			✓: Both elements *Risk Management ✓: Applying Relevant Content *Measurement and Scale	
4 Mapping Death				
5 John Snow		A: Using Evidence		
6 Contaminated Water	✓: Designing Investigation			
7 Chlorination	A: All elements			A: Both elements

Note. "Variable"=construct. * Indicates content concepts assessed.

each item—this was easier for the item developers, but more difficult for the teachers, so it was decided to stick to the item type that was more difficult to develop but easier to use (see Wilson & Sloane, 2000, for more information about the IEY items).

It is interesting to note that consideration of the depth of information required to use the scoring guide for the ET construct (shown in Fig. 1.6 and Table 3.1) helps one understand why some of these features are present (e.g., without the "please explain" of [i], one seldom gets sufficient information). However, such considerations are not sufficient to generate all of the IEY item features. This is generally true: Somewhat arbitrary decisions are typically made about the types of items used to measure a construct in any given case. Going back to the PF-10 items, here the other components of the items might be summarized as: (a) they must relate to physical activities that are performed across a wide range of the target population; (b) they must be capable of being considered reasonable responses to the question "Does your health now limit you in these activities? If so, how much?", and it must be reasonable to respond using one of the options given (e.g., "Yes, limited a lot," etc.); and (c) they must be items from the older Medical Outcomes Study (MOS) instrument (see Ware & Gandek, 1998, for an explanation of this list).

Any list of characteristics derived from a specific list of items from an instrument must necessarily be somewhat arbitrary—for example, neither of the two prior lists include "they must be in English," yet this is indeed one of the features of both sets. One of the most important ideas behind the items design is to decrease this arbitrariness by explicitly adopting a description of the item pool quite early in instrument development. This items design may well be modified during the instrument development process, but that does not diminish the importance of having an items design early in the instrument development. The generation of at least a tentative items design should be one of the first steps (if not the first step) in item generation. Items constructed before a tentative items design is developed should primarily be seen as part of the process of developing the items design. Generally speaking, it is much harder to develop an items design from an existing set of items than a set of items from an items design. The items design can (and probably will) be revised, but having one in the first place makes the resulting item set much more likely to be coherent.

3.3 ITEM FORMATS AND STEPS IN ITEM DEVELOPMENT

Different item formats can be characterized by their *different amounts of pre-specification*—that is by the degree to which the results from the use of the instrument are developed *before* the instrument is administered to a respondent. The more that is pre-specified, the less that has to be done after the response has been made. Contrariwise, when there is little pre-specified (i.e., little is fixed before the response is made) then more has to occur afterward. This is used as the basis for a classification of item types described next. Table 3.1 contains the whole story, which is narrated in the paragraphs that follow. This typology can also be seen as a way to describe the *development* of items, with each such effort starting off with low prespecification, and then proceeding to greater amounts of pre-specification, until the optimum amount (of prespecification) is reached.

The item format with the lowest possible level of prespecification would be one where the administrator had not yet formulated any of the item characteristics discussed earlier, or even perhaps the construct—the aim of the instrument. What remains is the intent to observe. This type of diffuse instrumentation is exemplified by the *participant observation* technique (e.g., Ball, 1985) common in anthropological studies. Another closely related technique is the "informal conversational interview" as described by Patton (1980):

> the researcher has no presuppositions about what of importance may be learned by talking to people.... The phenomenological interviewer wants to maintain maximum flexibility to be able to pursue information in whatever direction appears to be appropriate, depending on the information that emerges from observing a particular setting or from talking to one or more individuals in that setting. (pp. 198–199)

The measurer (i.e., in this case, usually called the *participant observer*) may not know the purpose of the observation, and "the persons being talked with may not even realize they are being interviewed" (Patton, 1980, p. 198). The degree of prespecification of the participant observation item format is shown in the first row of Table 3.2, which emphasizes the progressive increase in prespecification as one moves from participant observation to fixed-response formats.

TABLE 3.2
Levels of Prespecification in Item Formats

Item Format	Intent to Measure Construct "X"	Description of Item Components		Specific Items		Responses
		General	Specific	No Score Guide	Score Guide	
Participant Observations	**Before or After**	After	After	After	After	After
Topics guide (a) General	Before	**Before**	After	After	After	After
Topics guide (b) Specific	Before	Before	**Before**	After	After	After
Open-ended	Before	Before	Before	**Before**	After	After
Open-ended plus Scoring Guide	Before	Before	Before	Before	**Before**	After
Fixed response	Before	Before	Before	Before	Before	**Before**

Some may balk at considering a technique like participant observation as an example of an instrument and including it in a book on measurement. Yet it and the next technique are included here because (a) many of the techniques described in these chapters are applicable to the results of such observations, (b) these techniques can be useful within an instrument design (more on this at the end of this section), and (c) the techniques mark a useful starting point in thinking about the level of prespecification of types of item formats.

The next level of prespecification occurs when the aims of the instrument are indeed preestablished—in the terms introduced earlier, call this the *topic guide* format (second row of Table 3.2). In the context of interviewing, Patton (1980), labeled this the *interview guide* approach—the guide consists of:

> a set of issues that are to be explored with each respondent before interviewing begins. The issues in the outline need not be taken in any particular order and the actual wording of questions to elicit responses about those issues is not determined in advance. The interview guide simply serves as a basic checklist during the interview to make sure that there is common information that should be obtained from each person interviewed. (p. 198)

Two levels of specificity in this format are distinguished. At the more general level of specificity, the components—including the definition of the construct and the other components—are only specified to a summary level—the *general* topic guide approach, presumably, the full specification of these occur after observations have been made. At the higher level of specificity, the complete set of components, including the construct definition, is available before administration—hence, this is the *specific* topic guide approach. The distinction between these two levels is a matter of degree—one could have a vague summary and, alternatively, there could be a more detailed summary that was nevertheless incomplete.

The next level of prespecification is the *open-ended* format. This includes the common open-ended test and interview instruments mentioned at the beginning of this chapter. Here the items are determined before the administration of the instrument and are administered under standard conditions, including a predetermined order. In the context of interviewing, Patton (1980) labeled this the "standardized open-ended interview." Like the previous level of item format, there are two discernible levels within this category. At the first level, the response categories are yet to be determined. Most tests that teachers make themselves and use in their classrooms are at this level. At the second level, the categories that the responses are divided into are predetermined—call this the *scoring guide* level. The LBC chemistry instrument and the Good Education Interview (used as examples in previous chapters) are in this category.

The final level of specificity is the *standardized fixed-response* format typified by the multiple- choice and Likert-style items. Here the respondent chooses rather than generates a response to the item. As mentioned earlier this is probably the most widely used item form in published instruments. The SAQ and PF-10 instruments described in previous chapters are examples, as is any multiple-choice test or Likert-style attitude scale.

This typology is not only a way to classify the items in instruments that one might come across in research and practice. Its real strength lies in its nature as a guide to the *item-generation* process. I argue that every instrument should go through a set of developmental stages that approximate the columns in Table 3.2 through to the desired level. Instrument development efforts that seek to skip levels will always end up having to make more or less arbitrary decisions about item design components at some point in the development. For example, deciding to create a Likert-type attitude scale without first investigating the responses that people would make to open-ended prompts will leave the instrument with no defense against the criticism that the fixed-response format has distorted the measurement.

Because the motivation to create a new instrument is almost certainly that the measurer wants to go beyond what was done in the past, it is important that the measurer bring new sources of information to the development—beyond what is learned from a literature review. One important source of information can be found through exactly the sort of *participant observation* approach described in the previous section. The measurer should find situations where people who would be typical respondents to the planned instrument could be observed and interviewed in the informal mode of participant observation. That might include informal conversational interviews, collections of products, recordings of performances, and so on. Information from these processes are used to develop a richer and deeper background for the theory that the measurer needs to establish the construct (i.e., the levels of the construct reference component) and the contextual practices that are necessary to develop the distributional components of the instrument. The set of informants described in Section 1.5 would be of help in this process—some as participants and some as observers.

Following the initial idea-building and background-filling work of the literature review and the participant observations, the measurer should assay an initial stab at the items design *topics guide*. This is difficult to do in a vacuum of context, so it is also necessary to develop some initial drafts of items. This is even true if the plan is to leave the instrument at the topics guide level because it is essential to try out the guides in practice (i.e., that means actually doing some interviews, etc.). The development of the construct through the idea of construct map was already discussed in chapter 2. The development of the other components requires insights from the participant observation to know what to focus on and how to express the questions appropriately—some similar information may be gleaned from the literature review, although usually such developmental information is not reported. The decision of whether to stop developing the topics guide at a summary level or go on to the finer grained specific topics guide depends on a number of issues, such as the amount of training the measurer devotes to the administrators of the instrument and the amount of time and effort that can be devoted to the analysis. If the aim is for the finer level, then inevitably the coarser level will be a step along the way.

Going on to an open-ended format will require either the generation of a set of items or the development of a method for automatically generating them in a standardized way. The latter is rather rare and quite specialized, so it will not be addressed here. Item development is a skill that is partly science and partly art. The science lies in the development of sound descriptions of the component; the art lies in the remainder. Every context is unique. If the aim is to develop fixed-response items, then a further step is needed. This step is discussed in the next chapter.

When items are organized into instruments, there are also issues of *instrument format* to consider. An important dimension of instrument design is the uniformity of the formats within the instrument. An instrument can consist entirely of one item format, such as is typical in many standardized achievement tests where all are usually multiple-choice items, and in many surveys, where Likert-type items are mostly used (although sometimes with different response categories for different sections of the survey). Yet more complex mixtures of formats are also used. For example, the portfolio is an instrument format common in the expressive and performance arts, and also in some professional areas. This consists of a sample of work that is relevant to the purpose of the portfolio, and so may consist of responses to items of many sorts and may be structured in a variety of ways more or less freely by the respondent according to the rules laid down. Tests may also be composed of mixed types—multiple-choice items as well as essays, say, or even performances of various sorts. Surveys and questionnaires may also be composed of different formats, true–false items, Likert items, and short-answer items. Interviews may consist of open-ended questions as well as forced-choice sections.

3.4 LISTENING TO THE RESPONDENTS

A crucial step in the process of developing an instrument, and one unique to the measurement of human beings, is for the measurer to ask the respondents what they are thinking about when responding to the items. In chapter 8 summative use of this sort of information is seen as a major tool in gathering evidence for the validity of the instrument and its use. In this section, formative use of this sort of information is seen as a tool for improving the instrument—in particular, the items of the instrument. There are two major types of investigations of response processes: the think aloud and the exit interview. Other types of investigation may involve reaction time (RT) studies, eye movement studies, and various treatment studies where, for example, the respondents are given certain sorts of information before they are asked to respond.

In the think aloud style of investigation, also called *cognitive labs* (American Institutes for Research, 2000), students are asked to talk aloud about what they are thinking while they are actually responding to the item. What the respondents say is recorded, and often what they do is being videotaped; other characteristics may also be recorded, such as having their eye movements tracked. Someone is at hand to prompt such self-reports and ask clarifying questions if necessary. Typically, respondents need a certain amount of training to know what it is that the researcher is interested in and also to feel comfortable with the procedure. The results can provide insights ranging from the very plain—"the respondents were not thinking about the desired topic when responding"—to the very detailed, including evidence about particular cognitive and metacognitive strategies that they are employing.

The exit interview is similar in aim, but is timed to occur after the respondent has made his or her responses. It may be conducted after each item or after the instrument as a whole, depending on whether the measurer judges that the delay will interfere with the respondent's memory. The types of information gained are similar to those from the think aloud, although generally they are not so detailed. This is not always a disadvantage; sometimes it is exactly the result of a respondent's reflection that are desired. Thus, it may be that a data-collection strategy that involves both think alouds and exit interviews is best.

An example of a summary from a cognitive lab is shown in Fig. 3.2—this is adapted (to maintain item security) from a report on a high school test developed for the California Department of Education (Levine & Huberman, 2000). Although it is not entirely clear from the material, the item is being evaluated with respect to whether it measures student achievement of a particular "standard" that asks whether the student can determine the approximate square root of an integer. In this case, the process was a combination of both think

```
Item: M00XXX
The square of a whole number is between 2,400 and 2,500.
The number must be between
     A     40 and 45.
     B     45 and 50.
     C     50 and 55.
     D     55 and 60.
```

Student performance:

Mastery	Performance		
	Correct	Incorrect	No Response (not reached)
No Mastery	2	1	1
Mastery	10	0	

Student mastery:

Two students who answered correctly had partial mastery but were unable to square 45 correctly. They got their correct answers through their ability to square 50—or just by being able to square 5.. This (50 squared, or 2,500) defines the upper limit of the range and identifies the option with 50 as the upper limit (option B) as the correct answer.

The student who got the item wrong did not know what the "square of a whole number" meant. He thought it meant the square root.

Cognitive processes:

Students would generally square the numbers in the options to identify a range. However, all that is required is the ability to recognize that the square root of 2,500 is 50. This defines the upper limit of the range—and the option B is the only option with 50 as the upper limit. At least two students who could not square 45 were able to get the correct answer because they could square 50.

Item problems:

This item could be correctly answered by a student who knows that 50 squared is 2,500—and cannot square the "harder" numbers. It does not really demand that a student be able to determine "between which two numbers the square root of an integer lies".

Recommendation:

Consider changing the numbers of ranges (e.g., 46-48; 49-51; 52-54; 55-58) even though it might be hard for some students to square these numbers without a calculator.

FIG. 3.2   A fictionalized report from an item cognitive lab
(adapted from Levine & Huberman, 2000).

aloud and exit interview. As part of the process, the interviewer was required to informally decide from the student interactions whether the student was indeed a master of the specific standard. Effectively, this interviewer decision constitutes a different form of an item focused on the same construct. This is an example of the usage of the concepts in the previous section—effectively, the consistency between two of the "steps in instrument development" is being used as an indicator of the quality of the more closed form. When the two-item formats are based on the same underlying construct and with two specific items designs, this is generally a sound idea, but it is less so in this instance because the decision made by the interviewer is simply an informal one based on no agreed-to components.

Information from respondents can be used at several levels of the instrument development process as detailed in this book. Reflections on what the respondents say can lead to wholesale changes in the idea of the construct; they can lead to revision of the construct component, the other components, and specific items and item types; and they can lead to changes in the outcome space and scoring schemes (to be described in the next chapter). It is difficult to overemphasize the importance of including procedures for tapping into the insights of the respondents in the instrument development process. A counterexample is useful here—in cognitive testing of babies and young infants, the measurer cannot gain insights in this way, and that has required the development of a whole range of specialized techniques to make up for such a lack.

Another issue that distinguishes measurement of humans from other sorts of measurement is that the measurer is obliged to make sure that the items do not offend the respondents or elicit personal information that would be detrimental to the respondent, ask them to carry out unlawful or harmful procedures, or unduly distress them. The steps described in the previous section prove informative of such matters, and the measurer should heed any information that the respondents supply and make subsequent revisions of the items. Simply noting such comments is not sufficient, however; there should be prompts that are explicitly aimed at addressing these issues because the respondents may think that such comments are "not wanted" in the think aloud and exit interview processes.

For example, to investigate whether items are offensive to potential respondents, it is useful to assemble a group of people who are seen as representing a broad range of potential respondents (which can have various titles, such as a *community review panel*). The specific demographic categories that should be represented in the group vary depending on the instrument and its audience, but likely demographic variables would be: age, gender, ethnicity, socioeconomic status (SES), and so on. This group is then asked to examine each item individually and the entire set of items as a group to recommend that items be deleted or amended on the grounds mentioned in the previous paragraphs, or any others that they feel are important. Of course it is up to the developer to decide what to do with such recommendations, but he or she should have a justification for not following any such recommendation.

3.5 RESOURCES

Apart from the creativity, insight, and hard work of the measurer, the general resources necessary to create an items design and actually generate the items are those already mentioned in previous chapters and in this one. In terms of specific resources, there is far too wide a range of potential types of constructs, areas of application, and item formats to even attempt to list particular sources here. Nevertheless, the background filling exercises at the end of chapter 1 should have resulted in useful leads to what has already been done and the range of item designs extant in a given area. Within the area of educational achievement testing, there are several useful resources for types of items and methods to develop them: Haladyna (1996, 1999), Nitko (1983), Osterlind (1998), and Roid and Haladyna (1982).

One greatly beneficial resource is the experience of professionals who have carried out instrument development exercises in related areas. Such people cannot only explain specific issues that arise in measuring in a particular area, but they can also explain how the many different sorts of information generated in the item development and critique process can be integrated to make better items.

3.6 EXERCISES AND ACTIVITIES

(following on from the exercises and activities in chaps. 1 and 2)

1. Generate lots of types of items and several examples of each type.

2. Write down your initial items design based on the preceding activities.
3. Give these draft items a thorough professional review at an "item panel" meeting—where key informants critique the items generated so far (see Appendix in chap. 3).
4. Write down your items design based on the preceding activities.
5. Following an initial round of item generation and item paneling, second or third rounds may be needed, and it may also involve a return to reconsider the construct definition or the definition of the other components.
6. Think through the steps outlined earlier in the context of developing your instrument, and write down notes about your plans.
7. Share your plans and progress with others—discuss what you and they are succeeding on and what problems have arisen.

APPENDIX : The Item Panel

1. How to prepare for the item paneling.
   (a) For each item you generate, make sure (i) you can explain its relationship to the framework, (ii) you can justify that it is appropriately expressed for the respondents, (iii) it is likely to generate the sort of information that you want, and (iv) the sorts of responses it elicits can be scored using your scoring guide.
   (b) If possible, first try out the items in an informal, but hopefully informative, small study using several of your informants. Ask them to take the instrument and comment on what they thought of it.
   (c) For each part of the framework that you have decided to measure, make sure that there are a sufficient number of items (remembering that a 50% loss of items between generation and final instrument is very likely). Note that if that will make for too many items to actually panel, also indicate a subset that will definitely be discussed in the panel.

2. Who should be on the item panel?
   The panel should be composed of the same profile of people as your informant group:
   (a) where possible, some potential respondents;

(b) professionals, teachers/academics, and researchers in the relevant areas;

(c) people knowledgeable about measurement in general and/or measurement in the specific area of interest; and

(d) other people who are knowledgeable and reflective about the area of interest and/or measurement in that area.

3. What to supply to the panelists.

At least a week ahead, send each panelist the following:

(a) The framework, along with suitable (but not overwhelming) background information;

(b) A description of how the instrument is administered and scored;

(c) A list of the items, with indications about what part of the framework each relates to and how it will be scored; and

(d) Any other relevant information (remember, for judged items, each panelist has to be a reasonable facsimile of a judge).

Offer to discuss any and all of this with the panelists if they have questions or difficulties understanding the materials

4. How to carry out the item paneling.

(a) You will chair the meeting. Your aim, as chair, is to help each panelist contribute in the most constructive way possible to creating the best set of items that well represent the framework. Each panelist needs to understand that that is the aim. Panelists are to be as critical as they can, but with the aim of being constructive as well. Disputes are to be left in the room at the end–the chair/item developer will decide what to do with each comment.

(b) Order of business:

(i) Explain the purpose of the panel in case some panelists are new to the procedure.

(ii) Give panelists a brief overview of the framework of the variable and context of the planned instrument, including the expected respondents and judges. Invite comments and questions.

(iii) Systematically discuss the items to be paneled, keeping in mind as you go the expected length of the meeting and the number of items to be paneled. Before passing on to the next item, be sure that you are satisfied that you are clear on the panel's recommended revisions for the current item (you may need to have someone else dedicated to the role of note taker because it can be difficult to chair the meeting as well as take notes).

(iv) After surveying all items, ask for general comments on the item set and, especially whether the item set comprehensively represents the framework for the variable.

(v) Collect the item sets and written comments from the panelists.

5. What to do after the panel meeting.
   (a) Immediately after the meeting:
      (i) Go over your notes (with the note taker) so that you are clear about recommended action for each item.
      (ii) Follow-up any matters that were not clear in your review of the notes.
   (b) Reflect on the revisions recommended by the panel members—bear in mind that their recommendations are not necessarily correct—decide which to accept and which to modify.
   (c) Carry out the revisions you have decided on (extrapolating to items not actually paneled) to items, framework, and other materials.
   (d) Send the revised items (and revised framework and background material, if that was recommended) to the panel for individual comments.
   (e) Make further changes depending on their responses and your own judgment.
   (f) If you are not sure that there has been sufficient improvement, repeat the whole exercise.

Chapter 4

The Outcome Space

4.0 CHAPTER OVERVIEW AND KEY CONCEPTS

outcome space
well-defined categories
finite and exhaustive categories
ordered categories
context-specific categories
research-based categories
scoring scheme

This chapter concentrates on how to categorize observations and then score them to be indicators of the construct. It introduces the idea of an *outcome space*, defining it as a set of categories that are well defined, finite and exhaustive, ordered, context-specific, and research-based. Each of these characteristics is then defined and exemplified. This is then followed by a section on scoring the categories in an outcome space. The chapter concludes with a description of two widely applicable strategies for developing both an outcome space and a scoring strategy.

4.1 THE ATTRIBUTES OF AN OUTCOME SPACE

The term *outcome space* was introduced by Marton (1981) to describe a set of outcome categories developed from a detailed (phenomenographic) analysis (see Section 4.2) of students' responses to standardized open-ended items such as the LBC item in Fig. 1.2. In much of his writing, Marton described the development of a set of outcome categories as a process of *discovering* the qualitatively different ways in which students respond to a task. In this book, the lead of Masters and Wilson (1997) is followed, and the term *outcome space* is adopted and applied in a broader sense to any set of qualitatively described categories for recording and/or judging how respondents have responded to items. Several examples of outcome spaces have already been shown in earlier examples. The LBC scoring guide in Fig. 1.5 defines how to categorize the responses to the LBC items attached to the visualizing matter construct—this is a typical outcome space for an open-ended item. The outcome spaces for fixed-response items look different—they are simply the fixed responses—for example, the outcome space for an evaluation item in the SAQ is:

I did not think about how effective my study efforts were.

I thought about whether I had put in enough time.

I thought about whether I had put in enough effort.

I thought about whether I had studied the material that was most important.

Although these two types of outcome space are quite different, it is important to see that they are strongly connected—the best way to construct a fixed set of responses is to construct an equivalent open-ended outcome space first, then decide how to choose representative responses as the fixed responses. Of course many considerations must be borne in mind while making those choices.

Inherent in the idea of categorization is an understanding that the categories that define the outcome space are *qualitatively distinct*. In fact all measures are based, at some point, on qualitative distinctions. Even fixed-response formats such as multiple-choice test items and Likert-style survey questions rely on a qualitative understanding of what constitutes different levels of response (more or less correct, or more or less agreeable, as the case may be). Rasch (1977) pointed out that this principle goes far beyond measurement in the social sciences: "That science should require observations to be measurable quantities is a mistake of course; even in physics, observations may be qualitative—as in the last analysis they always are" (p. 68). Dahlgren (1984) described an outcome space as a "kind of analytic map":

> It is an *empirical* concept which is not the product of logical or deductive analysis, but instead results from intensive examination of empirical data. Equally important, the outcome space is content-specific: the set of descriptive categories arrived at has not been determined *a priori*, but depends on the specific content of the [item]. (p. 26)

The remainder of this section contains a description of the requirements for a sound and useful outcome space—the account mainly follows that in Masters and Wilson (1997). The characteristics of an outcome space are that the categories are well defined, finite and exhaustive, ordered, context-specific, and research-based.

4.1.1 Well-Defined Categories

The categories that make up the outcome space must be well defined, including not only (a) a general definition of what is being measured by that item (i.e., in the approach described in this book, a definition of the construct), but also (b) background material; (c) examples of items, item responses, and their categorization; as well as (d) a training procedure. The LBC example displays all except the last of these characteristics: Fig. 1.1 gives a brief definition of the construct visualizing matter as well as a description of different levels of response; Fig. 1.5 shows the set of categories into which the item responses are to be categorized; and Fig. 1.6 shows an exemplary response (in this case, at score level 2) to the item shown in Fig. 1.2 (Wilson et al., 2000). The article cited in the description (Claesgens, Scalise, Draney, Wilson, & Stacey, 2002) gives a background discussion to the construct map, including many references to relevant literature.

What is not yet part of the LBC agenda is a training program to achieve high inter-rater agreement and usefulness for the results. To achieve high levels of agreement, it is necessary to go beyond written materials; some sort of training is usually required. One such method, called *assessment moderation*, is described in Wilson and Sloane (2000). In the context of education, this method has been found to be particularly helpful with teachers, who can bring their professional experiences to help in the judgment process, but who also have found the process to enhance their professional development. In this technique, teachers choose examples of responses from their own students or others and circulate the responses beforehand to other members of the moderation group. All the members of the group categorize the responses using all the materials available to them and then come together to moderate those categorizations at the moderation meeting. The aim of the meeting is for the group to compare their categorizations, discuss them until they come to a consensus about the scores, and discuss the instructional implications of knowing what categories the students have been categorized into. This process can be repeated a number of times with different sets of responses to achieve higher levels of initial agreement and to track teachers' improvement over time. The resulting outcome space may be modified from the original by this process.

One way to check that there is sufficiently interpretable detail provided is to have different teams of judges use the materials to categorize a set of responses. The agreement between the two sets of judgments provides an index of how successful the definition of the outcome space has been (although, of course, standards of success may vary). Marton (1986) gave a useful distinction between developing an outcome space and using one. In comparing the work of the measurer to that of a botanist classifying species of plants, he noted that

> while there is no reason to expect that two persons working independently will construct the same taxonomy, the important question is whether a category can be found or recognized by others once it has been described.... It must be possible to reach a high degree of agreement concerning the presence or absence of categories if other researchers are to be able to use them. (Marton, 1986, p. 35)

4.1.2 Research-Based Categories

The construction of an outcome space should be part of the process of developing an item and, hence, should be informed by research aimed at establishing the construct to be measured, and identifying and understanding the variety of responses students give to that task.

In the domain of measuring achievement, a National Research Council (2001) committee recently concluded:

> A model of cognition and learning should serve as the cornerstone of the assessment design process. This model should be based on the best available understanding of how students represent knowledge and develop competence in the domain.... This model may be fine-grained and very elaborate or more coarsely grained, depending on the purpose of the assessment, but it should always be based on empirical studies of learners in a domain. Ideally, the model will also provide a developmental perspective, showing typical ways in which learners progress toward competence. (pp. 2–5)

Thus, in the achievement context, a research-based model of cognition and learning should be the foundation for the definition of the construct, and hence also for the design of the outcome space and the development of items. In other areas, similar advice pertains—in psychological scales, health questionnaires, and even marketing surveys—there should be a construct to tie all of the development efforts together. There is a range of formality and depth that one can expect of the research behind such research-based outcome spaces. For example, the LBC constructs are based on a close reading of the relevant literature (Claesgens, Scalise, Draney, Wilson, & Stacey, 2002). The research basis for the PF-10 is documented in Ware and Gandek (1998), although the construct is not explicitly established. The set of categories that make up the outcome space for each of the IEY tasks was developed from an analysis of the variety of responses students give to pilot versions of those assessments (Wilson, Roberts, Draney, Samson, & Sloane, 2000) using the SOLO approach to cognition (Biggs & Collis, 1982).The SAQ was based on previous research that established the construct published by members of the research team (Thomas & Rohwer, 1993), as was the scoring scheme in the Good Education Interview (Commons et al., 1983, 1995).

4.1.3 Context-Specific Categories

In the measurement of a construct, the outcome space must always be specific to that construct and the contexts in which it is to be used. Sometimes it is possible to confuse the context-specific nature of an outcome space and the generality of the scores derived from that. For example, a multiple-choice item will have distractors that are only meaningful (and scoreable) in the context of that item, but the scores of the item ("correct"/"incorrect" or "1"/"0" are interpretable more broadly). Even when categories are superficially the same from context to context, their use inevitably requires a re-interpretation in each new context. The set of categories for the LBC tasks, for example, was developed from an analysis of students' answers to the set of tasks used in the pilot year of the assessment development project. The general scoring guide used for the LBC visualizing matter construct is supplemented by a specific set of exemplars for each task, such as the example in Fig. 1.6.

4.1.4 Finite and Exhaustive Categories

The responses to an open-ended item that the measurer obtains generally are a sample from a large population of possible responses. Consider a single essay prompt—something like the classic "What did you do over the summer vacation?" Suppose that there is a restriction to the length of the essay of, say, five pages. Think of how many possible different essays could be written in response to that prompt. It is indeed a large number (although because there is only a finite number of words in English, there is in fact a finite upper limit that could be estimated). Multiply this by the number of different possible prompts (again large, but finite), and then again by all the different possible sorts of administrative conditions (it can be hard to say what the numerical limit is here, perhaps infinite), and you end up with an even bigger number—perhaps infinite. The role of the outcome space is to bring order and sense to this extremely large and probably unruly bunch of potential responses. One prime characteristic is that the outcome space should consist of only a finite number of categories. For example, the LBC scoring guide categorizes all matter item responses into 10 categories, as shown in Fig. 1.5: an irrelevant response, describing (three levels), representing (three levels), relating, predicting and explaining. The PF-10 (Fig. 2.4) outcome space is just three categories: *Yes, limited a lot, Yes, limited a little,* and *No, not limited at all.*

The outcome space, to be fully useful, must also be exhaustive: There must be a category for every possible response. In the LBC example, the categories "no opportunity" and "irrelevant or missing" are designed to cope with two common types of difficult-to-classify responses. First, there are responses that arise in cases where the administrative conditions were not sufficiently standard; second, there are responses that do not conform with the expected range, like "Harry luvs Sally," "tests suck," and so on. Although such responses should not be ignored because they sometimes contain information that can be interpreted in a larger context, and may even be quite important in that larger context, they do not inform the measurer about the respondent's location on the matter construct. In fixed-response item formats like the PF-10 scale, the finiteness and exhaustiveness are forced by the format. One common measurer mistake is making the descriptions of the categories too content-specific, and thus not exhaustive. They think of all the mistakes they can think of, or that fit their theory, and then make a category for each one, not realizing that respondents will come up with many more mistakes than they have ever dreamed of, including a bunch that have nothing to do with their particular theory.

4.1.5 Ordered Categories

For an outcome space to be useful in defining a construct that is to be mapped, the categories must be capable of being ordered in some way. Some categories must represent lower levels on the construct, and some must represent higher ones. In traditional fixed-response item formats like the multiple-choice test item and the true–false survey question, the responses are ordered into just two levels—in the case of true–false questions (obviously), into "true" and "false"; in the case of multiple-choice items, into the correct category for choosing the correct distractor, and into the false category for choosing one of the false distractors. In Likert-type survey questions, the order is implicit in the nature of the choices: The options *strongly agree*, *agree*, *disagree*, and *strongly disagree* give a four-level order for the responses. A scoring guide for an open-ended item needs to do the same thing—the scores shown in Fig. 1.5 for the LBC item give 10 ordered categories scored 0 to 5, respectively (including the "–" and "+" scores).

Depending on circumstances, it may or may not be useful to assign the category "X" to the lowest of these score levels or to an unordered missing data level. This ordering needs to be supported by both the theory behind the construct and empirical evidence—the theory behind the outcome space should be the same as that behind the construct. Empirical evidence can be used to support the ordering of an outcome space—and is an essential part of both pilot and field investigations of an instrument. The ordering of the categories does not need to be complete. An ordered partition (i.e., where several categories may have the same rank in the ordering) can still be used to provide useful information (Wilson & Adams, 1995).

4.2 RELATING THE OUTCOME SPACE
BACK TO THE CONSTRUCT MAP: SCORING

Most often the set of categories that comes directly out of an outcome space is not sufficient for measurement. One more step is needed—the categories must be related back to the responses side of the generating construct map. This can be seen as the process of providing numerical values for the ordered levels of the outcome space (i.e., scoring of the item-response categories), but the deeper meaning pertains to the relationship back to the construct map from chapter 1. In many cases, this process is seen as integral to the definition of the categories, and that is indeed a good thing because it means that the categorization and scoring work in concert with one another. Nevertheless, it is important to be able to distinguish the two processes, at least in theory because (a) the measurer must be able to justify each step in the process of developing the instrument, and (b) sometimes the possibility of having different scoring schemes is useful in understanding the construct.

In most circumstances, especially where the measurer is using an established item format, the question of what scoring procedure to use has been established by long-term practice. For example, with multiple-choice test items, it is standard to score the correct distractor as 1 and the incorrect ones with 0. This is almost universally the way that multiple-choice items are scored. Likert-style response questions in surveys and questionnaires are usually scored according to the number of response categories allowed—if there are four categories like *strongly agree*, *agree*, *disagree*, and *strongly disagree*, then these are scored as 0, 1, 2, and 3 respectively (or sometimes 1, 2, 3, and 4). With questions that have a negative orientation, the scoring is generally reversed to be 3, 2, 1, and 0.

With open-ended items, the outcome categories must be ordered into qualitatively distinct, ordinal categories, such as was done in the LBC example. Just as for Likert-style items, it makes sense to think of each of these ordinal levels as being scored by successive integers, just as they are in Fig. 1.5, where the successive ordered categories are scored thus:

explaining = 5,

predicting = 4,

relating = 3,

representing = 2,

describing = 1,

irrelevant response = 0.

This can be augmented where there are finer gradations available—one way to represent this is by using "+" and "–," as was done in the LBC example; another way is to increase the number of scores to incorporate the extra categories. The category of "no opportunity" is scored as "X" in Fig. 1.5. Under some circumstances—say, where the student was not administered the item because it was deemed too difficult on an a priori basis—it would make sense to score the "X" consistently with that logic as a 0. However, if the student were not administered the item for reasons unrelated to that student's measure on the construct—say, that he or she was ill that day—it would make sense to maintain the "X" and interpret it as indicating missing data.

Under some circumstances, it can be interesting, and even enlightening, to consider alternative ways of scoring outcome categories. For example, in the case of multiple-choice items, there are sometimes distractors that are found to be chosen by "better" examinees than some other distractors (in the sense that the examinees obtained higher scores on the test as a whole or on some other relevant indicator). When this difference is large enough and when there is a way to interpret those differences with respect to the construct definition, it may make sense to try scoring these distractors to reflect partial success. For example, consider the multiple-choice test item in Fig. 4.1: A standard scoring scheme would be A or C or D = 0; B = 1. Among these distractors, it would seem reasonable to think that it would be

Q. What is the capitol city of Belgium?
   A. Amsterdam
   B. Brussels
   C. Ghent
   D. Lille

FIG. 4.1 An example of a multiple-choice test item that would be a candidate for polytomous scoring.

possible to assign a response C to a higher score than A or D because Ghent is also in Belgium and the other two cities are not. Thus, an alternative hypothetical scoring scheme would be: A or D = 0, C = 1, B = 2. A similar analysis could be applied to any other outcome space where the score levels are meaningful.

4.3 GENERAL APPROACHES TO CONSTRUCTING AN OUTCOME SPACE

The construction of an outcome space depends heavily on the specific context, both theoretical and practical, in which the measurer is developing the instrument. It should begin with the definition of the construct, proceed to the definition of the descriptive components of the items design, and require the initial development of some example items. The following describes two general schema developed for this purpose: (a) phenomenography (Marton, 1981),which was mentioned previously, and the SOLO Taxonomy (Biggs & Collis, 1982). At the end of this section, a third method, applicable to noncognitive contexts and derived from the work of Guttman, is described.

4.3.1 Phenomenography[1]

Phenomenography is a method of constructing an outcome space for a cognitive task based on a detailed analysis of student responses. Phenomenographic analysis has its origins in the work of Marton (1981), who described it as "a research method for mapping the qualitatively different ways in which people experience, conceptual-

---

[1]This section is based on Masters and Wilson (1997).

ize, perceive, and understand various aspects of, and phenomena in, the world around them" (Marton, 1986, p. 31).

Phenomenographic analysis usually involves the presentation of an open-ended task, question, or problem designed to elicit information about an individual's understanding of a particular phenomenon. Most commonly, tasks are attempted in relatively unstructured interviews during which students are encouraged to explain their approach to the task or conception of the problem.

A significant finding of these studies is that students' responses invariably reflect a limited number of qualitatively different ways to think about a phenomenon, concept, or principle (Marton, 1988). An analysis of responses to the question in Fig. 4.2, for example, revealed just a few different ways to think about the relationship between light and seeing. The main result of phenomenographic analysis is a set of categories describing the qualitatively different kinds of responses students give.

The data analyzed in studies of this kind are often, but not always, transcripts of interviews. In the analysis of students' responses, an attempt is made to identify the key features of each student's response to the assigned task. A search is made for statements that are particularly revealing of a student's way of thinking about the phenomenon under discussion. These revealing statements, with details of the contexts in which they were made, are excerpted from the transcripts and assembled into a *pool of quotes* for the next step in the analysis.

The focus of the analysis then shifts to the pool of quotes. Students' statements are read and assembled into groups. Borderline

On a clear, dark night, a car is parked on a straight, flat road. The car's headlights are on and dipped. A pedestrian standing on the road sees the car's lights. The situation is illustrated in the figure below which is divided into four sections. In which of the sections is there light? Give reasons for your answer.

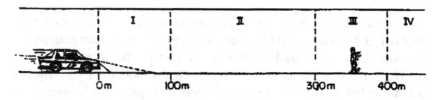

FIG. 4.2   An open-ended question in physics (from Marton, 1983).

statements are examined to clarify differences between the emerging groups. Of particular importance in this process is the study of contrasts.

> Bringing the quotes together develops the meaning of the category, and at the same time the evolving meaning of the category determines which quotes should be included and which should not. This means, of course, a tedious, time-consuming iterative procedure with repeated changes in the quotes brought together and in the exact meaning of each group of quotes. (Marton, 1988, p. 198)

The result of the analysis is a grouping of quotes reflecting different kinds of understandings. These groupings become the outcome categories, which are then described and illustrated using sampled student quotes. Outcome categories are "usually presented in terms of some hierarchy: There is a *best* conception, and sometimes the other conceptions can be ordered along an evaluative dimension" (Marton, 1988, p. 195). For Ramsden et al. (1993), it is the construction of hierarchically ordered, increasingly complex levels of understanding and the attempt to describe the logical relations among these levels that most clearly distinguishes phenomenography from other qualitative research methods.

We now consider an outcome space based on an investigation of students' understandings of the relationship between light and seeing (see Fig. 4.3). The concept of light as a physical entity that spreads in space and has an existence independent of its source and effects is an important notion in physics and is essential to understanding the relationship between light and seeing. Andersson and Kärrqvist (1981) found that few ninth-grade students in Swedish comprehensive schools understand these basic properties of light. They observed that authors of science textbooks take for granted an understanding of light and move rapidly to treatments and systems of lenses. Teachers similarly assume an understanding of the fundamental properties of light: "Teachers probably do not systematically teach this fundamental understanding, which is so much a part of a teacher's way of thinking that they neither think about how fundamental it is, nor recognize that it can be problematic for students" (Andersson & Kärrqvist, 1981, p. 82).

To investigate students' understandings of light and sight more closely, 558 students from the last four grades of the Swedish comprehensive school were given the question in Fig. 4.2, and follow-up interviews were conducted with 21 of these students (Marton, 1983). On the basis of students' written and verbal explanations, five different ways to think about light and sight were identified. These are summarized in the five categories in Fig. 4.3.

Reading from the bottom of Fig. 4.3 up, it can be seen that some students give responses to this task that demonstrate no understanding of the passage of light between the object and the eye: according to these students, we simply "see" (a). Other students describe the passage of "pictures" from objects to the eye; (b) the passage of "beams" from the eye to the object with the eyes directing and focusing these beams in much the same way as a flashlight directs a beam; (c) the passage of beams to the object and their reflection back to the eye; and (d) the reflection of light from objects to the eye (e).

Each of these responses suggests a qualitatively different understanding. The highest level of understanding is reflected in category (e), the lowest in category (a). Marton (1983) did not say whether he considered the five categories to constitute a hierarchy of five levels of understanding. His main purpose was to illustrate the process of

(e) The object reflects light and when the light reaches the eyes we see the object.

(d) There are beams going back and forth between the eyes and the object. The eyes send out beams which hit the object, return and tell the eyes about it.

(c) There are beams coming out from the eyes. When they hit the object we see (cf. Euclid's concept of "beam of sight").

(b) There is a picture going from the object to the eyes. When it reaches the eyes, we see (cf. the concept of "eidola" of the atomists in ancient Greece).

(a) The link between eyes and object is "taken for granted". It is not problematic: 'you can simply see'. The necessity of light may be pointed out and an explanation of what happens within the system of sight may be given.

FIG. 4.3   A phenomenographic outcome space.

constructing a set of outcome categories. Certainly, Categories (b), (c), and (d) reflect qualitatively different responses at one or more intermediate levels of understanding between Categories (a) and (e). No student in the sixth grade and only 11% of students in the ninth grade gave responses judged as Category (e).

4.3.2 The SOLO Taxonomy

The Structure of the Learning Outcome (SOLO) taxonomy is a general theoretical framework that may be used to construct an outcome space for a task related to cognition. The taxonomy, which is shown in Fig. 4.4, was developed by Biggs and Collis (1982) to provide a frame of reference for judging and classifying students' responses.

The SOLO taxonomy is based on Biggs and Collis' observation that attempts to allocate students to Piagetian stages and then use these allocations to predict students' responses to tasks invariably results in unexpected observations (i.e., inconsistent performances of individuals from task to task). The solution for Biggs and Collis (1982) is to shift the focus from a hierarchy of stages to a hierarchy of observable outcome categories: "The difficulty, from a practical point of view, can be resolved simply by shifting the label from the *student* to his *response* to a particular task" (p. 22). Thus, the SOLO levels "describe a particular performance at a particular time, and are not meant as labels to tag students" (p. 23).

The example detailed in Figs. 4.5 and 4.6 illustrates the construction of an outcome space by defining categories to match the levels of a general theoretical framework. In this example, five categories

An *extended abstract* response is one that not only includes all relevant pieces of information, but extends the response to integrate relevant pieces of information not in the stimulus.

A *relational* response integrates all relevant pieces of information from the stimulus.

A *multistructural* response is one that responds to several relevant pieces of information from the stimulus.

A *unistructural* response is one that responds to only one relevant piece of information from the stimulus.

A *pre-structural* response is one that consists only of irrelevant information.

FIG. 4.4 The SOLO taxonomy.

The Function of Stonehenge

Stonehenge is in the South of England, on the flat plain of Salisbury. There is a ring of very big stones which the picture shows. Some of the stones have fallen down and some have disappeared from the place. The people who lived in England in those days we call Bronze Age Men. Long before there were any towns, Stonehenge was a temple for worship and sacrifice. Some of the stones were brought from the nearby hills but others which we call Blue Stones, we think came from the mountains of Wales.

Question: Do you think Stonehenge might have been a fort and not a temple? Why do you think that?

FIG. 4.5   A SOLO task in the area of history (from Biggs & Collis, 1982).

corresponding to the five levels of the SOLO taxonomy—pre-structural, unistructural, multistructural, relational, and extended abstract—have been developed for a task requiring students to inter-pret historical data about Stonehenge (Biggs & Collis, 1982). The history task in Fig. 4.6 was constructed to assess students' abilities to develop plausible interpretations from incomplete data. Students ages 7½ to 15 years were given the passage in Fig. 4.6 and a picture of Stonehenge; they were asked to give in writing their thoughts about whether Stonehenge might have been a fort rather than a temple.

This example raises the interesting question of how useful theo-retical frameworks of this kind might be in general. Certainly, Biggs and Collis demonstrated the possibility of applying the SOLO taxon-omy to a wide variety of tasks and learning areas, and other research-ers have observed SOLO-like structures in empirical data. Dahlgren (1984), however, believed that "the great strength of the SOLO tax-onomy—its generality of application—is also its weakness. Differ-ences in outcome which are bound up with the specific content of a particular task may remain unaccounted for. In some of our analyses, structural differences in outcome similar to those represented in the SOLO taxonomy can be observed, and yet differences dependent on the specific content are repeatedly found." Nevertheless, the SOLO taxonomy has been used in many assessment contexts as a way to get started. An example of such an adaptation was given earlier in the

4 Extended Abstract

e.g., 'Stonehenge is one of the many monuments from the past about which there are a number of theories. It may have been a fort but the evidence suggests it was more likely to have been a temple. Archaeologists think that there were three different periods in its construction so it seems unlikely to have been a fort. The circular design and the blue stones from Wales make it seem reasonable that Stonehenge was built as a place of worship. It has been suggested that it was for the worship of the sun god because at a certain time of the year the sun shines along a path to the altar stone. There is a theory that its construction has astrological significance or that the outside ring of pits was used to record time. There are many explanations about Stonehenge but nobody really knows.'

This response reveals the student's ability to hold the result unclosed while he considers evidence from both points of view. The student has introduced information from outside the data and the structure of his response reveals his ability to reason deductively.

3 Relational

e.g., 'I think it would be a temple because it has a round formation with an altar at the top end. I think it was used for worship of the sun god. There was no roof on it so that the sun shines right into the temple. There is a lot of hard work and labor in it for a god and the fact that they brought the blue stone from Wales. Anyway, it's unlikely they'd build a fort in the middle of a plain.'

This is a more thoughtful response than the ones below; it incorporates most of the data, considers the alternatives, and interrelates the facts.

2 Multistructural

e.g., 'It might have been a fort because it looks like it would stand up to it. They used to build castles out of stones in those days. It looks like you could defend it too.'

'It is more likely that stonehenge was a temple because it looks like a kind of design all in circles and they have gone to a lot of trouble.'

These students have chosen an answer to the question (i.e., they have required a closed result) by considering a few features that stand out for them in the data, and have treated those features as independent and unrelated. They have not weighed the pros and cons of *each* alternative and come to balanced conclusion on the probabilities.

1 Unistructural

e.g., 'It looks more like a temple because they are all in circles.'

'It could have been a fort because some of those big stones have been pushed over.'

These students have focused on one aspect of the data and have used it to support their answer to the question.

0 Prestructural

e.g., 'A temple because people live in it.'

'It can't be a fort or a temple because those big stones have fallen over.'

The first response shows a lack of understanding of the material presented and of the implication of the question. The student is vaguely aware of 'temple', 'people', and 'living', and he uses these disconnected data from the story, picture, and questions to form his response. In the second response the pupil has focused on an irrelevant aspect of the picture.

FIG. 4.6   SOLO outcome space for the history task (from Biggs & Collis, 1982).

IEY Using Evidence construct map (Fig. 2.4), which began as a SOLO hierarchy, but was eventually changed to the structure shown. Similar adaptations were made for all of the IEY constructs, which were adapted from the SOLO structure based on the evidence from student responses to the items. The same was true for the SAQ items. This may be the greatest strength of the SOLO taxonomy—its usefulness as a starting place for the analysis of responses.

In subsequent work using the SOLO taxonomy, several other useful levels were developed. A problem in applying the taxonomy was found—the multistructural level tends to be quite a bit larger than the other levels—effectively, there are lots of ways to be partially correct. To improve the diagnostic uses of the levels, several intermediate levels within the multistructural one have been developed by the Berkeley Evaluation and Assessment Research (BEAR) Center, and hence the new generic outcome space is called the BEAR taxonomy. Fig. 4.7 gives the revised taxonomy.

4.3.3 Guttman Items

A general approach to the creation of outcome spaces in areas such as attitude and behavior surveys has been the Likert style of item. The most generic form of this is the provision of a stimulus statement (sometimes called a *stem*) and a set of standard options among which the respondent must choose. Possibly the most common set of options is *strongly agree*, *agree*, *disagree*, and *strongly disagree*,

---

An *extended abstract* response is one that not only includes all relevant pieces of information, but extends the response to integrate relevant pieces of information not in the stimulus.

A *relational* response integrates all relevant pieces of information from the stimulus.

A *semi-relational* response is one that integrates *some* (but not all) of the relevant pieces of information into a self-consistent whole.

A *multistructural* response is one that responds to several relevant pieces of information from the stimulus, and that relates them together. but that does not result in a self-consistent whole.

A *plural* response is one that responds to more than one relevant piece of information, but that does not succeed in relating them together.

A *unitary* response is one that responds to only one relevant piece of information from the stimulus.

A *pre-structural* response is one that consists only of irrelevant information.

FIG. 4.7   The BEAR taxonomy.

with sometimes a middle neutral option. The set of options may be adapted to match the context. For example, the PF-10 Health Outcomes survey uses this approach (see Section 2.2.1). Although this is a popular approach, largely I suspect because it is relatively easy to come up with many items when all that is needed is a new stem for each one, there is certain dissatisfaction with the way that the response options relate to the construct. The problem is that there is little to guide a respondent in judging the difference between, say, *strongly disagree* and *agree*. Indeed respondents may well have radically different ideas about these distinctions. This problem is greatly aggravated when the options offered are not even words, but numerals or letters such as "1," "2," "3," "4," and "5"—in this sort of array, the respondent does not even get a hint as to what it is that she is supposed to be making distinctions between.

An alternative is to build into each option set meaningful statements that give the respondent some context in which to make the desired distinctions. The aim here is to try and make the relationship between each item and the overall scale interpretable. This approach was formalized by Guttman (1944), who created his *scalogram* approach (also known as *Guttman scaling*):

> If a person endorses a more extreme statement, he should endorse all less extreme statements if the statements are to be considered a [Guttman] scale.... We shall call a set of items of common content a scale if a person with a higher rank than another person is just as high or higher on every item than the other person. (Guttman, 1950, p. 62)

Thus, for example, hypothesize four dichotomous attitude items that form a Guttman scale. If the order of Items 1, 2, 3, and 4 is in this case also the scale order, and the responses are *agree* and *disagree*, then only the responses in Table 4.1 are possible under the Guttman scale requirement. If all the responses are of this type, when they are scored (say, *agree* = 1, and *disagree* = 0), there is a one-to-one relationship between the scores and the set of item responses. A person with a score of 1 *must* have agreed with Item 1 and not the rest, and thus can be interpreted as being somewhere between Items 1 and 2 in her views. Similarly, a person who scored 3 must have agreed with the first three items and disagreed with the last, so can be interpreted as being somewhere between Item 3 and Item 4 in her views. Other responses to the item set, such as *disagree, disagree, agree, disagree*, would indicate that the items did not form a perfect Guttman scale.

TABLE 4.1
Responses to a Hypothetical Guttman Scale

	Item Number			
1	2	3	4	Score
Agree	Agree	Agree	Agree	4
Agree	Agree	Agree	Disagree	3
Agree	Agree	Disagree	Disagree	2
Agree	Disagree	Disagree	Disagree	1
Disagree	Disagree	Disagree	Disagree	0

Four items developed by Guttman using this approach are shown in Fig. 4.8. These items were used in a study of American soldiers returning from World War II—they have more than two categories, which makes them somewhat more complicated to interpret as Guttman items, but nevertheless they can still be thought of in the same way. Part of a scalogram is illustrated in Fig. 4.9, where only the first item is displayed. The eight types of responses to the four items that are consistent with the Guttman scalogram have been scored (ordinally) from 0 to 7 along the bottom of Fig. 4.9. The frequencies of each such response type (with all others deleted) is given in the next row. Then the region of the scalogram for the first item is shown in the top panel, with the percentages for each response category given. Thus, respondents who scored 3 overall would be expected to respond with Option (a) to Item 5, whereas those who scored 6 would be expected to choose Option (b).

Note how the diagram in Fig. 4.9 includes the same sorts of information that has been identified as belonging in a construct map, but it is "on its side." The top row of Fig. 4.9 is a set of item responses just like the right-hand side of a construct map. The two bottom rows are information about the respondents—the location of respondents with a particular score (on the bottom row), and the percentages of respondents at each location (in the middle row)—just like the left-hand side of a construct map.

One of the case studies (the one by Laik-Woon Teh) developed a set of Guttman items for the chosen topic, which was student satisfaction with the National Education (NE) classes in Singapore, which constitute a national civics program. Some example items from his

5   If you were offered a good job, what would you do?
(a) I would take the job
(b) I would turn it down if the government would help me to go to school
(c) I would turn it down and go back to school regardless

6   If you were offered some kind of job, but not a good one, what would you do?
(a) I would take the job
(b) I would turn it down if the government would help me to go to school
(c) I would turn it down and go back to school regardless

7   If you could get no job at all, what would you do?
(a) I would not go back to school
(b) If the government would aid me, I would go back to school
(c) I would go back to school even without government aid

8   If you could do what you like after the war is over, would you go back to school?
(a) Yes
(b) No

FIG. 4.8   Guttman's (1944) items.

Good Job	Would take a good job (70%)				If govt. aided would turn down good Job (20)%			Would turn down good job (10%)
Frequency	35%	15%	10%	10%	5%	5%	10%	10%
Score	0	1	2	3	4	5	6	7

FIG. 4.9   Scalogram of a Guttman item (adapted from Guttman, 1944).

instrument are shown in Fig. 4.10. Note how the options derive meaning from the options around them and from their order. For example, in Item 1, the option "I will attend the class" has its meaning focused by the surrounding two options. Laik also generated a set of Likert-style items. The Guttman items performed considerably better than the Likert items in one of the investigations pertaining to the interpretation of the construct (the correlation between the item order and expected order) and did about the same in terms of item consistency. Laik did report, however, that the Guttman items were harder to generate than the Likert items.

1. If the next class is a compulsory National Education (NE) class, what will you do?
    a. I will not attend the class.
    b. I will attend the class only if the topic sounds interesting.
    c. I will attend the class.
    d. I will attend the class with enthusiasm.

6. What do you usually do in an NE class?
    a. I do nothing in the class.
    b. I will participate in the class activity when called upon.
    c. I do enough just to get by.
    d. I do everything that is required by the teacher.
    e. I participate in all the class activities enthusiastically.

FIG. 4.10   Two sample Guttman items from the National Education student attitude survey.

4.4 RESOURCES

The development of an outcome space is a complex and demanding exercise. Probably the largest single collection of accounts of how it can be done is contained in the volume on phenomenography by Marton, Hounsell, and Entwistle (1984). The seminal reference on the SOLO taxonomy is Biggs and Collis (1982); extensive information on using the taxonomy in educational settings is given in Biggs and Moore (1993). The scoring of outcome spaces is an interesting topic. For studies of the effects of applying different scores to an outcome space, see Wright and Masters (1981) and Wilson (1992a, 1992b).

4.5 EXERCISES AND ACTIVITIES

(following on from the exercises and activities in chaps. 1–3)

1. For some of your items, carry out a phenomenographic study as described in Section 4.3.1.
2. After developing your outcome space, write it up as a scoring guide (as in Fig. 1.5), and incorporate this information into your construct map.
3. Carry out an Item Pilot Study as described in the appendix in chapter 5.

4. Try to think through the steps outlined earlier in the context of developing your instrument, and write down notes about your plans.
5. Share your plans and progress with others—discuss what you and they are succeeding on, and what problems have arisen.

APPENDIX : The Item Pilot Investigation

Before the Pilot Investigation

(a) Complete the item panel described in this appendix.
(b) Select a small group of respondents (say, 30–100) who represent the *range* of your target typical respondents. Note that it is not necessary for this group to be representative, but it is important that the full range on (especially) the construct and other important respondent demographics be included.
(c) Select subgroups for the think alouds and exit interviews.
(d) Try out the administration procedures for the pilot instrument to (i) familiarize the instrument administrator (probably yourself) with procedures, and (ii) iron out any bugs in the procedures. Practice the think aloud and exit interview procedures.
(e) Incorporate into your design opportunities to examine both validity and reliability (see chaps. 7 and 8). Use the "Research Report Structure" outlined next to help think about reporting on the pilot investigation.

The Pilot Investigation

(a) Administer the instrument just as you intend it to be used.
(b) For a subgroup, use a think aloud procedure and record their comments.
(c) Give all respondents an exit survey, asking them about their experience in taking the instrument and opinions about it.
(d) For another subgroup, administer an exit interview, asking them about each item in turn.

Follow-up to the Pilot Investigation

(a) Read and reflect on the records of the think alouds, exit interviews, and exit survey.

(b) Check with the instrument administrator to find out about any administration problems.

(c) Examine the item responses to look for any interesting patterns. Because there are just a few respondents, only gross patterns will be evident here, such as items that get no responses or responses of only one kind.

A Possible Structure for a Research Report on an Instrument

1. Background
   Motivation for the instrument
   Background/literature review
   Context in which the instrument is to be used

2. Design of instrument
   Definition of variable to be measured (chap. 2)
   Generating items for the instrument (chap. 3)
   Categorizing and scoring item responses (chap. 4)

3. Design of pilot data collection to calibrate/investigate instrument

4. Results from the pilot study
   Instrument calibration (chap. 5)
   Item and person fit (chap. 6)
   Reliability (chap. 7)
   Validity (chap. 8)

5. Discussion of results from data collection
   What was learned?
   What modifications would you make to the instrument?

Chapter 5

The Measurement Model

5.0 CHAPTER OVERVIEW AND KEY CONCEPTS

Rasch model
Wright map
item characteristic curve (ICC)
polytomous responses
standard error of measurement
respondent fit

The aim of this chapter is to describe a way to relate the scored outcomes from the items design and the outcome space back to the construct that was the original inspiration of the items (see Fig. 2.9)—the way we relate these is called the *measurement model*. There have been many measurement models proposed and used in the previous century. In this book, the main approach taken is to explain and use just one such model. Nevertheless, it is useful to know something of the historical background because that gives context to the basic ideas and terms used in measurement, and also because the general ideas that one first has when finding out about an area is influenced by the common general vocabulary possessed by professionals in that area. Hence, this first section of the chapter discusses two different approaches to measurement with the aim to motivate the use of the construct modeling approach. The account is didactic in nature, rather than an attempt to present an exhaustive historical analysis. While the researchers mentioned later were working, there were others working on similar ideas and similar approaches—choosing to not discuss them here is not intended to slight their contribution.

5.1 COMBINING THE TWO APPROACHES
TO MEASUREMENT MODELS

Suppose you ask a person who has no professional connection to the construction or use of instruments: "What is the relation between the thing we are measuring and the responses to the questions?" The answer is usually one of two types. One type of answer focuses on the items (e.g., in the context of the PF-10): "If a patient says that his or her vigorous activities are 'limited a lot,' that means he or she has less physical functioning," or "If someone can't walk one block, he or she is clearly in poor health." A second type of answer considers ways to combine the responses to the items: "If someone answers 'limited a lot' to most of the questions, then he or she has poor physical capabilities," or "If a person scores high on the test, he or she is in good physical health." Usually in this latter case, the idea of a score is the same as what people knew when they were in school, where the individual item scores are added to give a total (which might then be presented as a percentage instead, in which case the score is divided by the total to give a percentage). These two types of answers are indicative of two of the different approaches to measurement that novices express. The first approach focuses on the items and their relationship to the construct. The second approach focuses on the scores and their relationship to the construct. In the second approach, there is an understanding that there needs to be some sort of an aggregation across the items, but the means of aggregation is either left vague or assumed on the basis of historical precedent to be summation of item scores. The two different approaches have different histories. A brief sketch of each is given next.

Some elements of the history of the *item-focused approach* have already been described in foregoing chapters. The pioneering work of Binet and Simon, in which they grouped items into age-developmental levels, was described above in Section 2.2.5. The item-focused approach was made more formal by Guttman (1944, 1950) as described in the previous chapter (see Section 4.3.3). From this it should be clear that the item-focused approach has been the driving force behind the first three building blocks. However, the story does not end there. Although the logic of Guttman scale items makes for a straightforward relationship between the two sides of the construct map, as shown in Fig. 4.9, the use of Guttman scales has been found to be severely compromised by the problem of large numbers of response patterns that do not conform to the Guttman requirements. For example, here is what Kofsky (1966) had do say, drawing on extensive experience with using Guttman scale approach in the area of developmental psychology:

> ... the scalogram model may not be the most accurate picture of development, since it is based on the assumption that an individual can be placed on a continuum at a point that discriminates the *exact* [emphasis added] skills he has mastered from those he has never been able to perform.... A better way of describing individual growth sequences might employ probability statements about the likelihood of mastering one task once another has been or is in the process of being mastered. (pp. 202–203)

Thus, to successfully integrate the two aspects of the construct map, the issue of response patterns that are not strictly in the Guttman format must be addressed.

The intuitive foundation of the *instrument-focused* approach is what might be called *simple score theory*. There needs to be some sort of an aggregation of information across the items, but the means of aggregation is either left vague or assumed on the basis of historical precedent to be the summation of item scores. Simple score theory is more like a folk theory, but nevertheless exerts a powerful influence on intuitive interpretations.

The simple score theory approach was formalized by classical test theory (also known as *true score theory*). This approach was founded by the work of Edgeworth (1888, 1892) and Spearman (1904, 1907) in a series of papers at the beginning of the 20th century. They set out to explain an empirical phenomenon that had been observed: some sets of items seemed to give more consistent results than other sets of items. To do so, they borrowed a perspective from the fledgling statistical approach of the time and posited that an observed total score on the instrument, X, was composed of the sum of a "true score" T and an "error" E:

$$X = T + E, \tag{5.1}$$

where the true score would be the long-term average score that the respondent would get over many re-takings of the instrument (assuming the respondent could be "brainwashed" to forget all the preceding ones), and the "error" is not seen as something inherently wrong, but simply what is left over after taking out the true score—it is what is not modeled by T, hence in this approach it is the "noise." The explanation that Spearman found for the phenomenon was what is called the *reliability coefficient*—essentially the correlation between two forms of the instrument constructed to be equivalent (see chap. 7). The introduction of an error term allows for a quantification of inconsistency in observed scores, which is part of the solution to the problem with Guttman scales. The scores can also be *norm referenced*. That is, the relation between each score and the distribution on the scores can be established for a given population, allowing comparisons between individual measures in terms of their percentiles.[1] However, all this comes at a high price: The items have disappeared from the measurement model (see Eq. 5.1); there are no items present. Hence, without further elaboration of the true score theory approach, the efforts that have been expended on the first three building blocks might be in vain.

In summary, each of the approaches can be seen to have its virtues: Guttman scaling focuses attention on the meaningfulness of the results from the instrument (i.e., its validity), whereas classical test theory models the statistical nature of the scores and focuses attention on the consistency of the results from the instrument (i.e., its reliability). There has been a long history of attempts to reconcile these two approaches. One notable early approach is that of Thurstone (1925), who clearly saw the need to have a measurement model that combined the virtues of both and sketched out an early solution (see Fig. 5.1). In this figure, the curves show the cumulative empirical probability of success on each item for successive years of age. The ordering of these curves is essentially the ordering that Guttman was looking for, with chronological age

---

[1] The pth percentile (p between 0 and 100) is the score below which $p\%$ of the respondents fall.

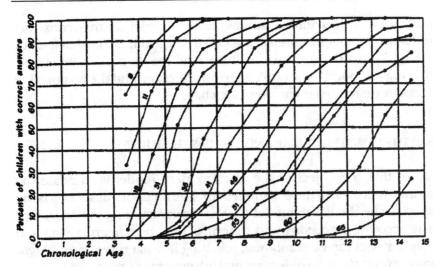

FIG. 5.1 Thurstone's graph of student success versus chronological age
(adapted from Thurstone, 1925).

standing in for score. The fact that they are curves rather than vertical lines corresponds to a probabilistic expression of the relationship between the score and success, which is an answer to Kofsky's
plea. Unfortunately, this early reconciliation remained an isolated,
inspired moment for many years. Thurstone (1928) also went beyond this to outline a further pair of requirements for a measurement model: "The scale must transcend the group measured. A
measuring instrument must not be seriously affected in its measuring function by the object of measurement" (p. 547).

The approach adopted in this volume (termed *construct modeling*) is indeed intended as a reconciliation of these two basic historical tendencies. Statistically and philosophically, it is founded on the
work of Rasch (1960), who first pointed out the important qualities
of the model that bears his name—the Rasch model (which is described in the next section). The usefulness of this model for measuring has been developed principally by Wright (1968, 1977) and
Fischer (see Fischer & Molenaar, 1995, for a thorough summary of
Fischer's contributions). Other researchers have developed similar
lines of research in what is usually termed *item-response theory*
(IRT), such as Lord (1952, 1980), Birnbaum (1968); (Bock & Jones,
1968; Samejima, 1969). The focus of this book is understanding the

purpose and mechanics of a measurement model; for that, construct modeling has been chosen as a good starting point. Note that it is not intended that the measurer will learn all that is needed by merely reading this book—the book is an introduction, and the responsible measurer needs to go further (see chap. 9).

5.2 THE CONSTRUCT MAP AND THE RASCH MODEL

Recall that the object of the measurement model is to relate the scored data back to the construct map. The focus of this section is the special role the Rasch model plays in understanding the construct. The account proceeds by considering how the construct map and Rasch model can be combined, resulting in what is termed a *Wright map*, and it then considers several advantages of doing so.

5.2.1 The Wright Map

The Rasch model differs from true score theory in several critical ways. First, it is expressed at the item level and the instrument level, not just the instrument level, as is true score theory. Second, it focuses attention on modeling the *probability* of the observed responses, rather than on modeling the responses, as does true score theory. That is, in Eq. 5.1, the observed score, X, was expressed in terms of T and E. In contrast, in the Rasch model, the form of the relationship is that the *probability* of the item response for item i, X_i, is modeled as a function of the respondent location θ (Greek "theta") and the item location δ_i (Greek "delta"). In achievement and ability applications, the respondent location is usually termed the respondent *ability*, and the item location is termed the item *difficulty*. In attitude applications, these terms are not appropriate, so terms such as *attitude towards something* and *item scale value* are sometimes used. To be neutral to areas of application, the terms used here are *respondent location* and *item location*—this is also helpful in reminding the reader that these parameters have certain graphical interpretations in terms of the construct map.

To make this more specific, suppose that the item has been scored dichotomously as "0" or "1" ("right"/"wrong," "agree"/"disagree," etc.)—that is, $X_i = 0$ or 1. The logic of the Rasch model is that the respondent has a certain amount of the construct, indicated by θ, and an item also has a certain amount, indicated by δ_i. The way the amounts work is in opposite directions—hence, the *difference* between them is what counts. We can consider three situations:

(a) when those amounts are the same, the probability of the response "1" is 0.5 (and hence the probability of "0" is the same, 0.5—see Fig. 5.2 panel [a]);
(b) when the respondent has more of the construct than the item has (i.e., $\theta > \delta_i$)—the probability of a 1 is greater than 0.5 (see Fig. 5.2, panel [b]); and
(c) when the item has more of the construct than the respondent has (i.e., $\theta < \delta_i$), then the probability of a "1" is less than 0.5 (see Fig. 5.2, panel [c]).

In the context of achievement testing, we would say that the ability of the respondent is (a) equal to, (b) greater than, or (c) less than the difficulty of the item. In the context of attitude measurement, we would say that (a) the respondent and the statement are equally positive, (b) the respondent is more positive than the item, and (c) the respondent is more negative than the item. Similar expressions would be appropriate in other contexts.

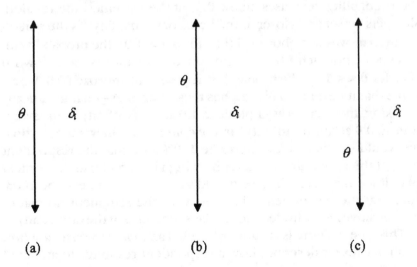

FIG. 5.2   Representation of three relationships between respondent location and the location of an item.

Note that these three situations—(a) $\theta = \delta_i$, (b) $\theta > \delta_i$, and (c) $\theta < \delta_i$ —correspond to the relationships (a) $\theta - \delta_i, = 0$, (b) $\theta - \delta_i, > 0$, and (c) $\theta - \delta_i, < 0$, respectively. This allows one to think of the relationship between the respondent and item locations as points on a line, where the *difference* between them is what matters. It is just one step beyond this to interpret that the distance between the person and item locations determines the probability. Putting this in the form of an equation, the probability of response $X_i = 1$ is:

$$\text{Probability } (X_i = 1 \mid \theta, \delta_i) = f(\theta - \delta_i), \qquad (5.2)$$

where f is a function defined in the next few paragraphs, and we have included θ and δ_i on the left-hand side to emphasize that the probability depends on both.

Graphically, we can picture the relationship between location and probability as in Fig. 5.3: The respondent locations, θ, are plotted on the vertical axis, and the probability of the response "1" is given on the horizontal axis. To make it concrete, it is assumed that the item location is $\delta_i = 1.0$. Thus, at $\theta = 1.0$, the person and item locations are the same, and the probability is 0.5 (check it). As the person location moves above 1.0 (i.e., for $\theta > 1.0$), the probability increases above 0.5; as the person location moves below 1.0 (i.e., for $\theta < 1.0$), the probability decreases below 0.5. At the extremes, the relationship gets closer and closer to the limits of probability: As the person location moves way above 1.0 (i.e., for $\theta >> 1.0$), the probability increases to approach 1.0; as the person location moves way below 1.0 (i.e., for $\theta << 1.0$), the probability decreases to approach 0.0. We assume that it never actually reaches these extremes—mathematically speaking, the curve is asymptotic to 1.0 at "plus infinity" and asymptotic to 0.0 at "minus infinity." In the context of achievement testing, we would say that we can never be 100% sure that the respondent will get the item right no matter how high her ability; in the context of attitude measurement, we would say that we can never be 100% sure that the respondent will agree with the statement no matter how positive her attitude (and similar statements at the other end).

This type of figure is customarily called an *item-response function* (IRF) because it describes how a respondent responds to an item.[2]

---

[2]Other common terms are "item characteristic curve" and "item response curve."

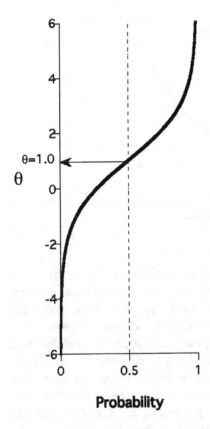

FIG. 5.3 Relationship between respondent location *(θ)* and probability of a response of "1" for an item with difficulty 1.0.

Those who have some experience in this area will perhaps be more familiar with an alternative orientation to the figure, with the respondent locations shown along the horizontal axis (see Fig. 5.4). The orientation used in Fig. 5.3 is used throughout this book, although it is not the most common, because it corresponds to the orientation of the construct map (as is seen later).

The complete equation for the Rasch model is:

$$\text{Probability } (X_i = 1 \mid \theta, \delta_i) = \frac{e^{(\theta - \delta_i)}}{1 + e^{(\theta - \delta_i)}} \qquad (5.3)$$

Notice that although the expression on the right-hand side is somewhat complex, it is indeed a function of $\theta - \delta_i$, as in Eq. 5.2. This makes it a rather simple model conceptually, and hence a good starting point for the measurement model. Remember, the probability of

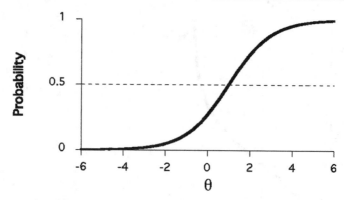

FIG. 5.4   Figure 5.3 reoriented so that respondent location is on the horizontal axis.

success in this model is seen as a function of the difference between the respondent parameter and the item parameter (i.e., the difference between the person location and the item location). This makes for a particularly intuitive interpretation on the construct map—the difference between a respondent's location and the item difficulty will govern the probability that the respondent will make that response. In particular, if the respondent is above the item difficulty (so that the difference is positive), they are more than 50% likely to make that response; if they are below the item difficulty (so that the difference is negative), they are less than 50% likely to make that response.

Equation 5.3, and the conceptualization of the relationship between the respondent and the item as a "distance," allows one to make the connection between the construct maps used in previous chapters and the equations of this chapter. What one would most like to do is stack the item-response functions for all the items in an instrument side by side on the figure. This has been done for an additional two items in Fig. 5.5. The full information one needs to relate respondent location to the item can be found in a figure like this. Yet, the problem is that, for an instrument of the usual length, even 10 or 20 items, the equivalent figure becomes cluttered with item-response functions and is uninterpretable. Thus, there is a practical problem of how to indicate where the item is on the construct map.

The solution used for this problem is to show on the construct map only critical points needed to interpret the item's location. For example, in Fig. 5.5, the items are shown on the construct map at only the point where the probability of choosing a response of "1" is 0.5 (i.e., that is the point in Fig. 5.3, labeled as "$\delta_i = 1.0$"). Hence, a response of "1" for Item i (indicated by "i.1" on the right-hand side under "Item Responses") is shown in Fig. 5.6 as being located at a value of 1.0 logit.[3] The interpretation of this symbol is for a respondent at the same point (e.g., the "X" at the same level on the left-hand side); for a respondent below that point (e.g., any of the "X"s lower down), the probability of responding "1" is less than 0.5; and for a respondent above that point, the probability is more than 0.5. The other two items are shown in the same manner—at 2.2 and 0.0 logits, respectively. By combining the construct map idea with the Rasch model, a particularly powerful means to interpret measure-

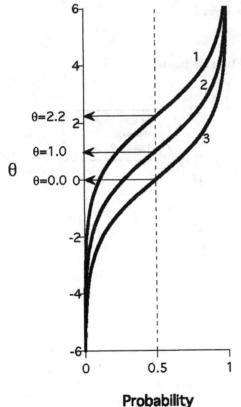

FIG. 5.5   Item-response functions for three items.

---

[3]A logit is the unit that is used along the construct (see later).

ments has been created. This combination is called a *Wright map* in this book in honor of its creator: Benjamin D. Wright of the University of Chicago.

There are a number of features of Fig. 5.6 that are worth pointing out. The central line is marked out in logits, which determine the relationship of the construct to the probability of response (calculations that are described in the next paragraph). On the left-hand side, under "Respondents," are noted the locations of several respondents, each indicated by an "X"—this is in the shape of an on-the-side histogram (with larger numbers of respondents, each "X" may indicate more than one respondent). Other symbols may be used to distinguish subgroups, and means and standard deviations of groups may also be added. The logits that mark out the units of the

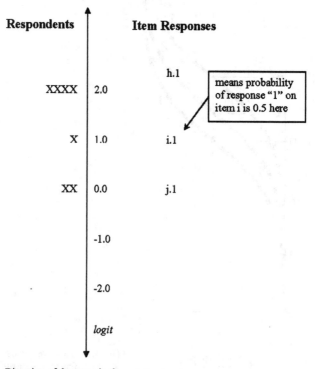

Direction of increase in the construct.

Respondents   **Item Responses**

h.1

XXXX | 2.0

means probability of response "1" on item i is 0.5 here

X | 1.0   i.1

XX | 0.0   j.1

-1.0

-2.0

logit

Direction of decrease in the construct.

FIG. 5.6   A generic Wright map. (Note: "X" = 1 respondent.)

construct are given immediately to the right of the central line. (Note that, in general, the respondents would not be located at round numbers of logits—they have been put there in this hypothetical example to make for simple calculations later.) On the right-hand side of the figure, under "Item Responses," are shown the locations of the items as described earlier. Note that the items may be denoted in other ways than that indicated here. For example, if it were clear that one were referring to the "1" responses, then the suffix ".1" could be left off, and the label could be changed to something more meaningful, such as an item name. Examples that use these different possibilities are shown in this and the following chapters.

Armed with Eq. 5.3, the relationship between the logits and the probability of response can be made clear. For the respondent at 1.0 logit in Fig. 5.3 or 5.6, the probability of responding "1" on Item i should be, as noted earlier, 0.5 (because the respondent and item are at the same location). To check this, note that

$$\Pr(X_i = 1 \mid 1.0, 1.0) = \frac{e^{(1.0-1.0)}}{1+e^{(1.0-1.0)}} , \qquad (5.4)$$

$$= \frac{e^{0.0}}{1+e^{0.0}}$$

$$= \frac{1}{1+1}$$

$$= 0.50 .$$

Compare this to the graph in Fig. 5.6—note where the IRF (item-response function) intersects a horizontal line drawn at $\theta=1.0$.

Similarly, for the respondents located at 2.0 logits, the probability of a "1" on Item I is greater than 0.5 because the respondents are higher than the item. To be exact, the probability is:

$$\Pr(X_i = 1 \mid 2.0, 1.0) = \frac{e^{(2.0-1.0)}}{1+e^{(2.0-1.0)}}$$

$$= \frac{e^{1.0}}{1+e^{1.0}}$$

$$= \frac{2.718}{1+2.718}$$

$$= 0.73 .^4$$

Again, compare this to the graph in Fig. 5.6—this time note where the IRF intersects $\theta=2.0$.

Similarly, for the respondents at 0.0 logits, the probability of a "1" is less than 0.5 because the respondent is lower than the item. To be exact, the probability is $e^{-1}/(1+e^{-1}) = 0.27$. In a similar fashion, the probabilities of the respondents at 0.0 of making the response "1" to Items b and k are 0.10 and 0.5, respectively (the items are at 2.2 and 0.0 logits). Again, compare this to the graph in Fig. 5.5—note where the IRF intersects $\theta = 0.0$. Thus, in the Wright map (vertical) distances relate to probability. It turns out that this is extremely helpful to the measurer in many ways—this is discussed in the following sections and in the next two chapters.

To get a feel for how the logits are related to probabilities, look at Table 5.1, which has been calculated using Eq. 5.3. To use the table, first find the difference between the respondent location and the item location, then look up the probability on the right-hand side, or, if the values in the table are not convenient, use your calculator to calculate the probability using your calculator and Eq. 5.3.

TABLE 5.1
Logit Differences and Probabilities for the Rasch Model

$\theta-\delta$	Probability
−4.0	0.02
−3.0	0.05
−2.0	0.12
−1.0	0.27
0.0	0.50
1.0	0.73
2.0	0.88
3.0	0.95
4.0	0.98

---

[4]Accurate to two decimal places. Note that e is approximately 2.718.

5.2.2 Modeling the Response Vector

In the previous section, the expression for the probability of a response of "1" was shown for the Rasch model. In this section, that is extended to show the probability for the entire set of responses by a person to the instrument, commonly called the *response vector*. Yet, in a dichotomous situation, a response vector might include responses of "0" as well as "1," so we also need to express that. This is relatively easy because the probabilities for X_i being 0 and 1 must sum to 1.0. Hence, Eq. 5.3 implies that

$$\text{Probability } (X_i = 0 \mid \theta, \delta_i) = 1 - \frac{e^{(\theta-\delta_i)}}{1+e^{(\theta-\delta_i)}} = \frac{1}{1+e^{(\theta-\delta_i)}} . \quad (5.5)$$

With this understood, the way the Rasch model works at the instrument level can be made concrete.

The way that the Rasch model (and other item-response models) calculates the probability of a response vector is to assume that, once you know the respondent's location and an item's parameters, each item's information contributes to the probability of the response vector as if the items were statistically independent—that is, you just calculate the product of the item probabilities. This is called the *conditional independence* assumption. As with many concepts, it becomes clearer when one considers noncases. A situation where one would suspect that conditional independence might not hold is where certain items share a common stimulus material. This is common in instruments such as reading comprehension tests, where a set of items asks comprehension questions about a single reading passage. If <u>all</u> the items share the same stimulus material, that does not raise the same issues.

As an example in the case where conditional independence does hold, suppose that the three items used in the previous section were used as an instrument, and that a respondent's response vector was (1, 1, 0) and the respondent is located at $\theta=0.0$. Then under the assumption of conditional independence, the probability of this particular response vector would be the product of the three probabilities:

$$\Pr(X = (1,1,0) \mid \theta, \delta_1, \delta_2, \delta_3) = \Pr(X_1 = 1 \mid \theta, \delta_1) \Pr(X_2 = 1 \mid \theta, \delta_2)$$
$$\Pr(X_3 = 0 \mid \theta, \delta_3) .$$

Substituting in Eqs. 5.3 and 5.5, that becomes

$$\frac{e^{(\theta-\delta_1)}}{1+e^{(\theta-\delta_1)}} \frac{e^{(\theta-\delta_2)}}{1+e^{(\theta-\delta_2)}} \frac{1}{1+e^{(\theta-\delta_3)}} = \frac{e^{(0-2.2)}}{1+e^{(0-2.2)}} \frac{e^{(0-1.0)}}{1+e^{(0-1.0)}} \frac{1}{1+e^{(0-0.0)}}$$

$$= \frac{e^{-2.2}}{1+e^{-2.2}} \frac{e^{-1.0}}{1+e^{-1.0}} \frac{1}{1+e^{0.0}}$$

$$= (0.10)(0.90)(0.50)$$

$$= 0.045 \,.$$

This is called *conditional independence* because all of the prior probabilities can only be calculated if you know the appropriate values of θ and δ_i. That is, they are conditional on knowing the relevant parameters—in this case θ and δ_i. This assumption means that the measurer believes that when calculating the probability of the whole response vector, the probability of each individual item response is simply multiplied by all the others.

Where do the locations come from? The equations given before for the Rasch model are not directly solvable for the θs and δs. Therefore, they are estimated using one of several statistical estimation approaches. The software used in the estimations for this book is called "GradeMap" (Wilson, Kennedy, & Draney, 2004). It was chosen because it can carry out all the statistical calculations needed in the following chapters. Discussion of estimation is beyond the scope of this book. Interested readers should consult the references noted at the end of Section 5.1. Another useful source on the Rasch model is Fischer and Molenaar (1995).

5.2.3 An Example: PF-10

The PF-10 scale has already been introduced and described in chapter 2. As described, there are three categories, but it can also make sense to consider just two, where the first two are collapsed together, and the third is left as it is—this makes the data dichotomous. Explicitly, this means coding the responses "Limited a lot" and "Limited a little" as "0" and recoding "Not limited at all" as "1." A large data set of patients' responses to these items has been collected (McHorney, Ware, Lu, & Sherbourne, 1994), and a Wright map calibrated from those data, dichotomized as described, is displayed in Fig. 5.7. Note that the full item set for the PF-10 is shown in Table 5.2, along with the abbreviations used in the figures and the text for each item.

Comparing this Wright map to the construct map in Fig. 2.3, we notice several ways in which they differ. First, this map is not just a sketch of the idea of the construct, but an empirical map based on respondents' self-reports. A histogram of the responses is shown on the left-hand side of the map. What is unusual for a histogram is that the spaces between the bars of the histogram are not evenly spaced. That is because the locations of the bars are the estimated locations of the respondents,[5] which can vary in a continuous way. Although each bar corresponds to a particular score, the estimation procedure can result in bars located at any point on the continuum—they are not located at integer values as are raw scores. The units for that continuous scale are shown on the far left-hand side in the column headed "Logits." The respondents range from those that are "less limited" at the top to those that are "more limited" at the bottom. Each location (i.e., each histogram bar) corresponds to a score on the instrument, ranging from 0 to 9.[6] (Note that no one scored 10 so it is not shown.) Tables showing the exact values of the respondent and item locations are included in Appendix 2.

The right-hand side of the map in Fig. 5.7 shows the *calibrated* item locations—these correspond to the δs in Eqs. 5.3, 5.5, and so on. Notice, for instance, that the respondents with a score of 6 are at almost the same point on the map as the "Bend" item. This means that they have approximately[7] a 0.50 probability of responding "Not limited at all" to that item. Noting that "SevStair" is about 1 logit above this location, we can see that for the respondents with a score of 6 the probability of getting the same response to that item is approximately .27. Noting that "WalkBlks" is about 1 logit below this location, we can say that the probability of respondents with a score of 6 giving the more positive response to that item is approximately .73.

---

[5]The estimation method used for the respondent locations is maximum likelihood (MLE).

[6]The general form of the MLE algorithm does not provide a finite estimate for a zero or perfect score, but the GradeMap program (Wilson, Kennedy, & Draney, 2004) uses a common correction to provide estimates for these scores (Wu, Adams, & Wilson, 1998).

[7]These probabilities are approximate because we are using the map to indicate logit differences—for a more exact probability, use the results in Appendix 2 to get exact values of θ and δ

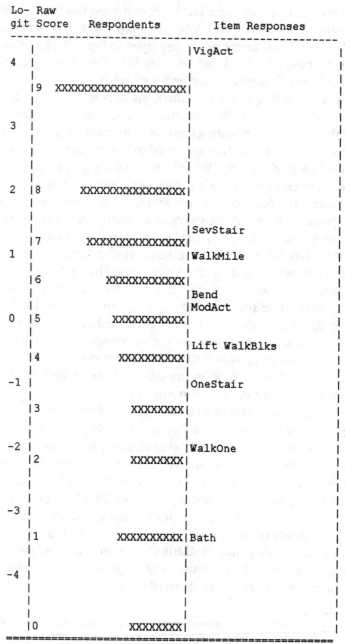

```
Lo-  Raw
git  Score   Respondents              Item Responses
     ----------------------------------------------------
       |                            |VigAct                    |
  4    |                            |                          |
       |                            |                          |
       |9   XXXXXXXXXXXXXXXXXXXXX|                          |
       |                            |                          |
  3    |                            |                          |
       |                            |                          |
       |                            |                          |
       |                            |                          |
       |                            |                          |
  2    |8    XXXXXXXXXXXXXXXX|                          |
       |                            |                          |
       |                            |                          |
       |                            |SevStair                  |
       |7    XXXXXXXXXXXXXX|                          |
  1    |                            |WalkMile                  |
       |                            |                          |
       |6        XXXXXXXXXXXX|                          |
       |                            |Bend                      |
       |                            |ModAct                    |
  0    |5        XXXXXXXXXXX|                          |
       |                            |                          |
       |                            |Lift WalkBlks             |
       |4        XXXXXXXXXXX|                          |
 -1    |                            |OneStair                  |
       |                            |                          |
       |3         XXXXXXXXX|                          |
       |                            |                          |
 -2    |                            |WalkOne                   |
       |2         XXXXXXXXX|                          |
       |                            |                          |
       |                            |                          |
       |                            |                          |
 -3    |                            |                          |
       |                            |                          |
       |1     XXXXXXXXXX|Bath                      |
       |                            |                          |
       |                            |                          |
 -4    |                            |                          |
       |                            |                          |
       |                            |                          |
       |                            |                          |
       |0        XXXXXXXXX|                          |
     ====================================================
```

Each case X is approx. 18 cases each row is 0.20 logits

FIG. 5.7   A Wright map for the dichotomized PF-10 instrument.

TABLE 5.2
Items in the PF-10

Item Number	Item Label	Item
1	VigAct	Vigorous activities, such as running, lifting heavy objects, or participating in strenuous sports
2	ModAct	Moderate activities, such as moving a table, pushing a vacuum cleaner, bowling, or playing golf
3	Lift	Lifting or carrying groceries
4	SevStair	Climbing several flights of stairs
5	OneStair	Climbing one flight of stairs
6	Bend	Bending, kneeling, or stooping
7	WalkMile	Walking more than a mile
8	WalkBlks	Walking several blocks
9	WalkOne	Walking one block
10	Bath	Bathing or dressing yourself

Using the benchmarks in Table 5.1, the reader can practice translating the logit differences implicit in Fig. 5.7 into probability statements about expectations for respondents giving a more positive response. Exact expressions can easily be worked out using a calculator to implement Eq. 5.3.

The relative locations of the items can also be examined to review how well the Wright map reflects the construct map. Comparing the right-hand side of Fig. 5.7 to the construct map in Fig. 2.3, we can see that "Vigorous activities" are indeed the most difficult, and that easy activities like "Bathing" and "Walk one block" are located at the easy end of the Wright map. More exact comparisons are limited by the inexactness of the specifications in the construct map. This sort of analysis, which is a variant of construct validity evidence, is given a more thorough examination in chapter 8, where a more exact prediction of the order in the construct map is used.

5.3 MORE THAN TWO SCORE CATEGORIES

The previous discussion and graphs provide some interesting ways to interpret output from the measurement model when the data are dichotomous (i.e., exactly two score categories). It is not immediately clear how to generalize this to the case where there is a greater number of score categories (called *polytomous* or, sometimes, *polychotomous* data), but indeed there is a fairly straightforward way to generalize the approach in the previous section. First, we need to develop a somewhat simpler way to express Eq. 5.3. Some algebra shows that the ratio of the expressions in Eqs. 5.3 and 5.5 is a relatively simple expression: $e^{\theta - \delta_i}$. Then taking the log of that, we get:

$$\log\left(\frac{\Pr(X_i = 1)}{\Pr(X_i = 0)}\right) = \theta - \delta_i \ . \tag{5.6}$$

Now the "odds" of an event is the proportion of times that event occurs compared to the times it does not occur, so this gives an expression for the log of the odds of a "1" (as opposed to a "0"). The log of the odds is often called the *logit*. Thus, Eq. 5.6 can be rewritten:

$$\text{logit}(1{:}0) = \theta - \delta_i \ . \tag{5.7}$$

This expression highlights the simple relationship between the person location and the item location in the Rasch model. One way to express it is to say that "the log-odds are linear in both the person location and item location."

This gives a way to generalize the dichotomous expression in Eq. 5.7 to a polytomous relationship. Consider the case of items with five ordered scores: 0, 1, 2, 3, and 4. Suppose that we assumed that the "logit" relationship in Eq. 5.7 held between scores 0 and 1:

$$\text{logit}(1{:}0) = \theta - \delta_{i1} \ , \tag{5.8}$$

where the item location δ_i has been relabeled δ_{i1}. Then just repeat this for the pair of scores 1 and 2:

$$\text{logit}(2{:}1) = \theta - \delta_{i2} \ . \tag{5.9}$$

Repeat this again for the subsequent pairs 2 and 3 and pairs 3 and 4:

$$\text{logit}(3{:}2) = \theta - \delta_{i3} \ , \tag{5.10}$$

$$\text{logit}(4{:}3) = \theta - \delta_{i4} \ . \tag{5.11}$$

It turns out that these four equations are sufficient to generalize the Rasch model to polytomous data in this case where there are five ordered response categories. The parameters δ_{ik} are known as "step parameters"—they govern the probability of making the "step" from score k-1 to score k (Wright & Masters, 1981). For example, look at Eq. 5.11: The relationship says that, if a respondent is in either score category 3 or 4, then the relative probability of being in score category 4 is a function of $\theta - \delta_{i4}$—that is, it is a function of the difference between the person location and the step parameter. In general, similar equations can be developed for any finite number of ordered categories, and there is one equation less than the number of categories (because, as earlier, they are related to the comparison between score categories k-1 and k, and there is one less step comparison than there are categories). See Wright and Masters (1981) for a lengthier discussion of these step parameters and their interpretation.

To develop a graphical expression for the polytomous case, we start with the item-response function for $X_i = 0$ in the dichotomous case. When considering the probabilities for each of the categories in turn, they can be called the *category response functions*. Remember that the probability of this category is (by definition) one minus the probability in Fig. 5.3. Thus, Fig. 5.8 results. In this figure, the probability of $X_i = 1$ is simply the distance to the right of the curve to 1.0. The equivalent for a polytomous item generalizes this, cutting up the probabilities into more than two segments.

Thus, an equivalent of Fig. 5.8 for a polytomous (in this case, five-category) item is shown in Fig. 5.9. Note that in this graph the curves are cumulative versions of the category response functions mentioned previously. That is, what is shown is the cumulative probability of being in successive score categories: first, being in score category 0, then being in score categories 0 and 1, then being in score categories 0, 1, and 2, and so on. Note that the probability of all responses except that of 0 is very small at the lower end of the scale; that the probability of 1, 2, and 3 first increases and then decreases as you get higher on the scale; and that the probability of 4 steadily increases, becoming close to 1.0 at the highest end of the scale. The first curve is just the probability of a score of 0, so the shape of the curve is similar to that in Fig. 5.8.

The critical points that are then mapped onto a Wright map for the polytomous item are the points where these cumulative curves intersect with the probability = .5 line, shown on Fig. 5.9. These

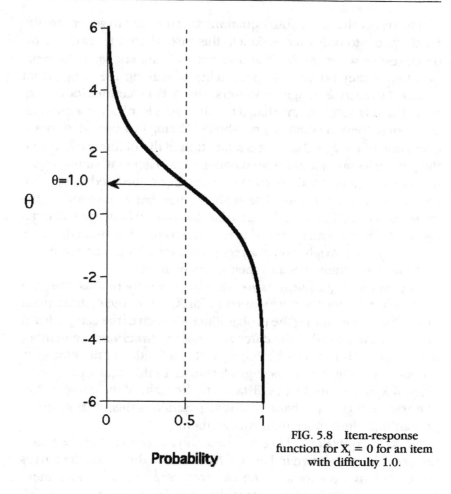

FIG. 5.8 Item-response function for $X_i = 0$ for an item with difficulty 1.0.

Probability

points are known as *Thurstone thresholds*: The kth Thurstone threshold can be interpreted as the point at which the probability of the scores below k is equal to the probability of the scores k and above (and that probability is .5). For example, the lowest intersection is the point at which Levels 1, 2, 3, and 4 together become more likely than Level 0; the next intersection up is the point at which Levels 2, 3, and 4 together become more likely than Levels 0 and 1; the next intersection up is the point at which Levels 3 and 4 together become more likely than Levels 0, 1, 2, and 3; and the highest intersection is the point at which Level 4 becomes more likely than all the rest together. Note that, except in the dichotomous

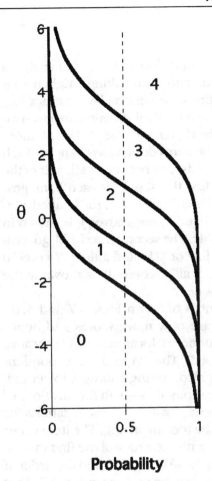

FIG. 5.9 The cumulative category response functions for a polytomous item.

case, the Thurstone thresholds in general are *not* the item parameters $\delta_{i1}, \ldots \delta_{i4}$ in Eqs. 5.8 to 5.11. Some people find this confusing, but we have chosen this way to represent the category response functions because it avoids some complexities that arise in interpreting the δ_{ik} parameters due to the fact that they are defined relative to pairs of categories. Note also that the probabilities given in Table 5.1 do not apply exactly for the Thurstone thresholds (because the curves in Fig. 5.9 do not have the same mathematical form as that in Fig. 5.3). Nevertheless, the relative locations of the Thurstone thresholds can be used for interpretive purposes (see examples in the next section).

5.3.1 The PF-10 Example Continued

The same data analyzed in a dichotomous format were also analyzed in their original trichotomous format, and the resulting Wright map is shown in Fig. 5.10. This map has the same general layout as for Fig. 5.7. In particular, note that the same types of information are given on the left-hand side of the map. Yet the right-hand side looks a bit more complicated—and that is because the items design has changed: Each item now has two Thurstone thresholds, one between each pair of the ordered response categories. The first threshold for each item, governing the transition from "Limited a lot" (scored 0) to "Limited a little" or "Not limited at all" (scored 1 and 2, respectively), is shown in the first column on the right-hand side. The second threshold, governing the transition from "Limited a lot" or "Limited a little" (scored 0 and 1, respectively) to "Not limited at all" (scored 0), is shown in the second column on the right-hand side.

There are a number of differences between Figs. 5.7 and 5.10. Looking from left to right, there are now more scores and hence more bars in the histogram of respondents' locations (this is because the categories are no longer collapsed). The shape of the respondent distribution is somewhat different also, having a longer, lower tail. The two columns have different locations also—with the locations of the thresholds for the first steps being lower than the locations for the second steps—this should not be too surprising. The item order differs within each of the columns, with the order of the first thresholds (0 vs. 1&2) being different than those in Fig. 5.7, and the order of the second thresholds (0&1 vs. 2) being the same as in Fig. 5.7. That the order of the thresholds is not consistent for the two sets of thresholds is not in itself a problem—it is an empirical result that the measurer may wish to try and explain or perhaps simply accept as a complexity of the way respondents react to specific items. However, if the threshold orders (for either threshold) were notably different from the predictions of the construct map, that would be a validity issue that the measurer should investigate (see chap. 8).

Just as for Fig. 5.7, one can gauge qualitative and approximate probability relationships between the items and persons using the map and Table 5.1. For example, we can see that even the lowest scoring respondents have about a 50% probability of responding above "Limited a lot" to Bath, but have a tiny probability of responding in the same way to SevStair (about 2%), and even less to VigAct.

```
Lo-  Raw                                    Item Responses
git  Score  Respondents          0 vs 1&2              0&1 vs 2
--------------------------------------------------------------
5  |                              |              VigAct         |
   |                              |                             |
   |                              |                             |
   |19 XXXXXXXXXXXXXXXXXXX|                             |
4  |                              |                             |
   |                              |                             |
   |                              |                             |
   |                              |                             |
   |18    XXXXXXXXXXXXXXX|                             |
3  |                              |                             |
   |                              |                             |
   |17    XXXXXXXXXXXXXX|                             |
   |                              |              SevStair        |
   |                              |                             |
2  |16       XXXXXXXXXXX|              WalkMile        |
   |                              |                             |
   |15      XXXXXXXXX|VigAct        Bend           |
   |                              |              ModAct         |
   |14       XXXXXXXXXX|                             |
1  |                              |                             |
   |13        XXXXXXXX|              Lift WalkBlks|
   |12         XXXXXX|                             |
   |                              |                             |
   |11         XXXXX|              OneStair        |
0  |                   |WalkMile                   |
   |10        XXXXX|SevStair                     |
   |9          XXXX|                             |
   |                   |              WalkOne        |
   |8          XXXX|WalkBlks                     |
-1 |7          XXXX|                             |
   |                   |ModAct                     |
   |6          XXXX|Bend                         |
   |                   |Lift                       |
   |5          XXXX|              Bath           |
-2 |                   |                             |
   |4           XXX|                             |
   |                   |OneStair WalkOne           |
   |3            XX|                             |
   |                   |                             |
-3 |                   |                             |
   |2            XX|                             |
   |                   |                             |
   |                   |                             |
   |                   |Bath                       |
-4 |1            XX|                             |
==============================================================
Each case X is approx. 17 cases each row is 0.2 logits
```

FIG. 5.10 A Wright map for the trichotomous PF-10.

Going to the other end, the highest scoring respondents have approximately a 95% probability of responding above "Limited a lot" to VigAct, but a less than 50% probability of responding "Not limited at all" to the same item. Looking at the relativities of item thresholds, we can see that responding above "Limited a lot" to VigAct is at about the same response level as "Not limited at all" for Bend.

5.4 RESOURCES

At several points in this chapter, the reader was referred to publications that give a more detailed and technical account of various measurement models, and these should be consulted by those who want a deeper account. Two that take a similar perspective to the one given here and are particularly readable are Wright and Stone (1979) and Wright and Masters (1981). The story here has deliberately taken a less comprehensive view, but has nevertheless attempted to offer some supports for intuitive understanding. See chapter 9 for guidelines on further reading.

5.5 EXERCISES AND ACTIVITIES

(following on from the exercises and activities in chaps. 1–4)

1. Read one of the classical works referred to in this chapter and summarize how it helped you understand one of the points made in the chapter (or any other point you think is interesting).
2. Check that the probabilities calculated in Section 5.2.1 are accurate using your own calculator.
3. Using the Wright map in Fig. 5.7, calculate approximate probabilities of a selected score level for five of the items.
4. Practice entering the data in Juan Sanchez's case study into a spreadsheet program such as Excel. Juan's data are given in his report in the Cases Archive (the filename is data.dbf). (If you already have your own data, use that as a second example.)
5. Check that you can carry out basic manipulations of the data, such as correcting values, finding frequencies, and getting the correlations between items.

6. Write out the data from the spreadsheet program as an ASCII or text file.
7. Follow the worked example in the GradeMap User's Guide included in the CD Appendix.
8. Use the data file you created as input for GradeMap—use Juan's control file as a model for your own (check what format your data are in). Check if you get the same output as Juan.
9. Think through the steps outlined earlier in the context of developing your instrument, and write down notes about your plans.
10. Share your plans and progress with others—discuss what you and they are succeeding on and what problems have arisen.

Part III

Quality Control Methods

Chapter 6

Choosing and Evaluating
a Measurement Model

6.0 CHAPTER OVERVIEW AND KEY CONCEPTS

requirements for a measurement model
standard errors
item fit
respondent fit

This chapter discusses two key issues that must be addressed when one is measuring. First, what measurement model should the measurer choose? Second, given that the choice has been made, how does the measurer decide whether the model is working for the specific data in hand?

6.1 REQUIREMENTS FOR THE MEASUREMENT MODEL

The requirements for a measurement model that is the last of these four building blocks are:

1. the measurement model must enable one to interpret the distance between respondent and response on the construct map, and
2. the measurement model must enable one to interpret distance between different responses on the construct map, and also the difference between different respondents (Wilson, 2004).

To make sense of these requirements, we must look carefully into what *distance* might mean in the context of a construct map. On a geographical map, distance and direction on the map have meaning on the surface of the earth: For example, 1 mile north might equal 1 inch "up" the map. On a construct map, distance between respondents and responses indicates the *probability* of making that response. To express this as an equation, assume that the respondent's position is represented by θ and the item response location is represented by δ. Then the probability of the response (Pr(response)) is given by some function (f) of the difference between the respondent and the response:

$$Pr(response) = f(\theta-\delta) . \tag{6.1}$$

That can be interpreted thus:
  (i)   zero distance between a person and a response would mean that that person is likely to endorse statement with a certain probability (say, 0.50),
  (ii) respondent *above* response would indicate a greater probability, and
  (iii) respondent *below* response would indicate a lesser probability.

Hence, we can say that the model must have qualitative features (i) to (iii). However, these qualitative features are not sufficient to preserve the idea of a "map." For that the requirements (ii) and (iii) would need to be more detailed, giving a specific metric form.

Consider now what that means for interpretations of the construct map. Figure 6.1 illustrates the situation for a person approximately in the middle of the construct. For this person, items that are at a similar level would be expected to elicit agreement at about a .50 probability, whereas items that are above would tend to result in a positive response with a lower probability and the opposite for those below. We can also consider distances between item responses. Figure 6.2 illustrates the distance between two item responses, considered by

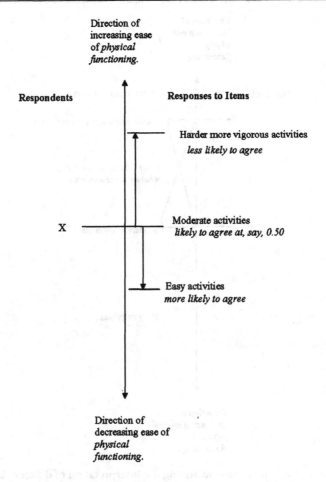

Direction of
increasing ease
of *physical*
functioning.

Respondents

Responses to Items

Harder more vigorous activities
less likely to agree

X

Moderate activities
likely to agree at, say, 0.50

Easy activities
more likely to agree

Direction of
decreasing ease of
physical
functioning.

FIG. 6.1   Construct map illustrating the interpretation of different item
locations with respect to a single person.

people at different points on the scale—say Persons X and Y. Note
that the distance between "harder and more vigorous activities" and
"moderate activities" is the same no matter whether you are looking
from the perspective of the people lower on the scale or those higher
on the scale. This is so obvious it seems odd to even point it out, but
it is fundamentally important to the sorts of interpretations one can
make using the map: The idea of location of an item response with
respect to the location of another item response only makes sense if

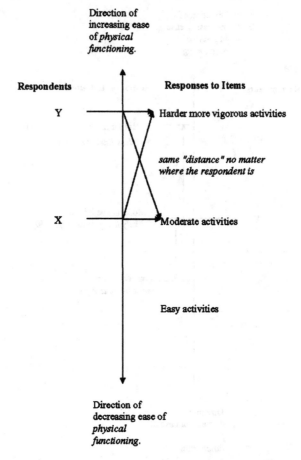

FIG. 6.2   Construct map illustrating the interpretation of different item
locations with respect to two persons.

that relative meaning is independent of the location of the respondent involved (i.e., the interpretation of relative locations needs to
be uniform no matter where the respondent is). Another way to put
this is that meaning is the same *no matter where you are on the map.*
This *invariance* requirement corresponds to the idea that an "inch
represents a mile" wherever you are on a geographical map.

One specific qualitative consequence of this is that the order (on the
map) of the item responses must remain the same for all respondents,
and the order of the respondents (on the map) must remain the same
for all item responses.[1] Yet recall Requirement 2—it is stronger: not just

---

[1]This is equivalent to double stochastic ordering—a concept used in nonparametric models.

order is preserved, but metric properties too. To achieve this in the framework of item-response modeling, the item model must have the property that the shape of the item-response function (IRF) is the same for all items, as in Fig. 6.3. In this figure, the items always have the same order in terms of probability no matter where the respondent is. For example, at θ=0.0, the lowest respondent location on the map, the items are ordered in difficulty (from highest to lowest) as Item 1, Item 2, and Item 3, respectively. Passing up to θ=1.0 and θ=2.2, one can see that the item difficulty order is identical. At the extremes, these differences become very small, eventually smaller than any given limit of accuracy. Nevertheless, in a mathematical sense, they are always ordered at any finite point on the scale. One can see that, for the relative item difficulty order to change, these IRFs would need to have different shapes.

Consider the context of item-response modeling, where the IRF is given a more complex relationship than that for the Rasch model—a so-called *two-parameter* logistic function:

$$\text{Probability }(X_i = 1 \mid \theta, \delta_i, \alpha_i) = \frac{e^{\alpha_i(\theta - \delta_i)}}{1 + e^{\alpha_i(\theta - \delta_i)}} \qquad (6.2)$$

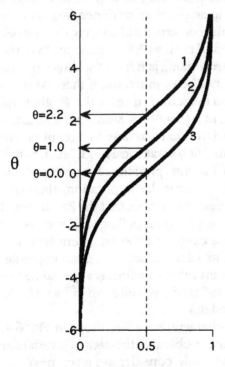

FIG. 6.3

where the θ and δ_i are as above, and the α_i is a slope parameter. In this context, having the same shape for all the IRFs implies that the α_i are all equal—that is, that we are requiring a Rasch model:

$$\text{Probability } (X_i = 1 \mid \theta, \delta_i) = \frac{e^{\theta-\delta_i}}{1 + e^{\theta-\delta_i}} . \qquad (6.3)$$

If the α_i are not equal, then the item responses will (at least somewhere) swap their order. This is illustrated in Fig. 6.4. In this figure, consider three persons at different locations on the scale: At −3.0, the order of the items is 1, 3, 2 (from hardest to easiest); at 0.0, the order of the items is 1, 2, 3; and at 4.0, the order of the items is 2, 1, 3.

The consequence of such differences in the shapes of the IRFs is that the invariant order implied by Requirements 1 and 2 are not present in the item set; hence, the interpretations afforded by the Wright map (and the construct map) are not available. Essentially, there is a different ordering of the items (i.e., a different scale) at different locations. This is impossible to represent in the way it was done earlier, so no figure is given that is the equivalent of 7.2 or 7.3. Going back to the analogy of a geographic map, having relative location of items depending on how high or low the respondent is on the construct is like saying that the distance between Berlin and Rome (and even which is to the north of the other) depends on whether you are looking at it from Washington or Istanbul. Geographic maps would not be of much use if there were inconsistencies of such an order, and the same is true for the Wright map. Hence, to summarize, the argument is that, if you want to use an interpretation tool like the Wright map, you have to have as a requirement for your items that they conform to ("fit") a statistical model such as that given in Eq. 6.3. Alternatively, if the interpretational strength of the Wright map were not wanted in a particular application, then one would not need to impose this requirement. Note that the Rasch model has other strong features, which many find compelling (e.g., see Fischer & Molenaar, 1995, for just such a case), but the argument here is a somewhat simpler one—the feature of the Rasch model being capitalized on is one that it shares with many others, including a special case of the probit model (the "equal slopes" case), as well as an infinity of others (including nonparametric models).

If an item set really did have characteristics like those in Fig. 6.4, what could one do to overcome the problem of this lack of invariance? Some possible strategies that one could consider are given next:

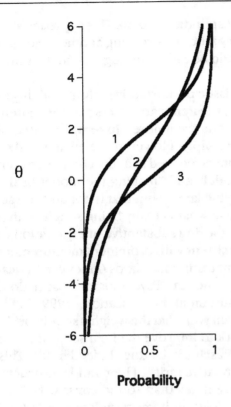

FIG. 6.4 Item-response functions—IRFs have different shapes.

(a) One could develop a more complex construct interpretation, where the underlying theory is (in fact predicts) that the order of the items should change for people at different points of the construct. This is a quite uncommon approach mainly because it involves making interpretations that are quite complex—more complex than are usually entertained in psychometric contexts. Some examples are: (i) Yen's (1985) interpretation of differences in slopes as evidence of "increasing cognitive complexity," and (ii) Wilson's extension of Rasch modeling to incorporate elements of Piagetian stages (the "saltus" model; Mislevy & Wilson, 1996; Wilson, 1989; Wilson & Draney, 1997). This could be called "make your construct more complex."

(b) One could pretend this issue does not matter and find ways to achieve something that looks the same. An example of this is given by the usage of the "Response Probability 80" (RP-80) convention (e.g., Kolstad, Cohen, Baldi, Chan, deFur, & Angeles, 1998). Under this convention, one uses the locations at which a person has a probability of responding of 0.80. This approach simply ignores the inconsistency with the ordering at other criterion levels of probability. This could be called "hiding behind the statistical complexity."

(c) One could ignore the issue of substantive interpretability of the item parameters. That is, the item parameters and their attendant probability interpretations are ignored in terms of internal construct validity—they are simply allowed to be whatever they turn out to be. This is sometimes referred to as the choice between "making the data fit the model" and "making the model fit the data" (with Option [c] being the latter), but that is not quite an accurate representation because what is really being sought is that the items fit the construct. Ignoring substantive interpretation of the item parameters is inconsistent with prominent measurement theories and also with current testing standards (American Educational Research Association, American Psychological Association, National Council for Measurement in Education, 1999). This could be called "let the data tell you what the weights should be."

(d) Finally, one could work to improve the item set so that the IRFs do not cross (e.g., the Rasch model does indeed hold). This makes sense in terms of the relative rarity of items and constructs; after all, there are many more items than sound constructs. This would be carried out by (i) deleting items with low slopes (i.e., those with low point biserial correlation coefficients), and/or (ii) adding new items that can be tested for reasonable slopes. This could be called "make the item set fit the construct."

Given that one is working in a "construct map" framework, (d) is the only viable alternative.

Thus, the consequences for measurement model are that the estimation of parameters of best fit needs to be done under the set of constraints implicit in Eq. 6.3. It does not matter that you might get better fit by estimating separate α_is—those models would not be *admissible* as part of the family of models that affords a construct map interpretation. This sort of position is not at all inconsistent with good statistical modeling practice. Consider the following:

> A criterion for a good model is one which "explains" a large proportion of this variability.... In practice this has to be balanced against other criteria such as simplicity. Occam's Razor suggests that a parsimonious model which describes the data adequately may be prefera-

ble to a complicated one which leaves little of the variability "unexplained." (Dobson, 1983, p. 8)

In fact the first strategy described by Dobson is really only a partial strategy—one must *always* consider the need for parsimony, as well as the need to base a statistical model on the interpretational context, which determines that some models are admissible and others are not.

Of course in carrying out Strategy (d), it is important that the constraint of equal α_i be reasonably well reflected in the data. That is why we need to test that particular fit aspect using techniques that investigate item slope, such as the "fit" statistics developed by Wright and his colleagues (e.g., Wright & Masters, 1981; Wright & Stone, 1979; also see the next section). These techniques pinpoint problem items, and can thus be helpful in diagnosing the causes of these problems, thus making it easier to come up with replacement items that do not have the same problems.

In review, the question of which measurement model to choose has been recast as a question of what are the a priori interpretational constraints that must be imposed on the model to have it make sense in the way that you want it to. This issue has been debated in the mainstream statistics literature. For example, consider what Gershenfeld had to say in 1998: "… the two central tasks are always choosing the functional form of the model and using the data to determine the adjustable parameters of the model" (p. 113). What we have concentrated on in this chapter is the former—the functional form of the model. Gershenfeld continued:

> Decreasing one kind of error is likely to increase the other kind. This is called a *bias/variance tradeoff*—if you want less bias in the estimate of a model parameter, it usually costs you some variance. A more flexible model that can better represent the data may also more easily be led astray by noise in the data. (Gershenfeld, 1998, p. 113)

Thus, the question becomes, should one make the model with constrained scores fit the data, or should one make the model with unconstrained scores fit the data? In other words, should you make the items fit the construct or the construct fit the items? Following the prior discussion, if the measurer wants to preserve the meaningfulness of the distance in a construct map, the measurer has no option but to seek item sets that fit the constrained model. In practice, within the item-response modeling area, this becomes a strategy of finding ways to use the Rasch family of models to deal with the many complexities of measurement situations. In theory, nonparametric models may also be used, but there are limits to what you can achieve with those models.

6.2 MEASURING

The purpose of the Wright map is to help interpret the locations of the respondents and the item thresholds on the construct. Yet the purpose of the instrument (usually) is to *measure* the respondents. On the map, each respondent can be located at a particular point on the logit scale—these are referred to in this book as the respondent *measures*. In Fig. 6.5, for example, respondents who scored 1 are located at −4.40 logits, whereas those who scored 19 are located at 4.78 logits. As mentioned earlier, these logits are often translated into different units before they are communicated to consumers. Any linear transformation preserves the probability interpretation of the logits given before. Some consumers prefer not to have to deal with negative numbers, and some do not like decimal fractions. Hence, a common translation is to make the new mean 500 and the new standard deviation 100—for most instruments, that keeps all numbers positive and eliminates the need for decimals.[2] All that is needed is a modified version of Table 5.1 that uses the desired units rather than logits.

6.2.1 Interpretations and Errors

The use of the item threshold locations to help with the *interpretation* of the measures has been discussed and illustrated earlier. This framework for making the location estimates meaningful is one of the most important features of the construct modeling approach to measurement—in fact one might even say that it is the purpose of a construct modeling approach. Further features of the item calibration and the person measures are described in the following chapters (chaps. 7 and 8 on reliability and validity); several of these can also be used to interpret the meaning of respondents' locations. For further exemplary maps, see the Cases Archive.

Recall that each location is an estimate. That means that it is subject to a degree of uncertainty. This uncertainty is usually characterized using the standard error of the location—the so-called

---

[2]For an interesting exception, see Dawson (1998).

```
Lo-  Raw    Confidence            Item Responses
git  Score  Interval          0 vs 1&2            0&1 vs 2
------------------------------------------------------------------
 5  |                        |                    VigAct       |
    |                        |                                 |
    |                        |                                 |
    | 19                     |                                 |
    |                        |                                 |
 4  |                        |                                 |
    |                        |                                 |
    |                        |                                 |
    |                        |                                 |
    | 18                     |                                 |
 3  |                        |                                 |
    |                        |                                 |
    | 17                     |                                 |
    |                        |                    SevStair     |
    |                        |                                 |
 2  | 16                   2 |                    WalkMile     |
    |                      2 |                                 |
    | 15                   2 | VigAct             Bend         |
    |                      1 |                    ModAct       |
    | 14                   1 |                                 |
 1  |                      1 |                                 |
    | 13                   X |                    Lift WalkBlks|
    | 12                   1 |                                 |
    |                      1 |                                 |
    | 11                   1 |                    OneStair     |
 0  |                      2 | WalkMile                        |
    | 10                   2 | SevStair                        |
    | 9                    2 |                                 |
    |                        |                    WalkOne      |
    | 8                      | WalkBlks                        |
-1  | 7                      |                                 |
    |                        | ModAct                          |
    | 6                      | Bend                            |
    |                        | Lift                            |
    | 5                      |                    Bath         |
-2  |                        |                                 |
    | 4                      |                                 |
    |                        | OneStair WalkOne                |
    | 3                      |                                 |
-3  |                        |                                 |
    | 2                      |                                 |
    |                        |                                 |
    |                        |                                 |
    |                        | Bath                            |
-4  | 1                      |                                 |
==================================================================
Each case X is approx. 17 cases each row is 0.2 logits
```

FIG. 6.5   A Wright map for the trichotomous PF-10 instrument, showing 67% and 95% confidence intervals for a respondent with a score of 13.

standard error of measurement.[3] This quantity tells the measurer how accurate each estimate is. For example, if a respondent scored 13 on the PF-10, his or her location is .87 logits, and the standard error of the respondent's location is .59. This is usually interpreted by saying that the measurer is uncertain about the exact location of the respondent, but that it is centered approximately on .87 logits and distributed around there with an approximately normal or Gaussian distribution with standard deviation of .59. Hence, in this case, the measurer can say that his or her (approximate) 67% confidence interval is .87±.59 (.28, 1.46). Alternatively, the 95% confidence interval is .87±1.96*.59 (−.29, 2.03).

See Fig. 6.5 for an illustration of this—the 67% confidence interval is indicated by the "1"s around the "X," and the 95% confidence interval is indicated by the "2"s. This second range looks quite wide—it is 2.36 logits, which shows that, although the respondent scored 13 on the instrument, the range of their true locations might be anywhere from the equivalent logits for about a score of 9 to about 16. Alternatively, it might be interpreted as ranging from a bit above the location of the second threshold for WalkOne to approximately the location of the second threshold for WalkMile. Although this is indeed quite wide, it is still an improvement on no data at all about the respondent. To see this, assume that a person without an observed score must fall somewhere in the range from the minimum to maximum score—the full range of the respondent locations is 8.61 logits, so the 95% confidence interval for a person scoring at 13 is about 27% of that range. Hence, one could say, with a 95% confidence, that the measurer is better off by a factor of 4 than if he or she had had no data on the respondent (i.e., compared to knowing only that it was reasonable to use the instrument for this person). Of course this may be an underestimate because the measurer may not have reasonably known that the respondent could reasonably be expected to fall within the active range of the instrument. Quality control indexes for the instrument, based on the ideas introduced in this paragraph, are given in much more scope and detail in chapter 7—Reliability.

Similarly, the item locations also have a standard error. In typical measurement situations, where there are more respondents than

---

[3]The formula for the standard error of measurement, as implemented in GradeMap, is given in Adams, Wilson, and Wang, (1997).

items, the item standard errors are quite a lot smaller than the respondent standard errors. For example, the standard error of the first threshold of VigAct is 0.04. In many applications, the item standard errors are small enough to ignore when interpreting the respondent locations. However, it is important to keep in mind that they are estimates subject to error, just as are the respondent location estimates. One situation that requires use of the item standard error is the calculation of item fit statistics as in the next section.

6.2.2 Item Fit

There are several sorts of technical expectations that are built into the analysis of the instrument data using a Rasch model, and they need to be checked to ensure that the estimates being used are indeed appropriate ones for their purpose. Note that in formal terms, the measurer should check this before checking the match to content in the previous subsection. During formative iterations, however, this may be relaxed because approximations are still useful for the purposes of improving the instrument. Nevertheless, it is important to check that technical requirements are being met, and the earlier this is done during the developmental iterations, the better.

The gathering of evidence that the mathematical models being used are appropriate is generally termed the investigation of *fit*; here it is discussed with respect to items, whereas in Section 6.2.3 it is discussed with respect to respondents. There is more than one approach to investigating fit—each approach tends to emphasize one aspect of the model over the other. In this section, following the discussion in Section 6.1, the emphasis is on consideration of how well the shapes of the empirical item characteristic curves are captured by the curves generated by the estimated item parameters. Most fit investigations begin by examining the residuals—the difference between the observed score and the expected score for a particular person and item:

$$Y_{in} = X_{in} - E_{in} \qquad (6.4)$$

where Y_{in}, X_{in}, and E_{in} are the residual, observed score, and expected score for person n responding to item i, respectively. The expected score is given by:

$$E_{in} = \sum_{k=1}^{K_i} k \Pr(X_{in} = k \mid \theta, \delta) \qquad (6.5)$$

where K_i is the number of response categories for the item, and δ is a vector of the parameters for Item i. Although we do not expect every response of a respondent to an item to have a small residual, we do expect that the distribution of these residuals across the instrument will be well behaved. Thus, fit indexes usually consist of various ways of looking at the distribution of the residuals, their means and variances, and so on. For example, one way to detect differences from what we expect is to compare how much the actual residuals compared to how much we would expect them to vary if the data fit the model. This is just what we do to calculate the so-called *mean square fit statistic* (Wright & Masters, 1981). First, note that under the estimated model, the expected squared residual for Item i is:

$$W_{in} = \sum_{k=0}^{K_i} (k - E_{in})^2 \Pr(X_{in} = k \mid \theta, \delta) . \qquad (6.6)$$

Then the average of these over all respondents is:

$$\sum_{n=1}^{N} W_{in} / N .$$

This can be compared to the mean of the squares of the observed residuals:

$$\sum_{n=1}^{N} Y_{in}^2 / N.$$

Then, the mean square fit statistic results by taking the ratio of these two variances (i.e., the Ns cancel):

$$MS_i = \sum_{n=1}^{N} Y_{in}^2 \Big/ \sum_{n=1}^{N} W_{in} \qquad (6.7)$$

Note that when the observed residuals are varying about as much as we expect, these two statistics should be about the same; hence, their ratio—the mean square—should be about 1. When mean square values are greater than 1.0, the observed variance is greater than the expected, and that can be interpreted as implying that the slope (i.e., α_i) indicated by the data is flatter than expected. When mean square values are less than 1.0, the observed variance is less than the expected, and that can be interpreted as saying that the slope indicated by the data is steeper than expected. In considering the interpretation of these results, it is important to see that items with this first characteristic (i.e., mean square greater than 1) are those that contribute less toward the overall estimation of the latent variable, and hence are the ones that are most problematic in general.

There are several ways to create fit indexes like this—the one shown previously is often termed the *weighted* mean square (or sometimes the *infit* mean square). An alternative is the *unweighted* mean square (sometimes called the *outfit* mean square), which is calculated in a similar way except that the effect of respondents further from the item are more strongly represented.

As an effect size, there is no absolute limit to what is a good weighted mean square value, but previous researchers have indicated that .75 (=3/4) is a reasonable lower bound and 1.33 (=4/3) is a reasonable upper bound (Adams & Khoo, 1996). A second fit index, the *weighted t*, uses a transformation that attempts to make the weighted mean square into a standard normal distribution (Wright & Masters, 1981), and it is sometimes used to test the statistical significance of the mean square (Wright & Masters, 1981). Yet, with large sample sizes, one can expect this statistic to show significant values for many items, hence a safer strategy is to consider as problematic only those items that show as misfitting on both the infit mean square and the *t* statistics. The GradeMap software distributed with this book supplies a version of both the weighted and unweighted values for both the mean square and *t* statistics. This version was developed for the particular estimation approach used by GradeMap (Wu, 1997; Wu, Adams, & Wilson, 1998) called the Marginal Maximum Likelihood (MML) estimation method. The GradeMap software carries out a further manipulation of the fit results and provides these statistics for both the average item location and the relative step parameters for each item. Note that the average item location is given by the mean (over the categories) of the item step parameters, and the relative step parameters are then the deviations of the step parameters around this mean value.

With this background, look at Fig. 6.6, which shows the weighted mean square for the average item locations for the PF-10 data. The weighted mean square indicates that all of the items are fitting within reasonable bounds. Note that quite a few of the weighted t statistics for these average location parameters are significant at the $\alpha = 0.05$ level, but that is not sufficient. We would be interested in items where both the mean square and the t indicate problems. A similar observation is true for the relative step parameters (see Appendix 2). Thus, the overall finding is that the PF-10 data fit the Partial Credit model reasonably well.

If the measurer finds an item that exhibits poor item fit, the next step is to decide what to do about it. One way to picture misfit is, conditional on respondent location, to compare the expected proportion (based on the estimated item parameters) that chose each option with the actual proportion that did. A picture of this comparison is shown in Fig. 6.7. In this figure, the relatively worst-fitting item (Item 1—top panel) and a relatively good fitting item (Item 8—bottom panel) are shown. Note that this figure is produced not by using GradeMap, but another piece of software called ConQuest (Wu, Adams, & Wilson, 1998)—that is why it is in the more traditional horizontal orientation.[4] The continuous line shows the expected cumulative probabilities (the IRFs), and the dots show observed cumulative proportions that responded with each option. Of course where the dots lie along the line, the fit is good: As they depart from the line, the fit typically gets somewhat worse. The bottom half of the figure shows Item 8, and is thus an illustration of a well-fitting item (see Fig. 6.6, which shows that the weighted mean square for this item is near to a perfect 1.0). Note that it fits very well, although not

```
Weighted Mean square
=================================================================
         0.58 0.67 0.75 0.83 0.92 1.00 1.08 1.17 1.25 1.33 1.42 1.50
-------------+----+----+----+----+----+----+----+----+----+----+
VigAct            .                   |                   *  .
ModAct            .              *     |                      .
Lift              .               *    |                      .
SevStair          .                   |         *            .
OneStair          .         *         |                      .
Bend              .                   |    *                 .
WalkMile          .                   |            *         .
WalkBlks          .                *  |                      .
WalkOne           .     *             |                      .
Bath              .                *  |                      .
=================================================================
```

FIG. 6.6   Fit results for the PF-10 data (average item location).

---

[4]The current version of GradeMap does not produce this figure, but later ones will.

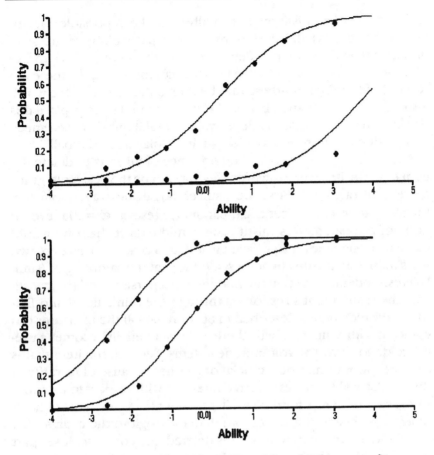

FIG. 6.7   Fit plots for Items 1 (upper panel) and 8 (lower panel).

all the dots are exactly on the line. For the top panel (Item 1, a somewhat poorly fitting item, although still less than the value 1.33), the dots for the 0 to 1/2 comparison are pretty close to the line, but the dots for the 0/1/ to 2 comparison are somewhat more distant from the line. It is most likely that this is the source of the somewhat large mean square for this item especially because there are a fairly high number of respondents at the upper end of the distribution (see Fig. 5.10)—the mean square statistic is sensitive to where the respondents are located. The deviations for the second transition (0/1 vs. 2) are noticeable, but look fairly small. There is no specific value that is a cut-off for an exploratory technique like this, but it is always interesting to see what misfit might actually look like. A possible conclusion might be: (a) the deviations are not particularly large, so it probably would not be justified to remove this item (especially because it is the one that is highest on the variable); and (b) there are some misfit problems—these may be due to the nature of the wording of the item. Perhaps a better alternative would be to replace this single item at the "vigorous" level with several items that each specified particular vigorous activities, such as "playing basketball."

A knee-jerk reaction to finding evidence of misfit is to delete the item from the item set. However, this may not be the best strategy for dealing with a poor fit. First, the result could be due to a random fluctuation—after all, in a set of 20 parameter tests at $\alpha = .05$, even if none of the parameters misfit, one would expect that one would come up as statistically significant just due to chance.[5] There are two ways to investigate this hypothesis: (a) repeat the sampling of (similar) respondents and see if the poor fit effect persists; and (b) investigate the respondent's responses through the think aloud and Exit Interview techniques described in Section 3.4—if the measurer can come up with a theory of why there is a misfit here, it becomes a useful guide for how to avoid it in new items. Second, the item that is showing poor fit may be a crucial one either because of its rarity in the item sample with respect to content or with respect to location. In the case of Item 1 for the PF-10 instrument, it is the most difficult to agree with, and it is a bit more than one logit to the nearest first threshold for another item—if it is deleted, the construct loses part of its definition. The best strategy in such a case is to first take steps as described earlier to confirm that there is indeed poor item fit. If the empirical evidence stands repeated samplings and there is a theory on which to base item redevelopment, more items should be developed of a similar nature. Unfortunately, such a strategy is not always possible—for a variety of reasons, it may be impossible to replace the affected item. Here the measurer must make a judgment as to whether there is more harm done by deleting the item or keeping it active. There are also technical strategies that can be applied to this problem—it may be that a somewhat different model would allow the item to fit—possibilities like this are beyond the scope of this book (see chap. 9).

---

[5]A careful analysis would include an examination of the family wise error rate across all of these test (see Holland and Copenhaver, 1988).

6.2.3 Respondent Fit

The concept of standard error of measurement is one that this approach shares with true score theory, but the newer approach also adds a new concept—*respondent fit*. Because this approach uses a specific mathematical model for how the respondents respond to the items, that same model can also be used to check whether those responses are consistent with the expectations of the model. This may be a bit confusing, but it does have its own logic. Consider an analogy—suppose the measurer was shown a warehouse full of tables and was asked to measure the areas of each table top. This proceeds quickly, with the measurer finding much use for the "length X width" formula recalled from school. Down in the back corner, she finds a triangular table! What to do? It does indeed have an area, but the usual formula will not work. The measurer must now make a judgment about what to do. The analogy to this in the situation of an instrument is that: (a) although most respondents will give a pattern of responses consistent with the item threshold difficulties (i.e., they will give more positive responses to the thresholds that are easier to respond positively to [those lower on the Wright map]) and fewer positive responses to those that are harder to respond positively to (i.e., those higher on the Wright map), (b) some respondents will give the opposite sorts of responses—more positive responses to the thresholds harder to agree with and less positive responses to thresholds that are easier to respond to.

Of course it is possible for any respondent to make a few such odd responses, and hence it would seem difficult to distinguish the truly unusual response patterns from mere random fluctuation. Yet that is one of the advantages of using a probabilistic model—it does indeed allow one to determine how unusual the response patterns are compared with the expectations derived from the respondent and item threshold locations.

These concepts can be illustrated by considering some particular respondents to the PF-10 scale. Three have been chosen, and their responses to the items are shown in Table 6.1. All three have a score of 9 on the PF-10 items and a common estimated location at –.41 (see Fig. 5.10). In this table, the expected scores for a respondent at –.41

---

[6]For those who want to check these cases in the data file, check the following case numbers: 397 is id no. 0200351, 381 is 620285H, and 375 is 432336S.

TABLE 6.1
Three Response Patterns for the PF-10 Scale

Response #	Score	Wgt. MS	Items in Difficulty of Order									
			10	9	5	3	2	8	6	7	4	1
Exp.	9	–	1.80	1.52	1.27	1.04	.87	.87	.86	.64	.54	.16
397	9	1.07	2	1	1	2	1	0	1	0	1	0
375	9	0.51	2	2	1	1	1	1	1	0	0	0
381	9	2.55	0	2	2	0	0	2	0	2	1	0

are shown in the top row. The items are listed in order of difficulty (i.e., by the order of the expected scores)—this makes it easier to see the pattern of orderliness. As one might intuitively expect, the scores range from high to low as the items become more difficult to agree to from left to right. For the first response pattern (#397[6]), a response that has a "typical" amount of orderliness is shown. The scores generally progress from higher (2) to lower (0) as the reader looks from left to right along the columns—this is what is expected. Yet the ordering is not completely strict—there has been some random variation—this too is what is expected in a probabilistic approach. It looks like the response to Item 8 and maybe Items 9, 4, or 3 have shown some of the random fluctuation that is to be expected. Note that, without the expected score to compare to, it often would be hard to say which item is the one that has fluctuated—in this case, absent the expected score, there is no reason to say whether the response to, say, Item 2 or Item 8 is more surprising, but looking at the expected score it looks like Item 8 is more surprising. Contrast this first response with the next response (#375). Here the ordering is consistent with the difficulty order—it proceeds from 2 to 0 with no fluctuations at all. In this case, we do not observe the sort of random fluctuations that we expect "on average" in a probabilistic situation. Now consider the last response pattern (#381): Here the fluctuations are greatly exaggerated—there seems to be little relation between the responses observed and the sorts of patterns that were expected. Also this respondent seems to be giving more extreme responses (or, equally, fewer 1s) than the other two.

The patterns in Table 6.1 can be displayed graphically as in Fig. 6.8. Each of the rows of Table 6.1 is displayed as part of a modified

```
        KIDMAP: 397                    KIDMAP: 375                    KIDMAP: 381
        Infit ms: 1.07                 Infit ms: 0.51                 Infit ms: 2.55
----Reached----Not Reached    ----Reached----Not Reached    ----Reached----Not
Reached

        1.2                            1.2                            1.2

        4.2                            4.2                            4.2
        7.2                            7.2              7.2

        1.1 6.2                        1.1 6.2                        1.1 6.2
        2.2                            2.2 8.2                        2.2
        8.2                            3.2 8.2          8.2           3.2

        5.2                            5.2              5.2
        7.1                            7.1              7.1
                                       4.1             4.1
    3.2                                                9.2
                                                       8.1
  - - - - - - |XXX| - - - - -   - - - - |XXX| - - - - -   - - - - |XXX| - - - - -
        4.1                      ........                  ........        2.1 6.1
                                                                           3.1
  9.2                            9.2                                       10.2
  8.1 ........                   8.1
                    2.1 6.1                    5.1 9.1
  2.1 6.1                        3.1
  3.1                            10.2
  10.2                           5.1 9.1
  5.1 9.1

  10.1                           10.1                            10.1
======================================================================

Note: Each row is 0.316 logit

FIG. 6.8   Kidmaps for three response patterns to the PF-10.
```

135

Wright map called a *kidmap* (Adams & Khoo, 1996; Mead, 1976), with the three respondents each taking up a vertical panel in the figure. The way each map is read is by noting that the left-hand side of the map shows which item responses were selected (or reached) by the respondent, and the right-hand side shows which were not reached. The notation "i.k," defined earlier, is used to indicate the item and response category, respectively. The horizontal "XXX" indicates the respondent's location. The dotted lines that extend out from them indicate a point beyond which the probabilities indicate some surprise; they could be called *surprise lines*. Remember the interpretation of the relative locations of persons and items described before: When a respondent is above an item threshold, it is more than 50% likely that she or he will respond in that category or below; when a respondent is below an item threshold, it is less than 50% likely that he or she will respond in that category or below. With this interpretation in mind, one should expect to see a pattern where the bottom left-hand quadrant and upper right-hand quadrant have most of the item thresholds in them. These kidmaps did not quite fit on a page, so some empty space has been cropped between the 1.2 and 4.2 marks in each one.

Looking at the kidmap for #397 in the left-hand panel, most of the thresholds are indeed in the expected quadrants. Only a few responses—the "2" for Item 3, the "2" for Item 9, and the "1" for Item 8—go beyond the surprise lines. Looking back at Table 6.1, we see that these are ones that one might see as being out of place there too: The expected score for 9 is closer to 2 than to 1, the expected score for 3 is closer to 1 than to 2, and the expected score for 8 is closer to 1 than to 0. Look now at the kidmap for #375 in the middle panel of Fig. 6.8. Here there are no thresholds that go out beyond the surprise lines; in fact the thresholds make just a single transition from left to right as the eye travels up the map. This corresponds to the strict ordering observed in Table 6.1. This orderliness is not necessarily a problem—even in a system with random fluctuations, some individuals may give, by chance, responses that are "orderly." Look now at the kidmap for #381 in the right-hand panel. Note that the "XXX" is at the same point as for #397; this is because they had the same score. Here there are many thresholds that extend beyond the surprise lines. This corresponds to the disorderliness of the last row in Table 6.1. Note that distance above or below the surprise lines indicates relative improbability. Hence, in this case, the most surprising results were the "2" for Item 7 and the "0" for Item 10.

Just as for items, fit indexes such as the weighted mean square and weighted t can be defined for respondents. The definitions are completely analogous to those for items. The values of the weighted mean squares for the respondents in Table 6.1 are shown in the third column. In interpreting fit results such as these, it is important to remember that the fit indexes only flag a pattern; they do not indicate anything causal. It could simply be the result of randomness. If the probabilistic model is indeed a good one for this context, then there should be *some* responses with poor fit that are due solely to random fluctuations, not to anything systematic. Consider the two types of poor fit shown in Table 6.1 and Fig. 6.8. On the one hand, there are respondents with low fit indexes such as #375 in Table 6.1. Such cases indicate that there is somewhat less randomness than the measurer should expect. This may be important when considering the overall fit of the model (see Section 6.3.1), but is usually not of great importance when measuring an individual response pattern (for an interesting exception, see Wilson, 1989). At worst the respondent responds to the construct with a somewhat more rigid order than was expected (i.e., there was less variation than our probabilistic model predicted).

On the other hand, there are those with high fit indexes, such as #381. Here the respondent gives a response indicating that the expected order may be wrong for him or her. For example, for Respondent #381, it looks like Items 7 and 8 are relatively easier to respond positively to than expected, and Items 2, 3, 5, and 10 are all relatively harder to respond positively to than expected. The best thing to do would be to interview this respondent to see what she or he is thinking. Absent that, one can speculate about the reasons for such a pattern. In this case, the WalkMile and WalkBlks items (Items 7 and 8) are surprisingly easy to give a positive response to than was expected, whereas the ModAct, Lift, Bend, and Bath (Items 2, 3, 5, and 10) are relatively difficult to give a positive response to than was expected. Perhaps a situation consistent with this pattern would be a person in a wheelchair who interprets *walk* to mean traveling in his or her wheelchair—a reasonable response to the question. Thus, positive responses were given to those questions. Yet Items 2, 3, 5, and 10 are all relatively difficult for that person, so they have answered less positively to those ones. Alternatively, there could have been a data entry error, or the respondent could have been choosing random responses. Although such interpretations are all possible, there is no way to choose among them without extra information.

Having the possibility of finding response patterns that are inconsistent with expectations is one of the most interesting advances in measurement in the last two decades. Although it is bureaucratically annoying to find such respondents, it is important from a perspective of understanding what the data tell us about the respondents. Where possible, all high-fit cases such as that discussed earlier should be examined in more detail to ensure that the measurements are useful. Effectively, this creates the possibility of using the pattern of item responses to establish a new class of respondents, those for whom we should treat their estimates as suspicious.

6.3 RESOURCES

The debate about what is the best measurement model is broad and deep: Just giving a comprehensive list of references would be exhausting. Some entry into the literature might be gained from reading the following: Andrich (in press), Bock (1977), Brennan (2001), Traub (1997), and Wright (1977). An excellent source for discussion and interpretations of misfit is Wright and Masters (1981).

6.4 EXERCISES AND ACTIVITIES

(following on from the exercises and activities in chaps. 1–5)

1. Read some of the sources listed in the "Resources" section, and think about how the ideas expressed there are reflected in issues that have arisen or ones you think might arise in developing your instrument. Write down a brief summary of your thoughts.
2. Look back at the GradeMap output from Juan's study. Check for item and person misfit following the procedures outlined in Section 6.2—do you agree with Juan's interpretations?
3. Think through the steps outlined earlier in the context of developing your instrument. Write down notes about your plans.
4. Share your plans and progress with others—discuss what you and they are succeeding on and what problems have arisen.

Chapter 7

Reliability

7.0 CHAPTER OVERVIEW AND KEY CONCEPTS

measurement error
standard error of measurement
reliability coefficient
internal consistency reliability
test–retest reliability
alternate forms reliability
inter-rater reliability

The aim of this chapter is to describe ways to investigate whether the instrument does, whatever it does, with sufficient consistency over individuals for the intended usage— that is, whether there is evidence for the reliability of the instrument's usage. Traditionally, reliability has been seen as a quality of the instrument separate from validity. It is seen here as an integral part of validity, but it is distinguished from the components that make up the next chapter because (a) the reliability of an instrument pertains to all of the validity characteristics, and (b) the tradition just mentioned.

7.1 MEASUREMENT ERROR

In creating a construct and realizing it through an instrument, the measurer has assumed that each respondent who might be measured has some amount of that construct and the amount is sufficiently measurable to be useful. This is what was symbolized by θ in chapters 5 and 6—the respondent's location on the Wright map. When a respondent actually gives a response and that response is scored, there are many influences on that score besides θ—all of these influences together mean that the estimated θ, labeled $\hat{\theta}$, will differ from the real θ for an individual—and that difference is the *measurement error*—let us call it ε. Then we can write: $\hat{\theta} = \theta + \varepsilon$, which is analogous to the expression $X = T + E$ from true score theory. There are many possible sources of measurement error: (a) there are influences associated with the individual respondent, such as their interest in the topic of the instrument, their mood, and their health; (b) there are influences associated with the conditions under which the instrument is being responded to, such as the temperature of the room, the noisiness of the environment, and the time of day; (c) there are influences associated with the specifics of the instrument, such as the selection of items and the style of presentation; and (d) there are influences associated with scoring, such as the training of the raters and the consistency of the raters. Note that there is nothing inherently wrong with these errors—it is a normal and expected part of measuring—the term *error* is used to mean the residual (cf. Eq. 6.4), that is, what is left unexplained after accounting for what the model (e.g., Eqs. 5.3, 5.5, etc.) has explained. However, the measurer does want to avoid having a lot of such error in the results.

There is no exhaustive and final way to classify all these potential errors—that is their nature—they are, by definition, whatever is not being modeled, and hence are not completely classifiable. Nevertheless, investigating their influence is important because an instrument with little or no consistency across the different conditions mentioned earlier will generally not be useful no matter how sound the other parts of the argument are for its validity. One way to conceptualize measurement error is to carry out a thought experiment, sometimes called the *brainwashing* analogy. Imagine that the respondent forgets that she or he has responded to an item (or set of items) immediately after making a response (that is the brainwashing) and then repeatedly asks them to respond and give them scores under all possible combinations of the varied conditions, such as those listed in the previous paragraph—one could then take the mean across all of these (possibly infinite number of) scores as giving the true location for that respondent (i.e., θ). Then the variance of the distribution of the observed locations, the variance of θ, is the variance of the errors ε. Of course it is unlikely that a respondent would actually forget his or her responses, but this thought experiment is one way to interpret the θ, the $\hat{\theta}$, and the ε.

One index of measurement error for respondents, the standard error of measurement $(sem(\theta)$[1]$)$, has already introduced in chapter 6 (Section 6.2.1). In using this index, the measurer is making use of the brainwashing analogy by assuming each item is a "little instrument" independent of the rest. When using a measurement on an individual respondent, the sem is the most important tool for assessing the usefulness of that estimate of location. If the sem is too large, the measurer will not be able to make intelligible interpretations of the results. For example, in chapter 6 (Section 6.2.1), the 95% confidence interval based on the sem was 2.36 logits wide—about 27% of the width of the entire Wright map from maximum to minimum locations. As was pointed out in the discussion there, this is certainly more information than one had before getting the data from the respondent. However, it is not accurate for individual usage—to see this, recall that the confidence interval spans (for the second threshold) the range from above "WalkOne" to "WalkMile," a wide range of physical functioning indeed. Thus, this short instrument is probably not very useful for accurate clinical diagnosis of individuals, but it may well be useful for initial screening or as a basis for group measures.

The $sem(\theta)$ varies depending on the respondent's location.[2] This is displayed for the PF-10 example in Fig. 7.1. The relationship is typically a "U" shape, with the minimum near the mean of the item thresholds and the value increasing toward the extremes. The reason for this can be seen by looking back at the IRF in Fig. 5.3 and noting that the steeper the tangent[3] to the IRF at a particular point, the

---

[1] Note that this is also called the *conditional standard error* when the focus is on the classical approach.

[2] Note that the estimates of sem(θ) and Inf(θ) produced by GradeMap are calculated assuming that the values of the item parameters are known rather than estimated, which can result in some inaccuracy for sem(θ) and Inf(θ).

[3] The tangent to a curve is the straight line that touches (but does not intersect) the curve at just one point, and hence its slope is the slope of the curve at exactly that point.

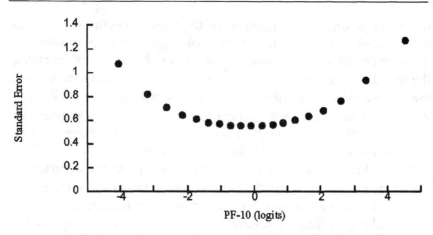

FIG. 7.1   The standard error of measurement for the PF-10 instrument
(each dot represents a score).

more the item can contribute to finding the respondent's location.
Yet the IRF is steepest at the item's location, where the probability of
response is 0.50. Hence, there is a general conclusion: The closer the
respondent is to an item, the more the item can contribute to the estimation of the respondent's location. Now apply this to the situation for a typical instrument like the PF-10 (see Fig. 5.10). The
respondents in the middle will always have more items near them
than those at the extremes, hence the *sem(θ)* will be smaller in the
middle than at the end. Note that this logic applies whenever the
item thresholds are distributed in anything between a bell-shape and
a uniform way over the construct—if the item threshold distribution
is bimodal, with a large distance between the modes, then the relationship between the respondent location and the *sem(θ)* can be
more complex.

Another way to express this relationship *is to use the Information
(Inf(θ))*, which is the reciprocal of the square of the *sem(θ)* (Lord,
1980):

$$Inf(\theta) = 1/sem(\theta)^2 . \tag{7.1}$$

This index is used in calculating the *sem(θ)* for hypothetical instruments, which capitalizes on the feature that the information for the
whole instrument is the sum of the information for each item, *Inf$_i$ (θ)*
(Lord, 1980):

$$Inf(\theta) = \sum_{i-1}^{I} Inf_i(\theta) \qquad (7.2)$$

This allows one to hypothesize that the information contribution from a typical item is the mean of the information for the whole instrument:

$$\overline{Inf(\theta)} = Inf(\theta) / I. \qquad (7.3)$$

The equivalent of Fig. 7.1 in terms of information, is shown in Fig. 7.2. Note that, as it is usually presented, true score theory assumes that the graph in Fig. 7.1 is a horizontal straight line, and hence, so would be the curve in the equivalent of Fig. 7.2.

These graphs are useful in designing an instrument. In the case of the PF-10 scale, they show that the most sensitive part of the instrument is from approximately –2.0 to +2.0 logits. If this is indeed the target range of the instrument, then that is a good thing. Looking back at the Wright map for PF-10 (Fig. 5.10), this corresponds to approximately the range of all the first thresholds (0 vs. 1&2) for all the items except for three (i.e., Bath, OneStair, WalkOne) and eight of the second thresholds too (0&1 vs. 2). Thus, the instrument's range of maximum sensitivity makes general sense with respect to the item-response categories. However, the distribution of the respon-

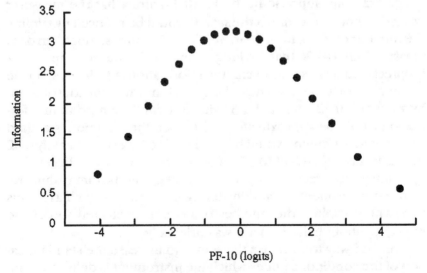

FIG. 7.2   The information for the PF-10 instrument.

dents in Fig. 5.10 shows that many respondents in this sample are above 2.0 logits—hence, the instrument is not functioning optimally for quite a large proportion of this sample. Of course it depends on the ultimate purpose of the instrument—if it is to be used on similar samples as this one, it probably should be augmented with more items up at the VigAct end. If it is intended for a sample that is generally lower in physical functioning than the current sample, then the current set of items will likely suffice. If the measurer wanted to look carefully at a sample with low functioning, it would be best to add new items at the low end (near Bath).

The shape of the graph is not the only important feature of Figs. 7.1 and 7.2. So too is the average height of the graph. Changing that (down for 7.1 and up for 7.2) can result in increased consistency. The most general way to accomplish this is to increase the number of items (assuming they are of a similar nature as the existing ones). This will almost always decrease the $sem(\theta)$: The only situation where the measurer might expect this not to result in greater consistency would be if the new items were of a diverse nature. One useful way to roughly approximate the hypothetical effect of adding similar items is to: (a) choose a location that makes a convenient reference point, (b) use Eq. 7.3 to estimate the contribution of a typical item, (c) adjust the whole instrument Information using Eq. 7.2, and (d) convert that back to the standard error of measurement using Equation 7.1.

For example, suppose in the PF-10 example that the measurer wished to know how much the $sem(\theta)$ could be reduced by tripling the number of items from 10 to 30. The minimum standard error of measurement is 0.56 (hard to judge from Fig. 7.1, but see Appendix 2 for precise values), so the maximum information is 3.19 based on the existing set of 10 items. Thus, the typical information contribution by an item is 0.32. Hence, for 30 similar items, the maximum information would be approximately 9.60. Then the minimum standard error of measurement would be predicted to be approximately 0.32 or a little more than half (0.57) of the current minimum. Because of the nature of the relationship, there will generally be diminishing returns on investments in administering more items—such as in this case where tripling the number of items is predicted to cut the $sem(\theta)$ to about half of what it was originally.

A second way to decrease the sem is to increase the standardization of the conditions under which the instrument is delivered. The likelihood of increasing consistency with this strategy, which is historically quite common, must be balanced against the possibility of decreasing the validity of the instrument by narrowing the descriptive and construct-reference components of the items design. A classic example of the perils of this strategy arose in the area of writing assessment. Here it was discovered that one could increase the consistency of scores on a writing test by adding multiple-choice items at the expense of decreasing the actual writing that respondents did. The logical conclusion of that observation is to eliminate the writing from the writing test and use only multiple-choice items. This was indeed what happened—at one point, many prominent writing tests had no request for writing in them whatsoever. The response from among educators who teach writing was one of horror—students could pass the test without actually writing! After considerable debate, the situation has swung back to a point where some writing tests now include only a single essay and deliver only a single score, which risks taking a student's measure on a sample of topics of size one. Unfortunately, this is not a good situation either—the best resolution lies in finding balance among the competing validity demands, as discussed in the next chapter.

7.2 SUMMARIES OF MEASUREMENT ERROR

To develop quality-control indexes of consistency, the traditional approach has been to find ways to compare how much of the observed variance in respondent locations is attributable to the model as a proportion of the total variance. There are several ways to consider this in terms of: (a) proportion of variance accounted for by the model, (b) consistency over time, and (c) consistency over different sets of items (i.e., different forms). These constitute three different perspectives on measurement error and are termed *internal consistency*, *test—retest*, and *alternate forms*, respectively. Another issue that arises is consistency between raters, and this is also discussed. The various summaries of measurement error are summarized in Table 7.1.

7.2.1 Internal Consistency Coefficients

The consistency coefficients described in this section are termed *internal consistency* coefficients. This is because the basis for their cal-

TABLE 7.1

Summary of Various Measurement Error Summaries (Reliability Indicators)

Name	Function
Internal consistency indicators	
Kuder–Richardson 20/21	Used for true score theory approach (raw scores) Used for dichotomous responses.
Cronbach's Alpha	Used for true score theory approach (raw scores) Used for polytomous responses.
Separation Reliability	Used for true score theory approach (raw scores) Used for polytomous responses.
(Spearman–Brown Formula)	Allows calculation of hypothetical reliabilities
Test–retest indicators	
Test-retest correlation	Used when same respondents are measured again.
Alternate forms indicator	
Alternate forms correlation	Used when there are two sets of items with a similar structure.
Inter-Rater consistency indicators	
Exact agreement proportion	Used when a rater is compared to a reference.

culation is the information about variability that is contained in the data from a single administration of the instrument—effectively they are investigating the proportion of variance accounted for by the estimator of a respondent's location. This variance explained formulation is familiar to many through its use in analysis of variance and regression methods. It is also directly applicable in the construct-reference approach adopted here: It can be used as a basis for calculating the *separation reliability* (Wright & Masters, 1981), *r*. To calculate this, first note that the observed total variance of the estimated locations, *Var(θ̂)*, is

$$Var\left(\hat{\theta}\right) = \frac{1}{N-1}\sum_{n=1}^{N}\left(\hat{\theta}_n - \bar{\theta}\right)^2 \qquad (7.4)$$

where $\bar{\theta}$ is the mean estimated location over the respondents. In the PF-10 example, the total variance is calculated to be 4.47. The variance accounted for by the errors can be calculated as the mean square of the standard errors of measurement (MSE):

$$MSE = \frac{1}{N} \sum_{n=1}^{N} sem(\theta_n)^2 \qquad (7.5)$$

In the PF-10 example, the MSE is calculated to be .67. Then the variance accounted for by the model, Var(θ), is the difference between these two:

$$Var(\theta) = Var(\hat{\theta}) - Var(\hat{\sigma}) . \qquad (7.6)$$

Thus, for the PF-10 example, this variance works out to be 3.79. The proportion of variance accounted for by the model, r, is then given by

$$r = Var(\theta)/ Var(\hat{\theta}) , \qquad (7.7)$$

which gives a reliability coefficient of .85 for the PF-10 scale. Note that this is not the only way to calculate a reliability estimate for these data—other possibilities are discussed in chapter 9.

This value illustrates one of the shortcomings of reliability coefficients—the lack of any absolute standards for what is acceptable. It is certainly true that a value of 0.90 is better than 0.84, but not so good as 0.95. At what point should one reject the instrument? At what point is it definitely acceptable? There are industry standards in some areas of application. For example, the State of California at one point endorsed a reliability coefficient of 0.90 as a minimum for achievement tests used in schools for individual testing, but this level has not been consistently applied. One reason that it is difficult to set a single uniform acceptable standard is that instruments are used for multiple purposes. A better approach is to consider each type of application individually and develop specific standards based on the context. For example, where an instrument is to be used to make a single division into two groups ("pass/fail," "positive/negative," etc.), then a reliability coefficient may be quite misleading, using, as it does, data from the entire spectrum of the respondent locations. It may be better to investigate false-positive and false-negative rates in a region near the cut location.

This reliability coefficient is an equivalent of the classical reliability indexes (Kuder-Richardson 20 and 21 [Kuder & Richardson, 1937] for dichotomous responses and coefficient alpha [Cronbach, 1951] for polytomous responses), although it is calculated in this case in the metric of the respondent locations rather than in the traditional score metric. One can also calculate the expected score for each person using Eq. 6.5 and use that to calculate an "expected score" reliability using the classical approach, but there is no particular advantage to doing so.

7.2.2 Test–Retest Coefficients

As described in the previous section, there are many sources of measurement error that lie outside a single administration of an instrument. Each such source could be the basis for calculating a different reliability coefficient. One type of coefficient that is commonly used is the *test–retest* reliability coefficient. In a test–retest reliability coefficient, the measurer first arranges to have the same respondents give responses to the questions twice, then the reliability coefficient is calculated simply as the correlation between the two sets of respondent locations. (In the classic approach, the same approach is applied to the raw scores.)

In observation of the brainwashing analogy, the test and retest should be so far apart that it is reasonable to assume that the respondents are not answering the second time by remembering the first, but are genuinely responding to each item anew. This may be difficult to achieve for some sorts of complex items, which may be quite memorable. However, because the aim is to investigate variation in the locations due to the instrument, not due to real change in respondents' locations, the measurements should be close enough together for it to be reasonable to assume that there has been little real change. Obviously, this form of the reliability index will work better where a stable construct is being measured with forgettable[4] items, as compared with a less stable construct being measured with memorable items.

---

[4]Many would say that forgettable items were not good items, but here is a case where they are quite useful.

7.2.3 Alternate Forms Coefficients

Another type of reliability coefficient is the *alternate forms* reliability coefficient. With this coefficient, the measurer arranges to develop two sets of items for the instrument, each following the same series of steps through the four building blocks as in chapters 2 through 5. The two alternate copies of the instrument are administered and calibrated, and then the two sets of locations are correlated to produce the alternate forms reliability coefficient. This coefficient is particularly useful as a way to check that the use of the four building blocks in chapters 2 through 5 has indeed resulted in an instrument that represents the construct in a content-stable way. This approach can be used for more than just calculating a reliability coefficient. For example, it can be used to investigate the robustness of construct validity evidence: When linked using the technique in Appendix 9A, the validity results can be compared using a Wright map.

Other classical consistency indexes have also been developed, and they have their equivalents in the construct modeling approach. For example, in the so-called *split-halves* reliability coefficient, the instrument is split into two different (nonintersecting) but similar parts, and the correlation between them is used as a reliability coefficient after adjustment with a factor that attempts to predict what the reliability would be if there were twice as many items as in each half. The adjustment is a special case of the Spearman–Brown formula:

$$r' = \frac{Lr}{1 + (L - 1)r}, \tag{7.8}$$

where L is the ratio of the number of items in the hypothetical test to the number of items in the real one (i.e., if the number of items were to be doubled, $L = 2$). To carry this out in the construct modeling approach, it is only necessary to make two different estimations of each respondent's location using the two different sets of items and then correlate the two and make the same adjustment.

These reliability coefficients can be calculated separately, and the results are quite useful for understanding the consistency of the instrument's measures across each of the different circumstances. In practice, such influences will occur simultaneously, and it would be better to have ways to investigate the influences simultaneously. Such methods have indeed been developed: (a) generalizability theory (e.g., Shavelson & Webb, 1991) is an expansion of the analysis of variance (ANOVA) approach mentioned earlier, and (b) facets analysis (Linacre, 1989; Wilson & Hoskens, 2001) is an expansion of the item-response modeling approach introduced previously.

7.3 INTER-RATER CONSISTENCY

Where the respondents' responses are to be scored by raters, another source of measurement error occurs—inconsistencies between the raters. There are many forms that such inconsistency can take: (a) there are raters who do not fully accommodate the training and so never apply the scoring guides in a correct way; (b) there are differences in rater severity—that is, some raters tend to score the same responses higher or lower than others; (c) there are differences in raters use of the score categories, such as raters who use the extremes more often than others or not as often as others, as well as more complex patterns; (d) there are raters who exhibit "halo effects"—that is, their scores are affected by recent scores; (e) there are raters who drift in their severity, their tendency to use extreme scores, and so on; and (f) there are raters who are inconsistent with themselves for a variety of reasons.

The most important steps to take to reduce rater inconsistency are: a program of sound rater *training*, and a *monitoring* system that helps both the administrators and raters know that they are keeping on track. A good training program includes:

1. background information on the concepts involved in the construct;
2. an opportunity for the raters to examine and rate a large number and wide range of responses, including both examples that are clearly within a category and examples that are not clear;
3. opportunities for the raters to discuss their ratings on specific pieces of work, and justifications for those ratings, with their fellow raters;
4. systematic feedback to the raters telling them how well they are rating prejudged responses; and
5. a system of rater calibration steps that either results in a rater being accepted as calibrated or being returned for further training and/or support.

Although a system like that just described constitutes a sound foundation for a rater, it has been found that they can soon drift away from even a sound beginning (see e.g., Wilson & Case, 2000). To deal with this problem, it is important to have a monitoring program in place also. There are essentially three ways to monitor the work of the raters: (a) scatter prejudged responses among them, (b) re-rate (by experts) some of their ratings, and (c) compare the records of (all of their) ratings to the ratings for all raters. Discussing these in any detail is beyond the scope of this volume (see, e.g., Wilson & Case, 2000, for some specific procedures).

Once the ratings have been made, they need to be summarized in ways that help the measurer see how consistent the raters have been. There are ways to carry this out using the construct modeling approach (see e.g., Wilson & Case, 2000) and also using generalizability theory, but they are beyond the scope of this volume, so more elementary methods are described. To apply these elementary methods, the first step is to gather a sample of ratings based on the same responses for the raters under investigation. Then they are either (a) compared to the ratings of an expert (or panel of experts) or, where that is not available, (b) compared to the mean ratings for the group. In either case, these are referred to as the *reference* ratings.

A comprehensive way to display the consistency of a rater with the reference ratings is shown in Table 7.2. In this hypothetical example, there are four score levels possible. The ratings for rater r are given in the first column, and the reference ratings are displayed at the heads of the next four columns. The number of cases of each possible pair is recorded in the main body of the table—n_{st} being the number of responses scored s by rater r and t by the reference rating. The appro-

TABLE 7.2
Layout of Data for Checking Rater Consistency

Rater r's Ratings	Reference Ratings 0	1	2	3	Total
0	n_{00}	n_{01}	n_{02}	n_{03}	$n_{0\cdot}$
1	n_{10}	n_{11}	n_{12}	n_{13}	$n_{1\cdot}$
2	n_{20}	n_{21}	n_{22}	n_{23}	$n_{2\cdot}$
3	n_{30}	n_{31}	n_{32}	n_{33}	$n_{3\cdot}$
Total	$n_{\cdot 0}$	$n_{\cdot 1}$	$n_{\cdot 2}$	$n_{\cdot 3}$	$n_{\cdot\cdot}$

priate marginals are also recorded and labeled using "•" to indicate whether the row or column (or both) are summed. A directly interpretable index of agreement is the proportion of exact agreement—the proportion of responses in the leading diagonal of entries n_{ss}:

$$p_{exact} = \sum_{s=1}^{4} n_{ss} / n_{..} . \qquad (7.9)$$

In cases where one wanted to control for the possibility that the matching scores might have arisen by chance, an alternative index called *Cohen's kappa* is available (Cohen, 1960). A less rigorous index of agreement is the proportion of responses in the same or adjacent categories. This is not recommended when the number of categories is small (as is the case in Table 7.1) because it can lead to overpositive interpretations. The table can also be examined for various patterns: (a) asymmetry of the diagonals would indicate differences in severity, and (b) relatively larger or smaller numbers at either end could indicate a tendency to the extremes or the middle. The table can also be examined with chi-square methods or log-linear analysis (see, e.g., Agresti, 1984) to test for independence and other patterns. Note that correlation coefficient can be a misleading way to examine the consistency between ratings because the standardization that is part of it will disguise differences in harshness between the raters.

7.4 RESOURCES

A well-rounded introduction to the classic perspective on measurement error and reliability can be found in Cronbach (1990). Included there are numerical examples of correlation-based reliability coefficients such as test–retest and alternate forms, as well as an explanation of how to calculate a correlation coefficient and a discussion on its interpretation. Further discussion of the interpretation of errors under the item-response modeling approach can be found in Lord (1980), Wright and Stone (1979), and Wright and Masters (1981).

7.5 EXERCISES AND ACTIVITIES

(following on from the exercises and activities in chaps. 1–6)

1. Look back at the GradeMap output you generated from Juan's data. Check the standard errors of measurement for the students in his study. Do they display the "U-shape" pattern mentioned earlier? Are they sufficiently small?
2. Locate the separation reliability and Cronbach's alpha in the GradeMap output. How do they compare?
3. Try to locate a data set containing either test–retest or alternate forms data and calculate a correlation coefficient to interpret as a reliability coefficient.
4. Write down your plan for collecting reliability information about your instrument.
5. Think through the steps outlined previously in the context of developing your instrument, and write down notes about your plans.
6. Share your plans and progress with others—discuss what you and they are succeeding on, and what problems have arisen.

Chapter 8

Validity

This is where quality meets quantity.

—Stephen Moore (April 2002)

8.0 CHAPTER OVERVIEW AND KEY CONCEPTS

test content
response processes
internal structure
external structure
consequences

The aim of this chapter is to describe ways to develop evidence as to whether the instrument does in fact accomplish what it is supposed to accomplish—that is, whether there is evidence for the *validity* of the instrument's *usage*. Traditionally, validity has been seen as composed of several different components, such as evidence related to criterion, content, and construct validities (American Educational Research Association, American Psychological Association, National Council for Measurement in Education, 1985; Cronbach, 1990) or, more recently, evidence based on test content, response processes, internal structure, relations to other variables, and consequences of testing (American Educational Research Association, American Psychological Association, National Council for Measurement in Education, 1999). This book's focus is on accumulating a specific set of arguments for an instrument, and each of these categories is used, in turn, as a source of possible evidence, either for or against the planned usage of the instrument. In general, the sequence of presentation follows that in the second list cited earlier.

The gathering of evidence of various types of validity, as described next, should not be seen as simply a once-and-for-all event. The purpose of validity evidence in instrument development is to help the measurer make the instrument work in a way that is more consistent with the intent, and evidence that the instrument is not doing so is not a dead end in this process. Instead such evidence is an important step forward—now there is some evidence of a problem. The trick is to find a way to make that evidence useful in the next iteration of the process.

8.1 EVIDENCE BASED ON INSTRUMENT CONTENT

To compile evidence based on an instrument's content, the measurer must engage in "an analysis of the relationship between a test's [instrument's] content and the construct it is intended to measure" (American Educational Research Association, American Psychological Association, National Council for Measurement in Education, 1999, p. 11) and interpret that analysis in an argument concerning the validity of using the instrument. This is exactly what was described in chapters 1 through 5. If the measurer carries out the steps outlined in those chapters, then he or she will have in place the desired analysis. Of course it is not required that the analysis stop there—more can be gained from more detailed analysis. Indeed a successful implementation of the steps in those chapters would result in a coherent account of the instrument's structure.

The results from carrying out the steps given in chapters 2 through 7 consist of the following: (a) definition of the construct (and a visual representation of that as a construct map)—the construct map; (b) a description of the set of items that comprise the instrument—the items design; (c) a strategy for coding the responses into an outcome space, and for scoring them—the outcome space; and (d) a technically calibrated version of the construct—the Wright map.

Thus, documentation of the steps taken as in chapters 2 through 5 constitute a thorough representation of the content validity evidence for the instrument (as well as the second aspect of validity, which is the topic of the next section). It also lays the foundations for the remaining aspects of validity evidence—in a sense, the evidence related to content is the target of the remaining evidence. The importance attached to this aspect of validity should be clear to the reader—it has taken center stage in four of the chapters of this book—every other aspect only gets a section of a chapter. Evidence based on instrument content is essential because it contains the realization of the construct, and that is what all the other aspects of validity play off (even reliability).

8.2 EVIDENCE BASED ON RESPONSE PROCESSES

To compile evidence based on response processes, the measurer must engage in a detailed analysis of individual responses, either while the individuals are taking the instrument or just after in an exit interview. A description of such activities has already been given in the context of instrument development in chapter 3 (Section 3.4). The evidence thus gathered, as well as evidence gathered in separate studies after the instrument has been developed, can all be used as part of the validity evidence for the instrument. It also makes sense to undertake such an investigation in the context of the item typology as given in chapter 3 (Section 3.3). The descriptions given in those sections are not repeated here, but that should not be interpreted as indicating that this sort of evidence is less important than others. Just as for the previous type of evidence, the importance of evidence based on response processes is not to be judged by the space this section occupies here. Rather, the fact that it has been deemed too important to leave to the end testifies to its fundamental importance.

Like the comments for the evidence related to content, the evidence gathered under this heading is extremely important for the soundness of the instrument: It sets up many of the expectations that are to be compared to outcomes during the investigations into other aspects of validity. In addition, it can stand directly as validity evidence in its own right.

8.3 EVIDENCE BASED ON INTERNAL STRUCTURE

To compile evidence based on internal structure, the measurer must first ensure that there is an intention of internal structure. Although this idea of intended structure may not be generally common among instruments designed in many areas, if the measurer has followed the steps outlined in chapters 2 through 5, indeed there must be an internal structure that is expected—it is the structure of the *construct* as described in chapter 2. If the measurer builds this construct following the steps in chapters 2 through 5, there will be an expectation that the levels of the construct will be in a certain order, running from high to low, easy to difficult, or positive to negative, as the case may be, as displayed in a construct map.

8.3.1 Did the Evidence Support the Construct Map?

The evidence that the content expectations have been fulfilled resides in the analysis of a field test of the data, analyzed using one of the measurement models in chapter 5 and displayed in a Wright map. The concordance between the theoretical expectations in the construct map and the empirical results in the Wright map reflects the support that the evidence offers.

For example, consider the construct map for the PF-10 instrument that is implicit in Fig. 8.1, which is taken from Raczek et al. (1998). Note that in this figure, the locations shown are for the average of the two-step parameters (see Eqs. 5.8–5.11). The order of items in this (sideways) construct map is (from low to high): Bath, WalkOne,

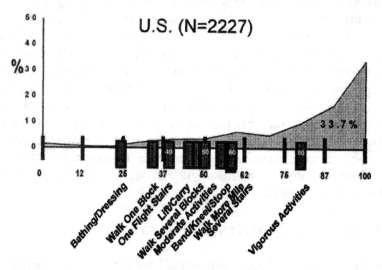

FIG. 8.1   The PF-10 construct map as it appears in the original article
(from Raczek et al., 1998, p. 1209).

OneStairs, Lift, WalkBlks, ModAct, Bend, WalkMile, SevStair, and VigAct. This particular set of expectations is based on empirical evidence. Often this is not the case; instead the construct map is developed based on theory and logical arguments, as well as empirical evidence. The measurer needs to compare that expected order to the estimated locations in the Wright map in Fig. 5.10 (based on data from McHorney et al., 1994). This can be illustrated as in Fig. 8.2, where the Raczek expectations are compared to the locations of the second threshold for each item. If the orders are the same, this graph should show a monotonically increasing slope from the first item to the last—in this case, that is true except there is a slight upturn between the sixth item (WalkBlks) and the seventh item (Lift), although this may be small compared with the item standard error. Clearly the orders are quite similar, but there are also some small qualitative differences—for example, the upturn noted previously corresponds to the observation that the locations of the thresholds for Lift (labeled as "Lift/Carry" in Fig. 8.1) and WalkBlks (labeled as "Walk Several Blocks" in Fig. 8.1) have been reversed.

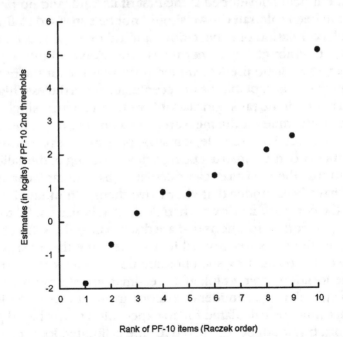

Rank of PF-10 items (Raczek order)

FIG. 8.2 Comparison of the expected threshold order from Fig. 7.1 (Raczek et al., 1998) and estimates from Fig. 5.10 (data from McHorney et al., 1994).

We can quantify the comparison of the estimates shown on the Wright map with the expectation of order shown in Fig. 8.1 using the Spearman rank-order correlation. The formula is:

$$\text{Spearman's } \rho = 1 - (6\Sigma D^2)/(I(I^2-1)) , \qquad (8.1)$$

where D is the rank difference of the items on the two maps, and I is the number of items. This works out to be 0.99 in this instance.[1] The two rankings are almost identical, and we can say that for all practical purposes they are the same. Note that usually an expectation like that shown in Fig. 8.1 will be a qualitative expectation based on theory—there will be at most a ranking of the expected locations, and so the rank correlation will be the appropriate index. The high correlation found here should not be much of a surprise—the expectations shown in Fig. 8.1 were based on the accumulation of experiences from many years, many researchers, and many studies (see Ware & Gandek, 1998, for a detailed discussion of this history).

In cases where there is no such history—where, for example, the instrument being developed is the first of its kind, and no previous data have been calibrated—we should not be surprised to find that the rank correlation of expectations and calibrations was considerably lower. Although low or negative correlations indicate a general problem, there is no predetermined positive value for the rank correlation that is acceptable or unacceptable. Nevertheless, higher is indeed better; if the rank correlation's value is embarrassingly low, it may be worthwhile for the measurer to reconsider his or her theory of the construct. For example, it may be possible to express an alternative theory of the construct using a new ordering of the calibrated items so that the measurer can calculate what the rank correlation would have been under that alternative theory. In other situations where the correlation is lower than desired, it is also useful to focus on the specific item locations that are discrepant—does this observation point the measurer toward items where the theory should be modified? In considering such possibilities, it is important to recall that the locations being ranked are estimates, not absolute values, and do indeed have a confidence interval around them. A confidence interval cannot be calculated for an expectation that is based purely on theory, but it can be calculated for the calibrated locations—this

---

[1]See appendix in chapter 8 for the calculations.

should be borne in mind when making interpretations (see next paragraph). Of course if the measurer does come up with a modified theory of the construct, then the best strategy is to return to the strategies of chapter 3 and rework the item set.

One might ask: What is the relationship of this iteration of the instrument development process to validity? Surely, all bets are off—the measurer has cheated the validity test by using empirical evidence to modify the target (the construct). Of course the correlation will be higher next time—how could it not be if you use strategies like the earlier ones to adjust the item set? This approach to interpreting validity evidence is somewhat common among commentators, but is in fact diametrically opposite to good practice. There are at least three different sorts of conclusions one can draw from negative evidence: (a) the original idea of the construct (theory of the construct) was in some way wrong (i.e., go back to chap. 2); (b) the items that were developed to match the construct are not working as intended (i.e., go back to chap. 3); or, (c) the scores that have been developed for the items are incorrect (i.e., go back to chap. 4).

Examples of each of these types of problems are included in the Cases Archive. The important thing to realize is that the steps outlined in chapter 1 and described in detail in chapters 2 through 7 are not ends in themselves. Any sound instrument is the result of several iterations, both part and whole, through those steps. The evidence (validity and reliability) that is gathered along the way is a means to achieve the goal of a sound instrument. Summative studies of validity evidence for an instrument are best conducted when the measurer has firm expectations that they will be positive based on a theory of the construct that has been built up in previous formative studies.

Sometimes the content expectation is based on an earlier calibration, such as the case in hand (i.e., comparing the McHorney et al. data with the Raczek et al. data), so we can also calculate a Pearson correlation. This takes into account slightly more information, such as the relative differences between the locations. In this case, it works out to be 0.99 also.[2] Thus, in this case, the two indexes give the same result. Sometimes one would like to look in a bit more detail at the relationship among the thresholds for specific parameters. For instance, in this case, it might be interesting to see whether the loca-

---

[2]The threshold locations for Fig. 9.1 are given in Raczek et al. (1998) in Table 3 under the heading "US." The threshold locations for Fig. 6.7 are given in Appendix 2.

tions for Lift and WalkBlks are significantly different in the calibrations from the two data sets. The Raczek results are provided in the original article (Raczek et al., 1998) and show the locations as being 47 and 45 on a translated logit scale with a standard error of 1 for both items. Thus, the 95% confidence intervals for the two locations are approximately (45, 49) and (43, 47): The overlap shows that we do not have evidence that the two items differ in this data set. Similar calculations can be carried out in the McHorney data using the item estimates in Appendix 2 to show that the two items are not distinguished in that data set either. What this means is that, given the data, we cannot say conclusively that one of the thresholds is above the other—they are at approximately the same location. Thus, it would have been more accurate to calculate the rank correlation counting these two as a tie (giving each a rank of 6.5, which would have resulted in a correlation of 1.0), and in particular one should not seek to interpret any difference between them.

There is a second way that the item calibration can indicate that the items have not fully realized the measurer's expectations. One aspect of the sorts of models introduced in chapter 5 is that they are more sensitive to respondents whose locations are near the item locations (as noted in chap. 6). This leads one to a general rule for a good instrument: The item parameters should "cover" the region of the scale where the respondents lay. Generally, the instrument is better when the item locations span the full range of the respondents. Large gaps in the coverage indicate areas where the respondents are being measured less well than elsewhere. In the case of the PF-10 results shown in Fig. 5.10, the item thresholds do indeed span the range of the respondents fairly well, with just the coverage of the extremes being less than one might want. The lower functioning people are covered by just one threshold for the "Bathing/Dressing" item. The best-functioning people are covered by just one threshold for the "Vigorous Activities" item. Thus, one piece of advice would be to add a few items that help out at the extremes, with some high- and low-functioning categories of response.

8.3.2 Did the Evidence Support the Items Design?

Construct validity issues are built into the items design as well as into the construct map. One requirement is that the items be consistent with the instrument as a whole. (This will, of course, be reversed for so-called *inverse* items that are expected to work the other way.) A second requirement is related to what is termed *differential item functioning*.

Item Analysis. One way that this consistency can be made manifest is that respondents higher on the construct would, in general, also score higher on each item. In terms of the Wright map, one could consider the locations of the respondents within each score group for a given item: If the *mean location* of each group tends to increase as the scores increase, it seems reasonable to say that this particular expectation that comes from the items design has been fulfilled. Consider the results for the PF-10 example shown in Table 8.1. In this table, the mean location of each score group is shown for the odd-numbered items (the results for the rest are quite consistent with these, so only a sample is shown). In every case, the mean increases as the score rises. If there were an item for which this were not true, that item should be examined to see whether there is an explanation (and the specific score that is inconsistent should give some hint). The point biserial correlation between the category (scored "0" and "1") and the raw score total on the instrument is also shown ("Pt-Biserial"). This more traditional indicator attempts to convey the same information, although it is not so clear in its interpretation. For example, for Item 9, the mean locations are increasing in the way that is expected, but the point biserial indicated that response categories 1 and 2 are indistinguishable. In general, I have found that the mean locations are more interpretable than the point biserial correlations.

Differential Item Functioning (DIF). Instruments are typically used across a wide spectrum of respondents—the second standard requirement of the items design is that, across important subgroups, items function in a similar way for respondents who are at the same location—that is, they should exhibit no evidence of differential item functioning (DIF). Here one is focusing on whether the items in the instrument behave in a reasonably similar way across different subgroups within the sample. Typically these subgroups are gender, ethnic, or socioeconomic groups, although other groupings may be relevant under particular circumstances. The technique can be applied to other subgroups, such as those identified in investigative

TABLE 8.1
Item Statistics for the PF-10 Example (for Selected Items)

Statistics	Response Categories		
	1	2	3
Item 1			
Count	1043	874	137
Percent (%)	50.8	42.6	6.7
Pt-Biserial	−.63	.53	.20
Mean Location	0.15	2.87	3.28
Std. Dev. of Locations	0.64	0.91	1.00
Item 3			
Count	213	615	1226
Percent (%)	10.4	29.9	59.7
Pt-Biserial	−.57	−.37	.70
Mean Location	−1.79	0.28	2.72
Std. Dev. of Locations	0.70	0.62	0.88
Item 5			
Count	137	511	1406
Percent (%)	6.7	24.9	68.5
Pt-Biserial	−.53	−.51	.76
Mean Location	−2.39	−0.29	2.56
Std. Dev. of Locations	0.76	0.60	0.85
Item 7			
Count	527	704	823
Percent (%)	25.7	34.3	40.1
Pt-Biserial	−.76	.07	.60
Mean Location	−1.04	1.48	3.19
Std. Dev. of Locations	0.64	0.68	0.97
Item 9			
Count	117	305	1632
Percent (%)	5.7	14.8	79.5
Pt-Biserial	−.51	−.52	.75
Mean Location	−2.56	−0.90	2.26
Std. Dev. of Locations	0.78	0.60	0.82

studies (e.g., respondents who use different cognitive strategies), or could even be composed of respondents with different sets of scores on the test—although these may be interesting for a variety of reasons, they are not specifically the focus of this section (American Educational Research Association et al., 1999).

It is necessary to make an important distinction. If the responses to an item have different frequencies for different subgroups, that is evidence of *differential impact* of the item on those subgroups. Although such results may well be of interest for other reasons, they are not generally the focus of DIF studies. Instead DIF studies focus on whether respondents at the same locations give similar responses across the different subgroups. Thus, in the PF-10 example, if two subgroups gave different rates of responses to a particular item—say that more working-class respondents found it more difficult to "Walk Several Blocks" than respondents from a managerial class—then that would constitute differential impact on the results of the measurement and could be an interesting result. Yet the issue of DIF would not necessarily be raised by such a result—it could be that the working-class respondents had suffered more injuries than those in the managerial class, and the instrument was accurately measuring that difference in physical functioning due to that and other causes. To make this distinction between differential impact and DIF, the measurer needs to control the comparison for the different levels of physical functioning between the two groups. In other words, the measurer needs to compare the item responses for respondents at the same location in the two groups. Thus, in the example, one would want to know whether respondents from the two groups *at the same location on the variable* were giving similar responses.

There are several different techniques available for investigating DIF, among them techniques based on linear and logistic regression, and techniques based on log-linear models (see Holland & Wainer, 1993, for an overview). The technique to be described here is based on the models described in chapter 5, so it fits in well with the approach of this book. In summary, the technique is quite simple—calibrate the variable separately in each of the two subgroups and examine the resulting item parameter estimates for important differences. Such differences indicate some form of DIF.

For example, consider the results of DIF analysis for the PF-10. The calibration has been repeated in two subgroups—male and female. The results for the first threshold are shown in Fig. 8.3 and for the second threshold in Fig. 8.4.[3] In both figures, the threshold estimates are visually quite close to the equality line. To decide whether any of these differences are evidence for DIF, we check to see if the 95% confidence intervals around the male and female thresholds overlap, as shown in the Appendix (Table 8A.2). Comparison of the confidence intervals for the males and females shows a distinct pattern—most of the first threshold differences show statistically significant DIF (all except those for Items 7 and 8), whereas the second thresholds do not. This is perhaps a little surprising because the differences between the logit values for the male and female thresholds, which are shown in the last column on the right-hand side of Table 8A.2, do not display this pattern. The explanation relates to the way that the thresholds are defined—as they increase (1st, 2nd, etc.), they represent the addition of information from successive steps, each of which is estimated with error, and, hence, the thresholds also tend to increase in their standard errors.

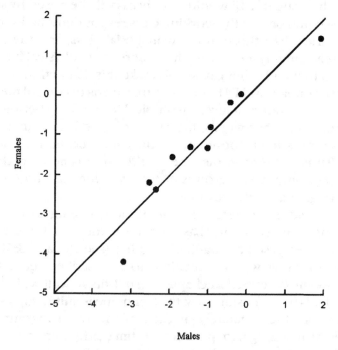

FIG. 8.3   Examining item DIF—comparing the first thresholds.

[3]The thresholds and their standard errors are given in Appendix 2.

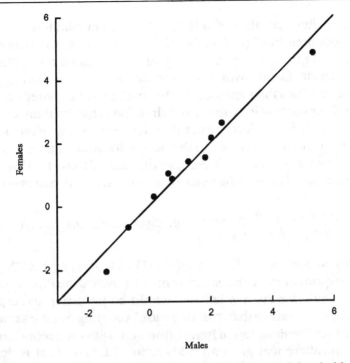

FIG. 8.4   Examining item DIF—comparing the second thresholds.

The findings concerning statistical significance need to be completed by considering effect size. In terms of DIF, a standard of effect size has been recommended by Longford, Holland, and Thayer (1993). This has been translated into the context of Rasch models by Paek (2002): A logit difference value less than .426 is "negligible," a value between .426 and .638 is "intermediate," and a value over .638 is "large." Applying these criteria to the statistically significant logit differences in Table 8A.2 shows that only one of the statistically significant threshold differences has intermediate DIF—the second threshold for Item 1—and only one has large DIF—the first threshold for Item 10. One way to offer an interpretation of these DIF results is to return to the step parameter estimates (see Appendix 2). In the case of the largest difference between the thresholds, the first step for Item 10, the step parameter estimates are −4.06 and −3.05 for females and males, respectively. Thus, it is about 1 logit easier for females than males (of the same overall physical functioning status) to agree that they are "limited a little" rather than "limited a lot" for "Bathing or dressing." (Remember that this applies to the Bath question, but not the other items.) It may be that males are more likely to express dissatisfaction with their serious problems in bathing and dressing activities than females, or that males have a higher expectation for their success in bathing and dressing activities than females. To get an idea of the effect size of this difference, the log of the odds is given by the difference between the person location and the relevant step parameter (see Eq. 5.13, etc.), so the ratio of these two log-odds can be calculated as the difference between those two expressions:

$$\log\left[\left(\frac{\text{"little"}_{male}}{\text{"lot"}_{male}}\right)\Big/\left(\frac{\text{"little"}_{female}}{\text{"lot"}_{female}}\right)\right] = (\theta - (-3.05)) - (\theta - (4.06)) = -1.01 \quad . \quad (8.2)$$

This corresponds to odds of ($\exp(-1.01)=$) 0.36:1, or 1:2.77—that is, for respondents at the same level of physical health, approximately 1 male for every 3 females would be predicted to respond "limited a little" rather than "limited a lot." Carrying out the same calculations for the first step of Item 1 (the item with the second largest threshold difference) gives an odds ratio of 1.51:1. That is, for respondents at the same level of physical health, males are selecting "limited a little" rather than "not at all" at a rate about one and a half times that of females—that is, men (at the same overall level of physical functioning) seem to be more likely to admit moderate problems with vigorous activities than females. These ratios are effect sizes and, as such, need a real-world context to decide whether they are important. In the case of Item 1, it may be questionable whether the DIF is important, but the result for Item 10 does seem to be a reasonably large difference, so one should not ignore it.

Once an item exhibiting DIF has been identified, the measurer must decide what to do about it. Recall that not all instances of empirical DIF threaten the item—as mentioned at the beginning of this subsection, the grouping characteristics may not be ones that are of concern for issues that have been determined to be important such as fairness, and so on. It is sobering to realize that, for each item, there will *always* be some grouping that could be constructed for which the item will exhibit DIF. The situation is analogous to that for a poorly fitting item, and the options are equivalent. First, it is necessary to establish that the DIF is indeed not a result of random fluctuations, and then the same steps are needed: (a) repeated samplings, and (b) development of a "theory of DIF" for that particular item. Given that the measurer is indeed confident that DIF is established, the best strategy is to develop alternative items that do not exhibit DIF. However, it may be that it is not possible to replace the DIF item in the instrument. Then the measurer must make a judgment about the best way to address the issue. Note that a technical solution is available here—the measurer can use the two different calibrations for the two groups, but this is seldom a chosen strategy because it involves complex issues of fairness and interpretation.[4]

8.4 EVIDENCE BASED ON RELATIONS TO OTHER VARIABLES

Where there are other external variables that the construct should (according to theory) predict, and also where another instrument is intended to measure the same or similar variable, a strong relation (or lack of a strong relation) between the instrument under scrutiny and these external variables can be used as validity evidence. Note that the latter case is somewhat rare, at least for the case where the other instrument is intended to measure the same construct, because a measurer would most likely use the preexisting instrument rather than develop a new one. Typical examples of these external variables are: (a) clinical judgments, records, and self-reports (for psychological and health variables), (b) scores on other tests and teachers ratings and grades (for educational achievement tests), and (c) supervisors' ratings and performance indicators (for business-related measures). Another source of external variables are treatment studies—where the measurer has good evidence that a treatment affects the construct; then the contrast between a treatment and a control group can be used as an external variable. Note that the relationship predicted from theory may be positive, negative, or null—that is, it is equally as important that the instrument be supported by evidence that it is measuring what it should measure (*convergent evidence*, which may be positive or negative depending on the way the variables are scored) as it is that it be supported by evidence that it is not measuring what it should not (*divergent evidence*, which would be indicated by a null relationship).

---

[4]To carry this out, use item estimates anchored (for the Non-DIF items) on the whole sample to estimate different estimates for the DIF items; then make sure that the two metrics are equated.

A reasonably straightforward indicator of this relationship is the Pearson correlation coefficient between the respondents' estimated locations and the external variable. When the external variable is a dichotomy, the relationship can be examined by considering the difference between the two means and can be tested using a t test. In addition to calculating this quantitative indicator, it is often useful to plot the relationship. For example, in the PF-10 data set, there is an indicator of the respondents' age. It is reasonable to say that, in general, physical functioning decreases as a person ages, although this is probably most true only in the senior years. Thus, we should look for an overall negative relationship between age and PF-10 location, with a relatively stronger negative relationship in later years and a relatively weaker relationship in younger years. The overall correlation is –0.26, which is statistically significantly different from 0.0 at the a=0.05 level.[5] This is indeed generally negative, although not strongly so. The relationship between the PF-10 estimates and age is shown in Fig. 8.5. The straight line is the best linear fit, the curved line is the best quadratic fit, and the dots show the array of data points. Note how the somewhat shallow general linear relationship becomes a steeper quadratic relationship for respondents over 60 years, just as was anticipated (convergent evidence). There is little relationship between the two in the younger and middle years, as was also anticipated (divergent evidence).

8.5 EVIDENCE BASED ON THE CONSEQUENCES OF USING AN INSTRUMENT

Regardless of all the other evidence gathered in the prior categories, if a general category of use of a particular instrument is found to have negative consequences, that is an overriding consideration that should be taken into account when deciding whether to use an instrument. To determine whether it is the particular instrument causing the problem, one would have to use an alternative instrument in the same place and get different results. If it were the case, for instance, that any instrument so used would have similar negative consequences, then the problem lies with the use of the construct, not the instrument per se. Putting that comment aside, this category of

---

[5]The approximate standard error of a correlation is $(N-3)^{-1/2}$ (where N is the sample size).

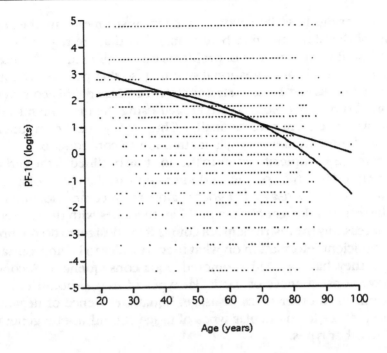

FIG. 8.5   Relationships (linear and quadratic) between the PF-10 scale and age.

validity evidence should be seen as the real-world complement of all the rest. Each validity argument composed of the various subarguments from the prior categories can only be a partial investigation of the large (probably infinite) number of potential threats to validity. This final category gives a (self-) critic the right to "20/20 hindsight" in deciding that good intentions and thorough methodology may sometimes be insufficient (see the discussion on this topic in Linn, 1997; Mehrens, 1997; Popham, 1997; Shepard, 1997).

Because there are always important consequences of using the instruments that measurers develop (otherwise they would not have developed them), it is important to maintain a constant monitoring of good usage and positive outcomes. One might say that this is a constant in any area where products are designed, but it is particularly so in this area of measurement. Consider an analogy—when an engineer builds a bridge and the bridge falls down, everyone can tell that there has been a failure. Yet in measuring in the types of contexts that are the focus of this book, it can be very hard for anyone to tell that "the bridge has fallen down." Often the instruments are the *only* basis for decisions and may be the only data that are regularly collected, so finding evidence of problems can be quite difficult. Often they are the basis of professional standing, so that people's reputations are in danger if the instruments are criticized (this comment applies both to people who are judged using the instruments and those who use them professionally). Thus, an essential component of sound measurement is vigilant attention to consequences.

There are a couple of caveats to the position outlined in the earlier paragraph. First, the comments do not apply to the abuse of an instrument—that is, usage that goes against the recommendations of the instrument designers—the problem there lies with the abusers, not necessarily the instrument. Of course if the designers do not provide sufficient information on what they consider to be appropriate usage, they have indeed promoted poor consequences. Second, positive consequences of particular types of usage should not be generalized to other types of usage. Equally, evidence of negative consequences for particular types of usage should not be generalized to other types.

8.6 CRAFTING A VALIDITY ARGUMENT

In creating a solid and integrated argument for the validity of an instrument, all of the prior forms of evidence should be used. Note that the forms are not merely a list of types of evidence—they bear important relationships to one another. The evidence regarding content is of a constructive nature: This form of evidence sets the structure against which other forms must bear. The evidence regarding response processes provides a microview on the cognitive processes that respondents are undergoing while responding to the instrument—this can both provide support for use of an instrument and information that leads to changes in the instrument. The evidence regarding internal structure is of paramount importance in showing that the structure—the construct—described in the content validity evidence is reflected in observations of the instrument in operation. Where there is solid theory and preexisting evidence regarding the relationship of the variable under examination to other external variables, then those relations can be used to test for validity also. Note that this form of argumentation can be somewhat tricky. For example, if all the internal validity evidence supported the use of the instrument, but one external variable was found not to be related, then the measurer might be justified in seeing this as a research finding rather than as evidence against validity. Finally, evidence drawn from consequential events can also be used as a way to check on all those many issues that were not examined in the original validity evidence plan—it is a good strategy of humility for the measurer to thus admit that the real world is more complex than she or he could anticipate.

8.7 RESOURCES

A prime resource for this chapter is the latest edition of the *Standards for Educational and Psychological Tests* (American Educational Research Association, American Psychological Association, National Council for Measurement in Education, 1999). An excellent account of a somewhat older, although still fundamentally sound, view on validity evidence is given in Cronbach (1990).

8.8 EXERCISES AND ACTIVITIES

(following on from the exercises and activities in chaps. 1–7)

1. Look back over the exercises in chapters 1 through 5 where you have written down descriptions of (a) the construct, (b) the construct map, (c) the items design, and (d) the construct map. Combine them to make up a comprehensive account of your evidence related to content validity.
2. Choose one of the case studies and read its account of how validity evidence was gathered and used. Write a critique of what was done.
3. Write down your plan for collecting validity evidence for your instrument—be sure to include each different type.
4. Think through the steps outlined earlier in the context of developing your instrument, and write down notes about your plans.
5. Share your plans and progress with others—discuss what you and they are succeeding on, and what problems have arisen.

APPENDIX:
Calculations for the Rank Correlation and for DIF

Rank Correlation

For the two rankings of the PF-10 second thresholds shown in Figs. 8.1 and 5.10 (which are referred to next as the Raczek and McHorney results, respectively), construct the following table and apply Eq. 8.1 as in Table 8A.1.

TABLE 8A.1
Calculations for the Rank Correlation Coefficient

	Rank		Rank Difference	
Thresholds	McHorney	Raczek	D	D^2
Vigorous Activities	1	1	0	0
Several Stairs	2	2	0	0
Walk More Mile	3	3	0	0
Bend/Kneel/Stoop	4	4	0	0
Moderate Activities	5	5	0	0
Lift/Carry	6	7	−1	1
Walk Several Blocks	7	6	1	1
One Flight Stairs	8	8	0	0
Walk One Block	9	9	0	0
Bathing/Dressing	10	10	0	0
TOTAL				2

$$
\begin{aligned}
r &= 1 - (6\Sigma D^2)/(l(l^2-1)) \quad\quad\quad (8A.1)\\
&= 1 - (6 \times 2)/(10(100-1))\\
&= 1 - 6/495\\
&= 1 - 0.0121212\\
&= 0.99
\end{aligned}
$$

DIF

To carry out the analysis needed to check for item DIF, lay out the results (means and standard errors of the item thresholds) from the two grouped analyses as in Table 8A.2. Usually the measurer would have to transform one of the scales to have the same metric as the other, but in this case the means and standard deviation of the parameters are close (see bottom of Table 8A.2) so that it was not considered necessary. The calculations for the 95% confidence interval are carried out in the usual way, and then the two confidence intervals are checked to see whether they overlap. In this case, only the first thresholds for Items 1 and 10 show a statistically significant difference.

TABLE 8A.2
Testing for DIF

| Item | Females | | | | Males | | | | Logit Difference |
	Threshold	Std. Err.	95% CI Lower	Upper	Threshold	Std. Err.	95% CI Lower	Upper	
Threshold 1									
1	1.47	0.06	1.36	1.58	1.88	0.07	1.75	2.02	-0.41
2	-1.30	0.06	-1.40	-1.19	-1.03	0.07	-1.18	-0.89	-0.27
3	-1.55	0.06	-1.65	-1.44	-1.95	0.07	-2.09	-1.80	0.40
4	-0.16	0.05	-0.26	-0.06	-0.45	0.07	-0.57	-0.32	0.28
5	-2.18	0.06	-2.30	-2.06	-2.56	0.08	-2.71	-2.40	0.38
6	-1.29	0.06	-1.40	-1.18	-1.48	0.07	-1.61	-1.35	0.19
7	0.06	0.06	-0.05	0.17	-0.18	0.07	-0.32	-0.04	0.24
8	-0.78	0.07	-0.91	-0.65	-0.95	0.08	-1.11	-0.79	0.17
9	-2.36	0.08	-2.51	-2.21	-2.39	0.10	-2.59	-2.20	0.03
10	-4.19	0.09	-4.36	-4.02	-3.23	0.11	-3.44	-3.01	-0.96

TABLE 8A.2 (continued)

Item	Females				Males				Logit
	Threshold	Std. Err.	95% CI Lower	Upper	Threshold	Std. Err.	95% CI Lower	Upper	Difference
Threshold 2									
1	4.86	0.15	4.57	5.15	5.37	0.18	5.01	5.73	-0.51
2	1.43	0.14	1.15	1.71	1.29	0.18	0.94	1.63	0.14
3	1.05	0.15	0.76	1.33	0.63	0.19	0.25	1.00	0.42
4	2.66	0.14	2.39	2.92	2.37	0.17	2.04	2.70	0.29
5	0.33	0.15	0.03	0.63	0.14	0.21	-0.26	0.55	0.19
6	1.56	0.14	1.27	1.84	1.84	0.18	1.49	2.18	-0.28
7	2.19	0.13	1.93	2.45	2.03	0.16	1.71	2.35	0.16
8	0.88	0.14	0.61	1.14	0.74	0.18	0.40	1.09	0.13
9	-0.64	0.17	-0.97	-0.31	-0.67	0.22	-1.10	-0.24	0.03
10	-2.03	0.22	-2.46	-1.60	-1.41	0.25	-1.91	-0.92	-0.62
Mean	0.00				0.00				
S.D.	2.09				2.07				

177

Part IV

A Beginning Rather Than a Conclusion

Chapter 9

Next Steps in Measuring

9.0 CHAPTER OVERVIEW AND KEY CONCEPTS

foundations in cognitive psychology
alignment of statistical models with the construct
the BEAR Assessment System

The aim of this chapter is to help the reader move beyond what has been described and discussed in the previous nine chapters. Reading about measurement issues, trying out your measurement ideas in practical context, and engaging in discussions about your measurement efforts and the theoretical issues that they provoke are all excellent activities that well define a first step into the measurement domain. Yet we have hardly scratched the surface of the deep debates, the modes of practice, and the literatures that make up the domain of measurement. The topics in this chapter represent several directions in which the reader can deepen and broaden his or her interests and experiences in measurement. One clear path is to look beyond each of the four building blocks that form the basis of the account in this book. For example,

1. one can look to cognitive psychology as a source of new construct maps or as the source of cognitive structures that are more

complex than, or perhaps inconsistent with, the idea of a construct map (see Section 9.1);

2. one can search among statistical models for ways to match the
constructs generated or incorporate measurement issues beyond those discussed in this book (see Section 9.2);

3. one can delve more deeply and thoroughly into an area of application—this requires investigating different items designs and
outcome spaces by looking more thoroughly at the specific application area in which the measurer is working. There are
many areas of application. It is not possible to cover them all in
this chapter, but instead an example is offered—the area of educational assessment (see Section 9.3); and

4. an expanded Resources Section is offered that looks beyond the
beginning theoretical perspective advanced here; it considers a
broader array of theoretical possibilities in measurement (see
Section 9.4).

For each of these directions, an orienting discussion and introduction is offered next.

9.1 BEYOND THE CONSTRUCT MAP:
CONNECTIONS TO COGNITIVE PSYCHOLOGY[1]

The theories of cognitive psychology are built up to explain how respondents develop knowledge structures, such as the ideas associated with a certain domain of knowledge or a subject matter
discipline, and ways of reasoning and problem solving. The discipline
of cognitive psychology seeks to understand how knowledge is en-
coded, stored, organized, and retrieved, and how different types of internal representations are created as people learn about a concept
(National Research Council, 1999). One major principle of cognitive
theory is that respondents actively construct their understanding by
trying to connect new data with their existing knowledge.

To cognitive psychologists, knowing is not merely the accumulation of factual information and routine procedures. Knowing means
being able to combine knowledge, skills, and procedures in ways
that are useful for interpreting new situations and solving problems.

---

[1]This section is adapted from Wilson (2003).

Thus, assessment of cognitive constructs should not over emphasize basic information and skills—these should be seen as resources for more meaningful activities. As Wiggins (1989b) pointed out, children learn a sport not just by practicing the component skills (e.g., in soccer, dribbling, passing, and shooting), but also by actually playing the sport.

Although the earlier differential (Carroll, 1993) and behaviorist (Skinner, 1938) approaches focused on the extent of knowledge possessed by a respondent, cognitive theory has emphasized what sort of knowledge a respondent has. Thus, from a cognitive perspective, one must not only assess how much respondents know, but also assess how, when, and whether they use what they know. From this perspective, traditional tests, which usually record how many items examinees answer correctly or incorrectly, fall short. What is needed are data about how they reach those answers and/or how well they understand the underlying concepts. For this, more complex tasks are required that reveal information about thinking strategies, and growth in understanding over time.

9.1.1 Implications for Measurement

Cognitive psychology theories focus on the way knowledge is represented, organized, and processed in the mind (National Research Council, 1999). Consideration is also given to social dimensions of learning, including social and participatory practices that support knowing and understanding (Anderson, Greeno, Reder, & Simon, 2000). The implication is that assessment practices need to include the more complex aspects of cognition as well as component skills and discrete bits of knowledge.

The mind's cognitive structure includes short-term (or working) memory, a limited system, and long-term memory, an almost limitless store of knowledge (Baddeley, 1986). In many contexts, what is most important is how well the respondent can utilize the knowledge stored in long-term memory and use it to reason efficiently about current information and problems. The contents of long-term memory include both general and specific knowledge, but much of what a respondent knows is domain- and task-specific and is organized into structures known as *schemas* (e.g., Cheng & Holyoak, 1985). Thus, assessments should evaluate what schemas a respondent has and under what circumstances the respondent regards the information as important. This evaluation should include how a respondent organizes acquired information, encompassing both strategies for problem solving and ways of chunking relevant information into workable units.

Studies of expert–novice differences in subject domains illuminate critical features of knowledge structures that should be the targets for assessment. Experts in a subject domain typically organize factual and procedural knowledge into schemas that support pattern recognition and the rapid retrieval and application of knowledge (Chi, Glaser, & Rees, 1982).

Metacognition—the process of reflecting on and directing one's own thinking—is one of the most important aspects of cognition (Newell, 1990). It is crucial to effective thinking and problem solving, and it is one of the principle features of expertise in specific areas of knowledge and skill. Experts use metacognitive strategies for monitoring understanding during problem solving and for performing self-correction (Hatano, 1990). The implication here is that measurements should seek to determine whether a respondent has good metacognitive skills.

Respondents learn in different ways and follow different paths to mastery. The growth process is not a uniform progression, nor is there invariant change from erroneous to optimal solution strategies, but a respondent's problem-solving strategies do become more effective over time and with practice (Siegler, 1998). The implication of this is that measurements should focus on identifying the range of strategies being used for problem solving, giving particular consideration to where those strategies fall on a developmental continuum of efficiency and suitability for a particular domain of knowledge and skill.

Respondents have rich intuitive knowledge of their world that undergoes significant alteration as they mature and change. Learning entails the transformation of naive understanding into more complete and accurate comprehension, and assessment can be used as a tool to facilitate this process (Case, 1992). Thus, measurements should focus on making respondents' thinking visible to both the measurer and, where appropriate, to the respondent. This way useful strategies can be selected to support an appropriate course for future growth.

Practice and feedback are crucial aspects of the development of skills and expertise (Rosenbloom & Newell, 1987). Thus, timely and informative feedback to a respondent during instruction and learning is one of the most important roles for measurement, ensuring that their practice of a skill and its subsequent acquisition will be effective and efficient.

Knowledge often develops in a highly contextualized and inflexible form, and hence does not transfer effectively. The possibility of transfer is dependent on the development of an explicit understanding of when to apply what has been learned (Bassok & Holyoak, 1989). When assessing achievement, then, the measurer needs to consider the prerequisite knowledge and skills needed to answer a question or solve a problem, including the context in which it is presented, and whether a task or situation is functioning as a test of zero, near, or far transfer.

9.1.2 The Situative Perspective

The situative or sociocultural perspective was, in part, prompted by concerns with the cognitive perspective's almost exclusive focus on the thinking of the individual respondent. Instead the situative perspective describes behavior at a different level of analysis—one oriented toward practical activity and context. Here *context* refers to engagement in particular forms of practice within particular communities. (A community can be any purposeful group, large or small, from the global society of professional archeologists to a local swimming club or classroom.) In these accounts, the fundamental unit of analysis is *mediated activity*—a person or group's activity mediated by cultural artifacts like tools and language (Wertsch, 1998). In this view, one learns to participate in the practices, goals, and habits of mind of a particular community.

One of the prime features of this approach is attention to the artifacts generated and used by people to shape the nature of cognitive activity. From a traditional cognitive perspective, physics is a particular knowledge structure—from the situative perspective of mediated activity, working in a physics laboratory is also strongly dependent on the participants' abilities to collaborate in such activities as formulating and understanding questions and problems (Ochs, Jacoby, & Gonzalez, 1994).

The situative perspective proposes that every assessment is, at least in part, a measure of the degree to which one can participate in a form of practice. From this perspective, filling in a Likert scale is a form of practice. There are some respondents who, by virtue of their histories, inclinations, or simple interests, are better prepared than others to participate effectively in this practice. Hence, simple assumptions about these or any other measurements as indicators of knowledge must be examined.

Discourse and interaction with others are the basis of much of what humans learn. Thus, knowledge is often embedded in particular sociocultural contexts, including the context of the assessments, and it encompasses understandings about the meaning of specific practices such as question asking and answering. The implication is that measurements need to examine how well respondents engage in communicative practices appropriate to a domain of knowledge and skill, what they understand about those practices, and how well they use the tools appropriate to that domain.

9.1.3 Future Perspectives

From the perspective outlined previously, one can see that models of cognition and learning provide a basis for the design and implementation of construct-driven measurement practices. Such programs and practices already exist and have been used productively in certain areas (e.g., Hunt & Minstrell, 1996; Marshall, 1995; White & Frederiksen, 1998; Wilson & Sloane, 2000). However, the vast majority of what is known has yet to be applied to the design of measurements for classroom or external evaluation purposes, and there are many subject areas where the cognitive foundations are not yet established. Therefore, further work is needed to utilize what is already known within cognitive science in measurement practice, as well as to develop additional cognitive analyses of domain-specific knowledge and expertise.

Many highly effective tools exist for probing and modeling a respondent's knowledge and for examining the contents and contexts of learning (such as reaction-time studies, computational modeling, analysis of protocols, microgenetic analysis, and ethnographic analysis; see National Research Council, 2001). The methods used in cognitive science to design tasks, observe and analyze cognition, and draw inferences about what a respondent knows are applicable to many of the challenges of designing effective measurements.

Contemporary assessment practices are, in general, not in concert with the situative perspective. There is good evidence to expect that a respondent's performance in an abstract measurement situation will not accurately reflect how well they would participate in organized, cumulative activities that may hold greater meaning for them. From the situative standpoint, measurement means observing and analyzing how respondents use knowledge, skills, and processes to participate in the real work of a community. For example, to assess performance in science education, one might look at how productively students find and use information resources; how clearly they formulate and support arguments and hypotheses; how well they initiate, explain, and discuss in a group; and whether they apply their conceptual knowledge and skills according to the standards of the discipline.

9.2 POSSIBILITIES FOR THE MEASUREMENT MODEL: SOURCES IN STATISTICAL MODELING[2]

Probably the most common form that the construct takes in measurement situations is that of a continuous latent variable—the construct is seen as a single progression from less to more or lower to higher. This is the basis for all three of the currently dominant approaches to measurement: classical test theory (CTT; see Lord & Novick, 1968, for a modern account), generalizability theory (GT; see Shavelson & Webb, 1991, for a recent introduction; Brennan, 2001, for a recent survey), and item response theory (IRT; see van der Linden & Hambleton, 1996, for a recent survey). In CTT, the continuous variable is termed the *true score* and is thought of as the long-run mean of the observed total score. In GT, the effects of various measurement design factors on this variable are analyzed using an ANOVA-like approach. In IRT, the focus shifts to modeling individual item responses: The probability of an item response is seen as a function of the underlying latent variable representing respondent competence (often denoted by θ) and parameters representing the item and the measurement context.

The most fundamental item parameter is the item difficulty, but others are also used where they are thought to be useful to represent

---

[2]This section is adapted from Wilson (in press).

the characteristics of the assessment situation. The difficulty parameter can usually be seen as relating the item responses to the construct (i.e., the θ variable). Other parameters may relate to characteristics of the observations. For example, differing item slopes can be interpreted as indicating when item responses are also possibly dependent on other (unmodeled) dimensions besides the θ variable (these slopes are sometimes called *discrimination parameters*, although that term can lead to confusion with the classical *discrimination index*). Parameters for lower and upper item asymptotes can be interpreted as indicating where item responses have floor and ceiling effects (where the lower asymptote is often called a *guessing* parameter). There is a debate in the literature about whether to include parameters beyond the basic difficulty parameters in the statistical model to make the model flexible, or whether to see them as indicating deviations from a certain regularity condition (i.e., specific objectivity) that sees them as threatening the interpretability of the results (Hambleton, Swaminathan, & Rogers, 1991; Wright, 1968, 1977).

A second possible form for the construct is a set of discrete classes, ordered or unordered depending on the theory. The equivalent psychometric models are termed *latent class* (LC) models (e.g., Haertel, 1990). In these models, the form of cognition, such as problem-solving strategy, only occurs within certain discrete classes, where there are no differences with respect to the construct among the respondents in those categories. An example might be strategy usage, where an LC approach would be seen as useful when students could be adequately described using only a certain number of different classes of strategies. These classes could be ordered by some criterion—say, cognitive sophistication—or they could have more complex relations to one another.

9.2.1 Adding Complexity to the Measurement Model

There are other complexities of the measurement context that can be added to these models. First, the construct can be seen as being composed of more than a single attribute. In the continuous construct approach, this possibility can be termed the *factor analysis* model when a classical approach is taken and a *multidimensional item response model* (MIRM) when starting from the continuum approach (e.g., Adams, Wilson, & Wang, 1997; Reckase, 1972). In contrast to the prior account, where parameters were added to the model when the item was being made more complex, here the model of the respondent is what is being enhanced. These models allow one to incorporate evidence about different constructs into the measurement situation.

Second, repeated measurements over time can be seen as indicators of a new construct—a construct related to patterns of change in the original construct (Bryk & Raudenbush, 1992; Collins & Wugalter, 1992; Embretson, 1996; Muthen & Khoo, 1998; Willet & Sayer, 1994; Wu, Adams, & Wilson, 1998). In another example, ANOVA-like effect parameters (Fischer, 1973; Linacre, 1989) similar to those available in GT can model observational effects such as rater characteristics and item design factors, but can also be used to model complexities of the construct (e.g., components of the construct that influence item difficulty, such as classes of cognitive strategies).

A third approach is to incorporate elements of the cognitive model in standard statistical models. The construct map described in chapter 2 is an example of this. A recent example, using the GradeMap software (Wilson, Kennedy, & Draney, 2004), is shown in Fig. 9.1, where the levels, called *criterion zones* in the figure, are those defined in Fig. 2.4. In this figure, one can see how an individual respondent's assessments over time can be displayed in a meaningful way in terms of the criterion zones. The same approach can be adapted for reporting group results of assessments and even large national surveys (e.g., Department of Employment, Education, and Youth Affairs, 1997). One can also examine individual students' pattern of results to help diagnose individual differences. An example is the Kidmap technique (described in chap. 6), which uses the discrepancy between the predicted response for a respondent on an item and the observed response (i.e., the residual) to flag respondents whose responses perhaps should not be summarized using a single location on a variable. An example, also from the GradeMap software, is shown in Fig. 9.2. Here an overall index of fit was used to flag that "Amy Brown's" responses need extra attention. Note that the format of this Kidmap is quite different from the ones shown in Fig. 6.7, but the information conveyed is the same. In this figure, the expected result for each item for "Amy Brown" are shown using the gray band across the middle, whereas the observed results are shown by the black shading. Clearly Amy has responded in surprising ways to sev-

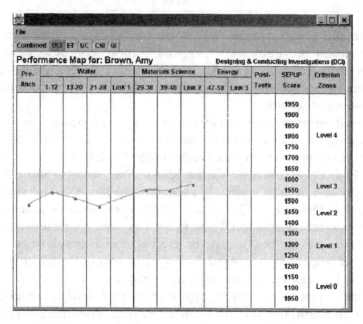

FIG. 9.1 A student's progress chart on one IEY construct
(produced using the GradeMap software; Wilson, Kennedy, & Draney, 2004).

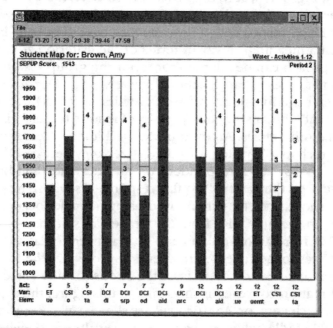

FIG. 9.2 A Kidmap for a student in the BEAR Assessment System
(produced using the GradeMap software; Wilson, Kennedy, & Draney, 2004).

eral items, and a content analysis of those items may prove interesting. An analogous technique has been developed by Tatsuoka (1990, 1995) with the advantage of focusing attention on specific cognitive diagnoses.

9.2.2 Adding Cognitive Structure Parameters to Statistical Models

One can go a step further than the previous strategy of incorporating interpretative techniques into the reporting—elements of the construct can be directly represented as parameters of the statistical model. From a statistical point of view, this would most often be the preferred tactic, but in practice it may add to the complexity of interpretation, so the merits should be considered for each application. A relatively straightforward example of this is the incorporation of differential item functioning (DIF) parameters into the statistical model. Such parameters adjust other parameters (usually item difficulty parameters) for different effects between (known) groups of respondents. Most often it has been seen as an item flaw needing to be corrected (e.g., Holland & Wainer, 1993). Yet in this context, such parameters could be used to allow for different construct effects, such as using different solution strategies (Lane, Wang, & Magone, 1996) or linguistic differences (Ercikan, 1998).

Another general strategy is the delineation of hierarchical classes of observation that group together the original observations to make them more interpretable. This can be seen as acting on either the respondent or item aspects of the statistical model. Looking from the respondent's side, this constitutes a way to split up the respondents into latent groups for diagnostic purposes (e.g., Haertel & Wiley, 1993; Junker, 2001). It could also be seen as a way to split up the items into classes, allowing interpretation of student results at the level of, say, classes of skills rather than at the individual item level (Janssen, Tuerlinckx, Meulders, & De Boeck, 2000). Continuum and latent class approaches may also be combined (Wilson, 1994b), thus allowing constructs that are partly continuous and partly discontinuous. For example, the *saltus model* (Mislevy & Wilson, 1996; Wilson, 1989) is designed to incorporate stagelike developmental changes along with more standard incremental increases in skill.

9.2.3 Generalized Approaches to Statistical Modeling of Cognitive Structures

Several generalized approaches have been proposed. One is the *unified model* (DiBello, Stout, & Roussos, 1995), which is based on the assumption that task analyses can classify respondents' performances into distinct latent classes. A second general approach, labeled M²RCML (Pirolli & Wilson, 1998), has been put forward based on a distinction between knowledge-level learning, as manifested by variations in solution strategies, and symbol-level learning, as manifested by variations in the success of application of those strategies (Dennett, 1988; Newell, 1982). This approach has been applied to data related to both learning on a LISP tutor (Draney, Pirolli, & Wilson, 1995) and a rule assessment analysis of reasoning involving the balance scale (Pirolli & Wilson, 1998).

A general approach to modeling such structures, called *Bayes nets*, has been developed by statisticians working in other fields (Andersen, Jensen, Olesen, & Jensen, 1989; Pearl, 1998). Two kinds of variables appear in a Bayes net for educational assessment: those that concern aspects of students' knowledge and skill, and others that concern aspects of the things they say, do, or make (Mislevy, 1996). All of the statistical models discussed in this section reflect this kind of reasoning, and all of them could be expressed (at least approximately) as particular implementations of Bayes nets. The models described earlier each evolved in their own special niches, with researchers in each gaining experience, writing computer programs, and developing a catalog of exemplars. Bayes nets have been used as the statistical model underlying such complex assessment contexts as intelligent tutoring systems (e.g., Martin & VanLehn, 1995; Mislevy & Gitomer, 1996).

9.2.4 Future Perspectives

The statistical models discussed earlier provide explicit, formal rules for integrating the many pieces of information that may be relevant to specific inferences drawn from observation of items. The statistical models currently available can support many of the kinds of inferences in a broad range of domains (such as educational and psychological assessment, etc.). In particular, it is possible to characterize respondents in terms of multiple constructs, rather than a single score; chart respondents' changes over time, instead of simply measuring the construct at a particular point in time; deal with multiple paths or alternative valued responses; model, monitor, and improve judgments based on informed evaluations; and model responses not only at the level of respondents, but also at the levels of groups, such as classes, schools, and states.

Unfortunately, many of the newer models and methods are not widely used because they are not easily understood or packaged in accessible ways for those without a strong technical background. Much hard work remains to focus psychometric model building on the critical features of models of cognition and learning and on observations that reveal meaningful cognitive processes in a particular domain. If anything the task has become more difficult because an additional step is now required—determining simultaneously the inferences that must be drawn, the observations needed, the tasks that will provide them, and the statistical models that will express the necessary patterns most efficiently. Therefore, having a broad array of models available does not mean that the measurement model problem is solved. More work is needed on relating the characteristics of measurement models to the specifics of theoretical constructs and types of observations. The long-standing tradition of leaving scientists, practitioners, instrument designers, and psychometricians to their own realms represents perhaps the most serious barrier to the necessary progress.

9.3 DEEPER PERSPECTIVES ON A PARTICULAR APPLICATION AREA: EDUCATIONAL ASSESSMENT[3]

One way to expand out from the material in the previous eight chapters is to explore more fully the possibilities for a particular area of application. There are a multitude of such areas, so one needs to be chosen to illustrate possibilities. Many areas have long and complex histories intertwining theoretical perspectives and measurement techniques—some have only a recent history. Educational assessment has been around for a long time; some of the earliest records of educational tests date from the second century BC from China (the

---

[3]This section is adapted from Wilson and Draney (2002).

Imperial Civil Service Examinations; Webber, 1989). Hence, the history of measurement in this area is "long and thick." Rather than attempt to direct the reader to a series of readings on this, instead I refer the reader to one particular source that is both authoritative and contains extensive references to related topics: Linn (1989).

The remainder of this section describes one particular contemporary approach to educational assessment as an instance of this deeper engagement with a particular area: The BEAR Assessment System (Wilson & Sloane, 2000), which can be summarized in terms of four principles: developmental perspective, quality evidence, match between instruction and assessment, and management by teachers. In particular, we examine one example of the application of the BEAR Assessment System—the IEY curriculum (Science Education for Public Understanding Program, 1995).

9.3.1 Developmental Perspective

The first principle of the BEAR Assessment System is that an educational assessment system should be based on a developmental perspective of student learning. Assessing the development of students' understanding of particular concepts and skills (as opposed to current status only) requires a model of how student learning develops over a certain period of (instructional) time. A developmental perspective helps us move away from one-shot testing situations and cross-sectional approaches to defining student performance toward an approach that focuses on the process of learning and on an individual's progress through that process.

The BEAR strategy to address this issue is to develop a set of progress variables (referred to in this book as *construct maps*) that mediate between the level of detail that is present in the content of specific curricula and the necessarily less precise descriptions in state standards and curriculum framework documents (Masters, Adams, & Wilson, 1990). Such progress variables can be defined at different levels of detail. At the most detailed level, every instructional unit would be seen as contributing in some way to student progress on at least one of these variables—every assessment would be closely aligned with one (or more) of the variables. At the classroom level, they might specify the intended content of a curriculum up to a level of detail that would allow, say, biweekly tracking of student progress through the curriculum. At a higher level, these might be aggregated into variables that are useful over a longer time span, perhaps over a semester or a year for a whole subject, such as biology or even science. This alignment allows the creation of a calibrated scale to map the growth of students so that teachers can track the progress of individual students and groups of students as they undergo instruction. At the higher levels, progress of a class over a semester or of a school over a whole year might be the target. This idea of a "cross-walk between standards and assessments" has also been suggested by Baker (cited in Land, 1997, p. 6). These variables also create a conceptual basis for relating the curriculum to standards documents to other curricula and to assessments not specifically related to that curriculum.

The IEY Example. An example of such a set of progress variables is taken from the Issues, Evidence, and You (IEY; Science Education for Public Understanding Program, 1995) middle school science curriculum described in Section 2.2.2. Following the developmental perspective principle, the BEAR researchers, along with the SEPUP curriculum developers, devised a framework of progress variables that embody the learning that students are expected to experience in the IEY year. The five IEY variables are shown in Fig. 9.3.

The first three variables—Understanding Concepts, Designing and Conducting Investigations, and Evidence and Trade-offs—are primary variables and are assessed most frequently. The traditional content of science tests has not been abandoned in this framework—traditional science content comes under the progress variable "Understanding Concepts." Thus, teachers using this system do not lose anything compared with what they would get from a traditional approach, but they can gain. Students' performance on Communicating Scientific Information can be assessed in conjunction with almost any activity or assessment depending on the teacher's interest in monitoring student progress on this variable. Opportunities in the course have been indicated for assessing students' skills in this area. The final variable, Group Interaction, is based on the SEPUP 4-2-1 model of instruction, which organizes student work into (a) groups of four for science investigations, (b) pairs for completing written reports of these investigations, and (c) individual students for responding to assessments (Science Education for Public Understanding Program, 1995), which can also be assessed throughout the year.

Understanding Concepts (UC)--understanding scientific concepts (such as properties and interactions of materials, energy, or thresholds) in order to apply the relevant scientific concepts to the solution of problems. This variable is the IEY version of the traditional "science content", although this content is not just "factoids".

Designing and Conducting Investigations (DCI)--designing a scientific experiment, carrying through a complete scientific investigation, performing laboratory procedures to collect data, recording and organizing data, and analyzing and interpreting results of an experiment. This variable is the IEY version of the traditional "science process."

Evidence and Tradeoffs (ET)--identifying objective scientific evidence as well as evaluating the advantages and disadvantages of different possible solutions to a problem based on the available evidence. This variable, and the two following are relatively new.

Communicating Scientific Information (CM)--organizing and presenting results in a way that is free of technical errors and effectively communicates with the chosen audience.

Group Interaction (GI)--developing skills in working with teammates to complete a task (such as a lab experiment) and in sharing the work of the activity.

FIG. 9.3   Progress variables in the IEY example.

9.3.2 Match Between Instruction and Assessment

The need to integrate assessment into the curriculum and instruction process (i.e., the classroom context) is often emphasized in discussions of current educational assessment practices. The second principle is that there must be a match between what is taught and what is assessed. This principle represents, of course, a basic tenet of content validity evidence (American Educational Research Association, American Psychological Association, National Council for Measurement in Education, 2001): that the items on a test are sampled appropriately from a domain that is defined by the content and level of cognitive processing expected in a given body of instruction. Traditional testing practices—in high-stakes or standardized tests as well as in teacher-made tests—have long been criticized for oversampling items that assess only basic levels of knowledge of content topics and ignoring more complex levels of understanding.

Concerns about the match among curriculum, instruction, and assessment have been discussed from both the curriculum development and assessment perspectives. From the curriculum perspective, efforts to emphasize new approaches to teaching and learning are inhibited by the form and content of accountability tests. Reports abound of teachers interrupting their use of their regular curricular materials to "teach the material" that students will encounter on the district- or state-wide tests. From an assessment perspective, advocates of assessment-driven reform hope to take advantage of the tendency to "teach to the test" by aligning high-stakes testing procedures to the goals of curricular reform. As Resnick and Resnick (1992) argued: "Assessments must be designed so that when teachers do the natural thing—that is, prepare their students to perform well—they will exercise the kinds of abilities and develop the kinds of skill and knowledge that are the real goals of educational reform" (p. 59).

The match between the instruction and assessment in the BEAR Assessment System is established and maintained through two major parts of the system: the progress variables described earlier, and the assessment tasks described next. In the previous section, the main motivation for the progress variables was that they serve as a framework for the assessments. However, the second principle makes clear that the framework for the assessments and the framework for the curriculum and instruction must be one and the same. This is not to imply that the needs of assessment must drive the curriculum, but rather that the two—assessment and instruction—must be in step (they drive one another). Using progress variables to structure both instruction and assessment is one way to ensure that the two are in alignment at least at the planning level. To make this alignment concrete, however, the match must also exist at the level of classroom interaction, and that is where the nature of the assessment tasks becomes so crucial.

Assessment tasks need to reflect the range and styles of the instructional practices in the curriculum. At the classroom level, they must have a place in the rhythm of the instruction, occurring at places where it makes instructional sense to include them. This is usually at points where teachers need to see how much progress his or her students have made on a specific topic (see Minstrell, 1998, for an elaboration of these kinds of occasions). One good way to achieve this is to develop both the instructional materials and assessment tasks at the same time—adapting good instructional sequences to produce accessible responses, and developing assessments into full-blown instructional events. At the higher levels of focus, such as between classes or schools, the tasks would reflect a sampling from those typically used across the range of contexts where the assessments are taking place.

The IEY Example, (cont'd). The IEY progress variables formed the framework for the development of almost all of the IEY curriculum—*both* the IEY instructional materials and the assessments were built around a core set of progress variables. Once the five progress variables were established, *all* instructional objectives for each activity and *all* of the assessment tasks were linked to one (or more) of the five IEY variables. The variety of assessment tasks used for assessment in IEY match in range the variety of instructional events: These include individual and group challenges, data processing questions, and questions following student readings. All assessment prompts are open ended, requiring students to fully explain their responses. For the majority of assessment tasks, the student responses are in a written format, reflecting the only practical way for teachers to attend to a classroom of student work.

An example of an assessment prompt is shown in Fig. 9.4. It is taken from IEY Activity 19: "Is Neutralization the Solution to Pollution?" It is typical of IEY embedded assessments in that it requires students to integrate information from readings they did in previous activities and labs (the "newspaper articles"), and it also asks them to explain their reasoning. It cannot be fully answered without access to the curricular materials that preceded it. It is related to the Evidence and Trade-offs variable. There is no one right answer. Rather students are required to make a statement or decision and then justify it with the information and evidence learned through the activities. Their performance is judged by the validity of the arguments they present, not simply the conclusion they draw.

To provide the sort of summative information typical of large-scale assessments, the BEAR researchers also developed "Link Tests," which are composed of fairly traditional-looking items. The items,

---

Based on everything you have learned about acid-base neutralization, do you think neutralization can be used as a solution to acid-base pollution? Explain your answer thoroughly. Describe both the advantages and disadvantages and other factors that must be considered before reaching a conclusion.

FIG. 9.4 An IEY assessment task.

each linked to at least one variable, are not curriculum-embedded like the assessment tasks and require short- to moderate-length written responses. An example is shown in Fig. 9.5.

Link Tests are a series of tests given at major transition points in the IEY course. Each test contains open-ended items related to the content of the course that further assess students' abilities with the IEY variables. Items on the Link Tests can also be used as an item bank for teachers to draw upon in designing their own end of unit or other tests to be administered during the year. Teachers can use the Link Test items as models of variable-linked, open-ended questions, or they may select specific items to be included in other teacher-made tests. The link tests are the analogue of large-scale assessment in the IEY context. Other types of assessments may be used where greater efficiency is desired, such as multiple-choice items.

9.3.3 Management by Teachers

The third principle of the BEAR Assessment is that teachers must be the managers of the system, and hence must have the tools to run it efficiently and use the assessment data effectively and appropriately. There are two broad issues involved in the Management by Teachers principle. First, it is the teachers who will use the assessment infor-

---

You run the shipping department of a company that makes glass kitchenware. You must decide what material to use for packing the glass so that it does not break when shipped to stores. You have narrowed the field to three materials: shredded newspaper, Styrofoam® pellets, and cornstarch foam pellets. Styrofoam® springs back to its original shape when squeezed, but newspaper and cornstarch foam do not. Both Styrofoam® and cornstarch foam float in water. Although Styrofoam® can be reused as a packing material, it will not break down in landfills. Newspaper can be recycled easily, and cornstarch easily dissolves in water.

Which material would you use? Discuss the advantages and disadvantages of each material. Be sure to describe the trade-offs made in your decision.

FIG. 9.5   A link item associated with the Evidence and Trade-offs Variable.

mation to inform and guide the teaching and learning process. For this function of assessment, teachers must be (a) involved in the process of collecting and selecting student work, (b) able to score and use the results immediately—not wait for scores to be returned several months later, (c) able to interpret the results in instructional terms, and (d) able to have a creative role in the way that the assessment system is realized in their classrooms. Only then will teachers really be able to use the assessment system.

Second, issues of teacher professionalism and teacher accountability demand that teachers play a more central and active role in collecting and interpreting evidence of student progress and performance (Tucker, 1991). If they are to be held accountable for their students' performance, teachers need a good understanding of what students are expected to learn *and* of what counts as adequate evidence of student learning. They are then in a better position, and a more central and responsible position, for presenting, explaining, and defending their students' performances and the outcomes of their instruction.

This perspective requires new views of the teaching and learning process, new roles for and demands on teachers, perhaps even a new assessment culture in the classroom (Brown, Campione, Webber, & McGilly, 1992; Cole, 1991; Resnick & Resnick, 1992; Torrance, 1995a, 1995b; Zessoules & Gardner, 1991). Preparing teachers to use these types of assessments in their classroom teaching may be a difficult challenge. Yet teacher understanding and belief in assessment determine the ultimate success of change (Airasian, 1988; Stake, 1991).

The IEY Example, (cont'd). For the information from assessment tasks and link items to be useful to IEY teachers, it must be couched in terms that are directly interpretable with respect to the instructional goals of the IEY variables. Moreover, this must be done in a way that is intellectually and practically efficient. The BEAR response to these two issues is the IEY Scoring Guide. IEY Scoring Guides define the elements of each variable and describe the performance criteria or characteristics for each score level of the element. There is one Scoring Guide for each of the five IEY variables, with each variable having between two and four elements (and the Scoring Guide is specific to each of these elements). A student's level of performance on an assessment task is determined by using the Scoring Guide(s) for the variable(s) being assessed. The guide is used throughout the entire course for all assessments relating to a particular variable. This means that there will inevitably be a need for interpretation of the Scoring Guide for any particular assessment. BEAR found that the combination of a uniform scoring guide, with examples for individual assessments, was much more efficient for teachers than having different Scoring Guides for each assessment. The scoring guides that are used by teachers in the classroom can also be the scoring guides used by raters in large-scale assessments. The exemplars differ with differing items used at the different levels, but public-release items can be used to share even that level of detail. In different situations, it may be better to have scoring guides that are specific to each item, although they should still be based on a common underlying concept.

Each IEY Scoring Guide uses a general logic (adapted from the SOLO Taxonomy; Biggs & Collis, 1982) based on discerning what would be under most circumstances a "complete and correct" response—this is coded a "3." Below this a student might give a partially correct response that leaves out at least one essential element—this is coded a "2." Below this, a student might give a response that is very low level, but is not entirely nonsensical—this is coded a "1." A response that has no relevant aspects is coded a "0," and a response that goes beyond a "3" in some significant way is coded a "4." All IEY Scoring Guides share this structure, but use specific criteria to adapt them uniquely to individual IEY variables. The Evidence and Trade-offs Variable Scoring Guide is found in Fig. 9.6. (Note that the right-hand side of this Scoring Guide constituted the example construct for IEY in chap. 2.)

To interpret each Scoring Guide, teachers need concrete examples—which BEAR calls "Exemplars"—of the rating of student work. Exemplars provide concrete examples of what a teacher might expect from students at varying levels of development along each variable. They are also a resource, available to the teachers as part of the Assessment System, which help them understand the rationale of the scoring guides.

Actual samples of student work, scored and moderated by teachers who pilot tested the BEAR Assessment System using IEY, are included with the documentation for IEY. These illustrate typical responses for each score level for specific assessment activities. An example of a Level 3 response from Activity 12 is shown in Fig. 9.7.

Evidence and Tradeoffs (ET) Variable

Score	Using Evidence: Response uses objective reason(s) based on relevant evidence to support choice.	Using Evidence to Make Tradeoffs: Response recognizes multiple perspectives of issue and explains each perspective using objective reasons, supported by evidence, in order to make choice.
4	Response accomplishes Level 3 AND goes beyond in some significant way, such as questioning or justifying the source, validity, and/or quantity of evidence.	Response accomplishes Level 3 AND goes beyond in some significant way, such as suggesting additional evidence beyond the activity that would further influence choices in specific ways, OR questioning the source, validity, and/or quantity of evidence & explaining how it influences choice.
3	Response provides major objective reasons AND supports each with relevant & accurate evidence.	Response discusses <u>at least two</u> perspectives of issue AND provides objective reasons, supported by relevant & accurate evidence, for each perspective.
2	Response provides <u>some</u> objective reasons AND some supporting evidence, BUT at least one reason is missing and/or part of the evidence is incomplete.	Response states at least one perspective of issue AND provides some objective reasons using some relevant evidence BUT reasons are incomplete and/or part of the evidence is missing; OR only one complete & accurate perspective has been provided.
1	Response provides only subjective reasons (opinions) for choice and/or uses inaccurate or irrelevant evidence from the activity.	Response states at least one perspective of issue BUT only provides subjective reasons and/or uses inaccurate or irrelevant evidence.
0	No response; illegible response; response offers no reasons AND no evidence to support choice made.	No response; illegible response; response lacks reasons AND offers no evidence to support decision made.
X	Student had no opportunity to respond.	

FIG. 9.6   Evidence and Trade-offs (ET) Scoring Guide.

9.3.4 Quality Evidence

The technical quality of performance assessments has been explored and debated primarily in the realm of high-stakes testing situations, such as state-wide assessment systems. For classroom-based alternative assessment procedures to gain "currency" in the assessment community, issues of technical quality have to be addressed as well.

Level 3	Uses relevant and accurate evidence to weigh the advantages and disadvantages of multiple options, and makes a choice supported by the evidence.

	Comment
"As an edjucated employee of the Grizzelyville water company, I am well aware of the controversy surrounding the topic of the chlorination of our drinking water. I have read the two articals regarding the pro's and cons of chlorinated water. I have made an informed decision based on the evidence presented the articals entitled "The Peru Story" and "700 Extra People May bet Cancer in the US." It is my recommendation that our towns water be chlorin treated. The risks of infecting our citizens with a bacterial disee

ase such as cholera would be inevitable if we drink nontreated water. Our town should learn from the country of Peru. The artical "The Peru Story" reads thousands of inocent people die of cholera epidemic. In just months 3,500 people were killed and more infected with the diease. On the other hand if we do in fact chlorine treat our drinking water a risk is posed. An increase in bladder and rectal cancer is directly related to drinking chlorinated water. Specifically 700 more people in the US may get cancer. However, the cholera risk far outweighs the cancer risk for 2 very important reasons. Many more people will be effected by cholera where as the chance of one of our citizens getting cancer due to the water would be very minimal. Also cholera is a spreading diease where as cancer is not. If our town was infected with cholera we could pass it on to millions of others. And so, after careful consideration it is my opion that the citizens of Grizzelyville drink chlorine treated water." | Both sides of the chlorinating issue have been presented and supported. The choice to chlorinate was made. |

FIG. 9.7 Exemplar for a Level 3 Response[4] on Activity 12, "The Peru Story."

Despite the plea of Wolf, Bixby, Glen, and Gardner (1991), the development of practical procedures for establishing the technical quality of classroom-based alternative assessments lags behind that for high-stakes assessment programs.

For classroom-based assessment to be useful in a coordinated system, BEAR contends that these assessments must be held to standards of fairness in terms of quality control. Teachers will continue to construct "teacher-made tests" and will rarely take the steps to establish the comparability or validity of these instruments. However, classroom-based assessment procedures can be developed for specific curricula and made available for teachers' use and adaptation. The evidence generated in the assessment process should be judged

---

[4]Element Scored: Using Evidence to Make Trade-offs.

by its suitability for purposes of individual assessment, student performance, instructional outcomes, and/or program effectiveness.

To ensure comparability of results across time and context, procedures are needed to (a) examine the coherence of information gathered using different formats, (b) map student performances onto the progress variables, (c) describe the structural elements of the accountability system—tasks and raters—in terms of the achievement variables, and (d) establish uniform levels of system functioning in terms of quality control indexes such as reliability.

Apart from traditional quality control indexes such as tables of reliability coefficients and standard errors, the BEAR Assessment System incorporates the four building blocks approach described in this book, using the term *progress map* in place of *construct map*. Progress maps have been used for both classroom and large-scale assessments (e.g., see Department of Employment, Education, and Youth Affairs, 1997). As a common means to display results, they add significantly to the coherence of the assessment system.

The IEY Example, (cont'd).   BEAR developed a variety of progress maps of the IEY variables. These are graphical representations of a variable, showing how it unfolds or evolves over the year in terms of student performance on assessment tasks. They are derived from empirical analyses of student data collected from IEY teachers' classrooms. The analyses for these maps were performed using the ConQuest software (Wu, Adams, & Wilson, 1998), which estimates multilevel and multidimensional Rasch-type models.

Once constructed, maps can be used to record and track student progress illustrate the skills a student has mastered and those on which the student is working. A map of an individual student's performance on the DCI variable can be found in Fig. 9.1. By placing students' performance on the continuum defined by the map, teachers can demonstrate students' progress with respect to the goals and expectations of the course. Therefore, the maps are one tool to provide feedback on how students as a whole are progressing in the course. They are also a source of information to use in providing feedback to individual students on their own performances in the course.

Maps, as graphical representations of student performance on assessment tasks, can be used by teachers for their own instructional planning and to show students, administrators, and parents how students are developing on the IEY variables over the year. As a result of teachers managing and using the BEAR Assessment System, maps can be produced that allow them to assess both individual and class progress. This can then be used to inform instructional planning. For instance, if the class as a whole has not performed well on a variable following a series of assessments, the teacher might feel the need to go back and re-address those concepts or issues reflected by the assessments. A progress map that reflects the performance of a group of students is shown in Fig. 9.8. Maps can also be used to portray the performances of groups of students in large-scale assessments, showing the whole distribution, not just the mean location. Thus, they can convey complex relationships such as when groups differ in mean, but overlap in range.

In this system, the traditional indexes of quality control for assessments are also available—for example, reliabilities for the link test for each part of the assessment system have been calculated and

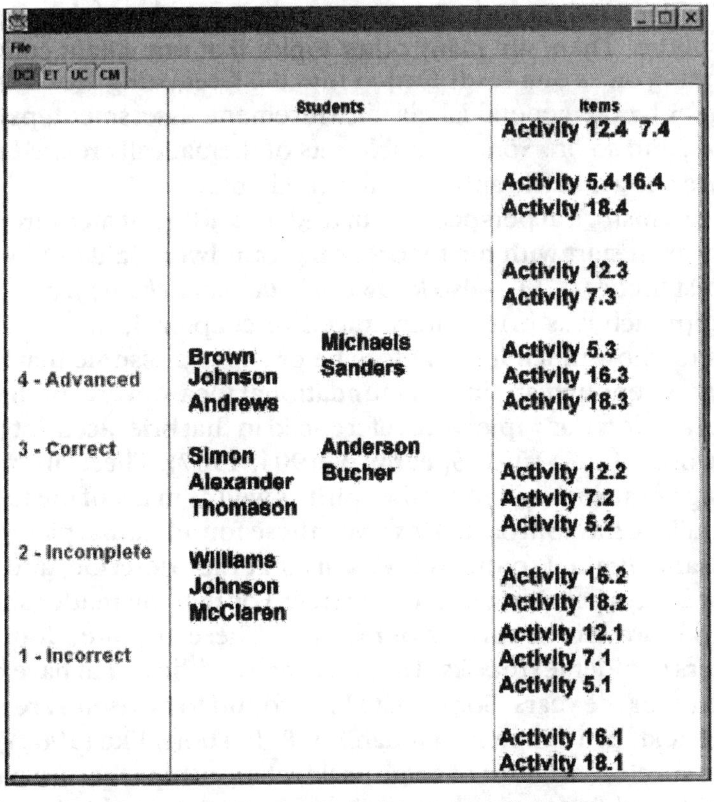

FIG. 9.8 A progress map for a group of students.

range from .65 to .85; values for the composite across all four dimensions range from .79 to .91. Standard errors of measurement are also available, which can be expressed on the IEY maps by indicating 95% confidence intervals directly on the maps.

9.4 RESOURCES: BROADER THEORETICAL PERSPECTIVES

The chapters herein have presented one particular approach to measurement. Concentration on one approach has allowed the reader to follow and apply the logic of that approach through the whole series of steps as represented by the four building blocks. However, this concentration has forced the account to devote little time to (a) historical perspectives on measurement, and (b) alternative ways of formulating measurement. A follow-up to this book would necessarily fill in these gaps and give the reader both a more historically complete understanding and a more comprehensive idea of the range of possibilities. There are many other topics that one might consider expanding on as one reads further into the fascinating area of study that goes by the general labels, measurement, assessment, psychometrics, and so on. Some possible sets of thematically related readings are shown in the appendix to this chapter.

From a historical perspective, an understanding of measurement theory must start with the theoretical groundwork laid out by classical test theory (CTT—also known as *true score theory*). Although this approach was briefly introduced in chapter 5, the measurer needs to know much more before he or she can assume that he or she knows enough about this foundational idea. Several of the pivotal articles on this topic were referenced in that brief account (e.g., Edgeworth, 1888, 1892; Spearman, 1904, 1907). These are worth reading because they convey the spirit as well as many of the technical details of the approach. However, these foundational papers are necessarily limited to the innovations that they describe, and they do not always provide a broad overview. For that the reader should turn to more recent surveys of the area: These are often found as chapters in older textbooks. There are many of these that have been written over the years: Some that I have found to be useful are mentioned next. In a chapter on reliability, R. L. Thorndike (1982) gave a quite succinct account of some basic relationships that are part of CST, although it does require some mathematical sophistication to follow the logic. An account that is somewhat more elementary, but also more comprehensive, is provided by Allen and Yen (1979). Of course the most authoritative account is that provided by Lord and Novick (1968).

The alternative approach, focused on the meaningfulness of measurement (following the argument in chapter 5—Section 5.1) has a more checkered history. The contribution of Guttman (1944, 1950) was mentioned earlier. A more recent take on the topic has been criterion-referenced testing, which has a number of manifestations. The essential idea, which is based on Glaser's (1963) seminal paper, is that the measurements should primarily be interpreted from the perspective of how they can inform the measurer about what the respondent can perform. The collection of papers in the volume by Berk (1980) gives some idea of the range of concerns raised by this approach. As argued by its inclusion in the Berk volume, *generalizability theory* (Cronbach, Gleser, Nanda, & Rajaratnam, 1972) can be seen as a way to inject more meaningfulness into measurement (see Shavelson & Webb, 1991, for a more recent and approachable account). A more recent perspective that is based on the same foundational argument about the importance of meaningfulness is provided by the National Research Council (2001) report, "Knowing What Students Know."

Although item-response modeling has been presented in this book as being based on this same meaningfulness perspective (i.e., through the use of construct maps and the other building blocks), that is not true for many who use it, and this other perspective arguably includes the most prominent uses of it. Instead item-response modeling is often seen as principally a solution to a broad range of technical scaling problems, in which case the argument presented in chapter 6 (Section 6.1) is largely ignored. A foundational account along these lines is provided by Birnbaum (1968), and a comprehensive account is given in Lord (1980). A recent pairing of accounts of these two views has been given by Bock (1997) and Wright (1997). For many in the area of measurement, an introduction to the area would essentially consist of an introduction to these technical topics. Clearly, the approach in this book takes a contrarian point of view of the best way to introduce the area of measurement. This does not imply that these technical issues are unimportant. Indeed one of the prime justifications of using models such as those described in chapters 5 and 6 is the power they have to deal with practical and technical issues. Recent general references are van der Linden and Hambleton (1996) and Fischer and Molenaar (1995).

9.5 EXERCISES AND ACTIVITIES

(following on from the exercises and activities in chaps. 1–8)

1. Reconsider the construct that you investigated—is there a more complex version of it that could not be represented as a construct map (or set of construct maps)?
2. Consider the range of statistical models described previously. Would use of one of them enhance the usefulness of your data analysis and reporting?
3. Attempt to design a BEAR Assessment System plan for your instrument. Write a brief account of this design using the four principles.

APPENDIX:
Readings on Particular Measurement Topics

9A.1 Measurement Ideas and Concepts in a Historical Context

Some historical accounts:

Cronbach, L. J. (1951). Coefficient alpha and the internal structure of tests. *Psychometrika, 16,* 297–334.
Edgeworth, F. Y. (1888). The statistics of examinations. *Journal of the Royal Statistical Society, 51,* 599–635.
Edgeworth, F. Y. (1892). Correlated averages. *Philosophical Magazine* (5th Series), *34,* 190–204.
Guttman, L. (1944). A basis for scaling qualitative data. *American Sociological Review, 9,* 139–150.
Rasch, G. (1960). *Probabilistic models for some intelligence and attainment tests.* [Reprinted by University of Chicago Press, 1980]
Rasch, G. (1977). On specific objectivity: An attempt at formalizing the request for generality and validity of scientific statements. *Danish Yearbook of Philosophy, 14,* 58–94.
Robinson, D. N. (1977). *Significant contributions to the history of psychology, 1750-1920, Series B Psychometrics and educational psychology, Volume 4, Binet, Simon, Stern, & Galton.* Washington, DC: University Press of America (pp. 9–14, 45–69, 261–273, all by Binet).

Spearman, C. (1904). The proof and measurement of association between two things. *American Journal of Psychology, 15,* 72–101.

Spearman, C. (1907). Demonstration of formulae for true measurement of correlation. *American Journal of Psychology, 18,* 161–169.

Thurstone, L. L. (1925). A method of scaling psychological and educational tests. *Journal of Educational Psychology, 16,* 433–451.

Some perspectives on the history:

Traub, R. E. (1997). Classical test theory in historical perspective. *Educational Measurement: Issues and Practice, 16*(4), 8–13.

Brennan, R. L. (1997). A perspective on the history of generalizability theory. *Educational Measurement: Issues and Practice, 16*(4), 14–20.

Bock, R. D. (1997). A brief history of item response theory. *Educational Measurement: Issues and Practice, 16*(4), 21–32.

Wright, B. D. (1997). A history of social science measurement. *Educational Measurement: Issues and Practice, 16*(4), 33–45.

9A.2 Consequential Validity

Linn, R. L. (1997). Evaluating the validity of assessments: The consequences of use. *Educational Measurement: Issues and Practice, 16*(2), 5–8.

Mehrens, W. A. (1997). The consequences of consequential validity. *Educational Measurement: Issues and Practice, 16*(2), 5–8.

Popham, W. J. (1997). Consequential validity: Right concern—wrong concept. *Educational Measurement: Issues and Practice, 16*(2), 9–13.

Shepard, L. A. (1997). The centrality of test use and consequences for test validity. *Educational Measurement: Issues and Practice, 16*(2), 5–8.

Wolf, D., Bixby, J., Glenn, J. III, & Gardner, H. (1991). To use their minds well: Investigating new forms of student assessment. *Review of Research in Education, 17,* 31–74.

9A.3 "Lake Wobegone": An Interesting Debate
About Measurement and Policy

Cannell, J. J. (1988). Nationally normed elementary achievement testing in America's public schools: How all 50 states are above the national average. *Educational Measurement: Issues and Practices, 7,* 5–9.

Phillips, G. W., & Finn, C. E., Jr. (1988). The Lake Wobegone effect: A skeleton in the testing closet? *Educational Measurement: Issues and Practices, 7,* 10–12.

References

Adams, R. J., & Khoo, S. T. (1996). *Quest*. Melbourne, Australia: Australian Council for Educational Research.

Adams, R. J., Wilson, M., & Wang, W. (1997). The multidimensional random coefficients multinomial logit model. *Applied Psychological Measurement, 21*, 1–23.

Agresti, A. (1984). *Analysis of ordinal categorical data*. New York: Wiley.

Airasian, P. W. (1988). Measurement-driven instruction: A closer look. *Educational Measurement: Issues and Practice, 7*, 6–11.

Allen, M. J., & Yen, W. M. (1979). *Introduction to measurement theory*. Monterey, CA: Brooks/Cole.

American Institutes for Research. (2000). *Voluntary National Test, Cognitive Laboratory Report, Year 2*. Palo Alto, CA: Author.

American Educational Research Association, American Psychological Association, National Council for Measurement in Education. (1985). *Standards for educational and psychological testing*. Washington, DC: American Psychological Association.

American Educational Research Association, American Psychological Association, National Council for Measurement in Education. (1999). *Standards for educational and psychological testing*. Washington, DC: American Educational Research Association.

Andersen, S. K., Jensen, F. V., Olesen, K. G., & Jensen, F. (1989). *HUGIN: A shell for building Bayesian belief universes for expert systems*. Aalborg, Denmark: HUGIN Expert Ltd.

Anderson, J. R., Greeno, J. G., Reder, L. M., & Simon, H. A. (2000). Perspectives on learning, thinking , and activity. *Educational Researcher, 29*, 11–13.

Andersson, B., & Kärrqvist, C. (1981). Light and its qualities (in Swedish). *EKNA-Rapport nr 8, Institutionen för Praktisk Pedagogik*. Gothenburg: Gothenburg University.

Andrich, D. (2004). Controversy and the Rasch model: A characteristic of a scientific revolution? *Medical Care, 42*(1 suppl.), 7–16.

Armon, C. (1984). *Ideals of the good life: Evaluative reasoning in children and adults*. Unpublished doctoral dissertation, Harvard University, Cambridge.

Baddeley, A. (1986). *Working memory*. Oxford: Clarendon.

Ball, S. J. (1985). Participant observation with pupils. In R. J. Burgess (Ed.), *Strategies of educational research: Qualitative methods* (pp. 23–56). London: The Falmer Press.

Bassok, M., & Holyoak, K. J. (1989). Interdomain transfer between isomorphic topics in algebra and physics. *Journal of Experimental Psychology: Memory, Learning, and Cognition, 15,* 153–166.

Berk, R. A. (1980). *Criterion-referenced measurement: The state of the art*. Baltimore, MD: Johns Hopkins Press.

Biggs, J. B., & Collis, K. F. (1982). *Evaluating the quality of learning: The SOLO taxonomy*. New York: Academic Press.

Biggs, J. B., & Moore, P. J. (1993). *The process of learning* (3rd ed.). New York: Prentice-Hall.

Binet, A., & Simon, T. (1905). Upon the necessity of establishing a scientific diagnosis of inferior states of intelligence. *L'Annee Psychologique,* 163–191. [Trans. from the French: D. N. Robinson (1977). *Significant Contributions to the History of Psychology, 1750–1920, Series B Psychometrics and Educational Psychology, Volume 4, Binet, Simon, Stern, & Galton.* Washington: UPA.]

Birnbaum, A. (1968). Estimation of an ability. In F. M. Lord & M. R. Novick (Eds.), *Statistical theories of mental test scores* (pp. 453–479). Reading, MA: Addison-Wesley.

Bock, R. D. (1997). A brief history of item response theory. *Educational Measurement: Issues and Practice, 16,* 21–32.

Bock, R. D., & Jones, L. V. (1968). *The measurement and prediction of judgment and choice*. San Francisco: Holden-Day.

Brennan, R. L. (2001). *Generalizability theory*. New York: Springer.

Brown, A. L., Campione, J. C., Webber, L. S., & McGilly, K. (1992). Interactive learning environments: A new look at assessment and instruction. In B. R. Gifford & M. C. O'Connor (Eds.), *Changing assessments* (pp. 121–211). Boston: Kluwer Academic Publishers.

Bryk, A. S., & Raudenbush, S. (1992). *Hierarchical linear models: Applications and data analysis methods*. Newbury Park, CA: Sage.

Cannell, J. J. (1988). Nationally normed elementary achievement testing in America's public schools: How all 50 states are above the national average. *Educational Measurement: Issues and Practices, 7,* 5–9.

Carroll, J. B. (1993). *Human cognitive abilities*. Cambridge: Cambridge University Press.

Case, R. (1992). *The mind's staircase: Exploring the conceptual underpinnings of children's thought and knowledge*. Hillsdale, NJ: Lawrence Erlbaum Associates.

Cheng, P. W., & Holyoak, K. J. (1985). Pragmatic reasoning schemas. *Cognitive-Psychology, 17,* 391–416.

Chi, M. T. H., Glaser, R., & Rees, E. (1982). Expertise in problem-solving. In R. J. Sternberg (Ed.), *Advances in the psychology of human intelligence* (Vol. 1, pp. 7–75). Hillsdale, NJ: Lawrence Erlbaum Associates.

Claesgens, J., Scalise, K., Draney, K., Wilson, M., & Stacey, A. (2002, April). *Perspectives of chemists: A framework to promote conceptual understanding of chemistry*. Paper presented at the annual meeting of the American Educational Research Association, New Orleans.

Cohen, J. (1960). A coefficient of agreement for nominal scales. *Educational and Psychological Measurement, 20*, 37–46.

Cole, N. (1991). The impact of science assessment on classroom practice. In G. Kulm & S. Malcom (Eds.), *Science assessment in the service of reform* (pp. 97–106). Washington, DC: American Association for the Advancement of Science.

Collins, L. M., & Wugalter, S. E. (1992). Latent class models for stage-sequential dynamic latent variables. *Multivariate Behavioral Research, 27*(1), 131–157.

Commons, M. L., Richards, F. A., with Ruf, F. J., Armstrong-Roche, M., & Bretzius, S. (1983). A general model of stage theory. In M. Commons, F. A. Richards, & C. Armon (Eds.), *Beyond formal operations* (pp. 120–140). New York, NY: Praeger.

Commons, M. L., Straughn, J., Meaney, M., Johnstone, J., Weaver, J. H., Lichtenbaum, E., Sonnert, G., & Rodriquez, J. (1995, November). *The general stage scoring system: How to score anything*. Paper presented at the annual meeting of the Association for Moral Education.

Cronbach, L. J. (1951). Coefficient alpha and the internal structure of tests. *Psychometrika, 16*, 297–334.

Cronbach, L. J. (1990). *Essentials of psychological testing* (5th ed.). New York: Harper & Row.

Cronbach, L. J., Gleser, G. C., Nanda, H., & Rajaratnam, N. (1972). *The dependability of behavioral measurement: Theory of generalizability for scores and profiles*. New York: Wiley.

Dahlgren, L. O. (1984). Outcomes of learning. In F. Martin, D. Hounsell, & N. Entwistle (Eds.), *The experience of learning* (pp. 19–35). Edinburgh: Scottish Academic Press.

Dawson, T. L. (1998). *A good education is … : A life-span investigation of developmental and conceptual features of evaluative reasoning about education*. Unpublished doctoral dissertation, University of California, Berkeley.

Dennett, D. C. (1988). *The intentional stance*. Cambridge, MA: Bradford Books, MIT Press.

Department of Employment, Education, and Youth Affairs. (1997). *National School English Literacy Survey*. Canberra, Australia: Author.

DiBello, L. V., Stout, W. F., & Roussos, L. A. (1995). Unified cognitive/psychometric diagnostic assessment likelihood-based classification techniques. In P. D. Nichols, S. F. Chipman, & R. L. Brennan (Eds.), *Cognitively diagnostic assessment* (pp. 361–389). Hillsdale, NJ: Lawrence Erlbaum Associates.

Dobson, A. J. (1983). *An introduction to statistical modeling*. London: Chapman & Hall.

Draney, K. L., Pirolli, P., & Wilson, M. (1995). A measurement model for a complex cognitive skill. In P. Nichols, S. Chipman, & R. Brennan (Eds.), *Cognitively diagnostic assessment* (pp. 103–126). Hillsdale, NJ: Lawrence Erlbaum Associates.

Edgeworth, F. Y. (1888). The statistics of examinations. *Journal of the Royal Statistical Society, 51*, 599–635.

Edgeworth, F. Y. (1892). Correlated averages. *Philosophical Magazine* (5th Series), *34*, 190–204.

Embretson, S. E. (1996). Multicomponent response models. In W. J. van der Linden & R. K. Hambleton (Eds.), *Handbook of modern item response theory* (pp. 305–322). New York: Springer.

Engelhard, G., & Wilson, M. (Eds.). (1996). *Objective measurement III: Theory into practice*. Norwood, NJ: Ablex.

Ercikan, K. (1998). Translation effects in international assessments. *International Journal of Educational Research, 29*, 543–553.

Fischer, G. H. (1973). The linear logistic test model as an instrument in educational research. *Acta Psychologica, 37*, 359–374.

Fischer, G. H., & Molenaar, I. W. (Eds.). (1995). *Rasch models: Foundations, recent developments, and applications*. New York: Springer-Verlag.

Gershenfeld, N. (1998). *The nature of mathematical modeling*. Cambridge: Cambridge University Press.

Glaser, R. (1963). Instructional technology and the measurement of learning outcomes: Some questions. *American Psychologist, 18*, 519–521.

Guttman, L. (1944). A basis for scaling qualitative data. *American Sociological Review, 9*, 139–150.

Guttman, L. A. (1950). The basis for scalogram analysis. In S. A. Stouffer, L. A. Guttman, F. A. Suchman, P. F. Lazarsfeld, S. A. Star, & J. A. Clausen (Eds.), *Studies in social psychology in World War II: Vol. 4. Measurement and prediction*. (pp. 60–90). Princeton: Princeton University Press.

Haertel, E. H. (1990). Continuous and discrete latent structure models for item response data. *Psychometrika, 55*, 477–494.

Haertel, E. H., & Wiley, D. E. (1993). Representations of ability structures: Implications for testing. In N. Frederiksen, R. J. Mislevy, & I. I. Bejar (Eds.), *Test theory for a new generation of tests* (pp. 359–384). Hillsdale, NJ: Lawrence Erlbaum Associates.

Haladyna, T. M. (1996). *Writing test items to evaluate higher order thinking*. New York: Pearson Education.

Haladyna, T. M. (1999). *Developing and validating multiple-choice items* (2nd ed.). Mahwah, NJ: Lawrence Erlbaum Associates.

Hambleton, R. K., Swaminathan, H., & Rogers, H. J. (1991). *Fundamentals of item response theory*. Newbury Park, CA: Sage.

Hatano, G. (1990). The nature of everyday science: A brief introduction. *British Journal of Developmental Psychology, 8*, 245–250.

Holland, B. S., & Copenhaver, M. (1988). Improved Bonferroni-type multiple testing procedures. *Psychological Bulletin, 104*, 145–149.

Holland, P. W., & Wainer, H. (1993). *Differential item functioning*. Hillsdale, NJ: Lawrence Erlbaum Associates.

Hunt, E., & Minstrell, J. (1996). Effective instruction in science and mathematics: Psychological principles and social constraints. *Issues in Education: Contributions from Educational Psychology, 2*, 123–162.

Janssen, R., Tuerlinckx, F., Meulders, M., & De Boeck, P. (2000). An hierarchical IRT model for mastery classification. *Journal of Educational and Behavioral Statistics, 25*, 285–306.

Junker, B. (2001). Some statistical models and computational methods that may be useful for cognitively-relevant assessment. In National Research Council, *Knowing what students know: The science and design of educational assessment* (Committee on the Foundations of Assessment. J. Pellegrino, N. Chudowsky, & R. Glaser, Eds., Division on Behavioral and Social Sciences and Education). Washington, DC: National Academy Press.

Kofsky, E. (1966). A scalogram study of classificatory development. *Child Development, 37*, 191–204.

Kolstad, A., Cohen, J., Baldi, S., Chan, T., deFur, E., & Angeles, J. (1998). *Should NCES adopt a standard? The response probability convention used in reporting data from IRT assessment scales*. Washington, DC: American Institutes for Research.

Kuder, G. F., & Richardson, M. W. (1937). The theory of the estimation of test reliability. *Psychometrika, 2*, 151–160.

Land, R. (1997). Moving up to complex assessment systems. *Evaluation Comment, 7*, 1–21.

Lane, S., Wang, N., & Magone, M. (1996). Gender-related differential item functioning on a middle-school mathematics performance assessment. *Educational Measurement: Issues and Practice, 15*, 21–28.

Levine, R., & Huberman, M. (2000). *High school exit examination: Cognitive laboratory testing of selected items*. Palo Alto, CA: American Institutes for Research.

Linacre, J. M. (1989). *Many-faceted Rasch measurement*. Chicago: MESA Press.

Linn, R. L. (1989). *Educational measurement*. New York: American Council on Education.

Linn, R. L. (1997). Evaluating the validity of assessments: The consequences of use. *Educational Measurement: Issues and Practice, 16*, 5–8.

Longford, N. T., Holland, P. W., & Thayer, D. T. (1993). Stability of the MH D-DIF statistics across populations. In P. W. Holland & H. Wainer (Eds.), *Differential item functioning* (pp. 67–113). Hillsdale, NJ: Lawrence Erlbaum Associates.

Lord, F. M. (1952). A theory of test scores. *Psychometric Monograph, 7*.

Lord, F. M. (1980). *Applications of item response theory to practical testing problems*. Hillsdale, NJ: Lawrence Erlbaum Associates.

Lord, F. M., & Novick, M. R. (1968). *Statistical theories of mental test scores*. Reading, MA: Addison-Wesley.

Marshall, S. P. (1995). *Schemas in problem-solving*. New York: Cambridge University Press.

Martin, J. D., & VanLehn, K. (1995). A Bayesian approach to cognitive assessment. In P. Nichols, S. Chipman, & R. Brennan (Eds.), *Cognitively diagnostic assessment* (pp. 141–166). Hillsdale, NJ: Lawrence Erlbaum Associates.

Marton, F. (1981). Phenomenography—Describing conceptions of the world around us. *Instructional Science, 10*, 177–200.

Marton, F. (1983). Beyond individual differences. *Educational Psychology, 3*, 289–303.

Marton, F. (1986). Phenomenography—A research approach to investigating different understandings of reality. *Journal of Thought, 21*, 29–49.

Marton, F. (1988). Phenomenography—Exploring different conceptions of reality. In D. Fetterman (Ed.), *Qualitative approaches to evaluation in education* (pp. 176–205). New York: Praeger.

Marton, F., Hounsell, D., & Entwistle, N. (Eds.). (1984). *The experience of learning*. Edinburgh: Scottish Academic Press.

Masters, G. N., Adams, R. J., & Wilson, M. (1990). Charting of student progress. In T. Husen & T. N. Postlethwaite (Eds.), *International encyclopedia of education: Research and studies. Supplementary Volume 2* (pp. 628–634). Oxford: Pergamon.

Masters, G. N., & Forster, M. (1996). *Developmental assessment: Assessment resource kit*. Hawthorn, Australia: ACER Press.

Masters, G. N., & Wilson, M. (1997). *Developmental assessment*. Berkeley, CA: BEAR Research Report, University of California.

McHorney, C. A., Ware, J. E., Rachel Lu, J. F., & Sherbourne, C. D. (1994). The MOS 36-item short-form health survey (SF-36): III. Tests of data quality, scaling assumptions, and reliability across diverse patient groups. *Medical Care, 32*, 40–66.

Mehrens, W. A. (1997). The consequences of consequential validity. *Educational Measurement: Issues and Practice, 16*, 5–8.

Messick, S. (1989). Validity. In R. L. Linn (Ed.), *Educational measurement* (3rd ed., pp. 13–103). New York: American Council on Education/Macmillan.

Metz, K. (1995). Reassessment of developmental constraints on children's science instruction. *Review of Educational Research, 65*, 93–127.

Minstrell, J. (2000). Student thinking and related assessment: Creating a facet-based learning environment. In National Research Council, *Grading the nation's report card: Research from the evaluation of NAEP* (pp. 44–73). Committee on the Evaluation of National and State Assessments of Educational Progress. N. S. Raju, J. W. Pellegrino, M. W. Bertenthal, K. J. Mitchell, & L. R. Jones (Eds.), Commission on Behavioral and Social Sciences and Education. Washington, DC: National Academy Press.

Mislevy, R. J. (1996). Test theory reconceived. *Journal of Educational Measurement, 33*, 379–416.

Mislevy, R. J., & Gitomer, D. H. (1996). The role of probability-based inference in an intelligent tutoring system. *User Modeling and User-Adapted Interaction, 5*, 253–282.

Mislevy, R. J., Steinberg, L. S., & Almond, R. G. (2003). On the structure of educational assessments. *Measurement: Interdisciplinary Research and Perspectives, 1*, 1–62.

Mislevy, R. J., & Wilson, M. (1996). Marginal maximum likelihood estimation for a psychometric model of discontinuous development. *Psychometrika, 61*, 41–71.

Mislevy, R. J., Wilson, M., Ercikan, K., & Chudowsky, N. (2003). Psychometric principles in student assessment. In D. Stufflebeam & T. Kellaghan (Eds.), *International handbook of educational evaluation* (pp. 489–532). Dordrecht, the Netherlands: Kluwer Academic Press.

Muthen, B. O., & Khoo, S. T. (1998). Longitudinal studies of achievement growth using latent variable modeling. *Learning and Individual Differences, 10*, 73–101.

National Research Council. (1999). *How people learn: Brain, mind, experience, and school* (Committee on Developments in the Science of Learning. J. D. Bransford, A. L. Brown, & R. R. Cocking, Eds., Commission on Behavioral and Social Sciences and Education). Washington, DC: National Academy Press.

National Research Council. (2001). *Knowing what students know: The science and design of educational assessment* (Committee on the Foundations of Assessment. J. Pellegrino, N. Chudowsky, & R. Glaser, Eds., Division on Behavioral and Social Sciences and Education). Washington, DC: National Academy Press.

Newell, A. (1982). The knowledge level. *Artificial Intelligence, 18*, 87–127.

Newell, A. (1990). *Unified theories of cognition*. Cambridge, MA: Harvard University Press.

Niaz, M., & Lawson, A. (1985). Balancing chemical equations: The role of developmental level and mental capacity. *Journal of Research in Science Teaching, 22*(1), 41–51.

Nitko, A. J. (1983). *Educational tests and measurement: An introduction*. New York: Harcourt Brace Jovanovich.

Ochs, E., Jacoby, S., & Gonzalez, P. (1994). Interpretive journeys: How physicists talk and travel through graphic space. *Configurations, 2*, 151–172.

Organization for Economic Co-operation and Development. (1999). *Measuring student knowledge and skills: A new framework for assessment*. Paris: OECD Publications.

Osterlind, S. J. (1998). *Constructing test items: Multiple-choice, constructed-response, performance, and other formats* (2nd ed.). New York: Kluwer Academic Publishers.

Paek, I. (2002). *Investigations of differential item functioning: Comparisons among approaches, and extension to a multidimensional context*. Unpublished doctoral dissertation, University of California, Berkeley.

Patton, M. Q. (1980). *Qualitative evaluation methods*. Beverly Hills, CA: Sage.

Pearl, J. (1988). *Probabilistic reasoning in intelligent systems: Networks of plausible inference*. San Mateo, CA: Kaufmann.

Phillips, G. W., & Finn, C. E., Jr. (1988). The Lake Wobegone effect: A skeleton in the testing closet? *Educational Measurement: Issues and Practices, 7*, 10–12.

Pirolli, P., & Wilson, M. (1998). A theory of the measurement of knowledge content, access, and learning. *Psychological Review, 105*, 58–82.

Plake, B. S., Impara, J. C., & Spies, R. A. (2003). *The fifteenth mental measurements yearbook*. Lincoln, NE: University of Nebraska Press.

Popham, W. J. (1997). Consequential validity: Right concern—wrong concept. *Educational Measurement: Issues and Practice, 16*, 9–13.

Raczek, A. E., Ware, J. E., Bjorner, J. B., Gandek, B., Haley, S. M., Aaronson, N. K., Apolone, G., Bech, P., Brazier, J. E., Bullinger, M., & Sullivan, M. (1998). Comparison of Rasch and summated rating scales constructed from the SF-36 Physical Functioning items in seven countries: Results from the IQOLA Project. *Journal of Clinical Epidemiology, 51*, 1203–1211.

Ramsden, P., Masters, G., Stephanou, A., Walsh, E., Martin, E., Laurillard, D., & Marton, F. (1993). Phenomenographic research and the measurement of understanding: An investigation of students' conceptions of speed, distance and time. *International Journal of Educational Research, 19*(3), 301–316.

Rasch, G. (1960). *Probabilistic models for some intelligence and attainment tests*. [Reprinted by University of Chicago Press, 1980.]

Rasch, G. (1977). On specific objectivity: An attempt at formalizing the request for generality and validity of scientific statements. *Danish Yearbook of Philosophy, 14*, 58–94.

Reckase, M. D. (1972). *Development and application of a multivariate logistic latent trait model*. Unpublished doctoral dissertation, Syracuse University, Syracuse, NY.

Resnick, L. B., & Resnick, D. P. (1992). Assessing the thinking curriculum: New tools for educational reform. In B. R. Gifford & M. C. O'Connor (Eds.), *Changing assessments* (pp. 37–75). Boston: Kluwer Academic Publishers.

Robinson, D. N. (1977). *Significant contributions to the history of psychology, 1750–1920, Series B Psychometrics and educational psychology, Vol. 4, Binet, Simon, Stern, & Galton*. Washington, DC: University Press of America.

Roid, G., & Haladyna, T. M. (1982), *Technology for test-item writing*. New York: Academic Press.

Rosenbloom, P., & Newell, A. (1987). Learning by chunking: A production system model of practice. In D. Klahr & P. Langley (Eds.), *Production system models of learning and development* (pp. 221–286). Cambridge, MA: MIT Press.

Samejima, F. (1969). Estimation of latent trait ability using a response pattern of graded scores. *Psychometrika Monograph Supplement, 18.*

Science Education for Public Understanding Program. (1995). *Issues, evidence, & you.* Ronkonkoma, NY: Lab-Aids.

Science Education for Public Understanding Program. (1995). *Issues, evidence and you: Teacher's guide.* Berkeley, CA: University of California, Berkeley, Lawrence Hall of Science.

Shavelson, R. J., & Webb, N. M. (1991). *Generalizability theory: A primer.* Newbury Park, CA: Sage.

Shepard, L. A. (1997). The centrality of test use and consequences for test validity. *Educational Measurement: Issues and Practice, 16,* 5–8.

Siegler, R. S. (1998). *Children's thinking* (3rd ed.). Upper Saddle River, NJ: Prentice-Hall.

Skinner, B. F. (1938). *The behavior of organisms: An experimental analysis.* New York: Appleton-Century-Crofts.

Spearman, C. (1904). The proof and measurement of association between two things. *American Journal of Psychology, 15,* 72–101.

Spearman, C. (1907). Demonstration of formulae for true measurement of correlation. *American Journal of Psychology, 18,* 161–169.

Stake, R. (1991). *Advances in program evaluation: Volume 1, Part A. Using assessment policy to reform education.* Greenwich, CT: JAI.

Stevens, S. S. (1946). On the theory of scales of measurement. *Science, 103,* 677–680.

Stinson, C., Milbrath, C., & Reidbord, S. (1993). Segmentation of spontaneous speech in therapy. *Psychotherapy Research, 31,* 21–33.

Tatsuoka, K. K. (1990). Toward an integration of item response theory and cognitive error diagnosis. In N. Frederiksen, R. Glaser, A. Lesgold, & M. G. Shafto (Eds.), *Diagnostic monitoring of skill and knowledge acquisition* (pp. 327–359). Hillsdale, NJ: Lawrence Erlbaum Associates.

Tatsuoka, K. K. (1995). Architecture of knowledge structures and cognitive diagnosis: A statistical pattern recognition and classification approach. In P. D. Nichols, S. F. Chipman, & R. L. Brennan (Eds.), *Cognitively diagnostic assessment* (pp. 327–360). Hillsdale, NJ: Lawrence Erlbaum Associates.

Thomas, J. W., & Rohwer, W. D., Jr. (1993). Proficient autonomous learning: Problems and prospects. In M. Rabinowitz (Ed.), *Cognitive science foundations of instruction* (pp. 1–32). Hillsdale, NJ: Lawrence Erlbaum Associates.

Thorndike, R. L. (1982). *Applied psychometrics.* Boston: Houghton-Mifflin.

Thurstone, L. L. (1925). A method of scaling psychological and educational tests. *Journal of Educational Psychology, 16,* 433–451.

Thurstone, L. L. (1928). Attitudes can be measured. *American Journal of Sociology, 33,* 529–554.

Torrance, H. (1995a). The role of assessment in educational reform. In H. Torrance (Ed.), *Evaluating authentic assessment* (pp. 144–156). Philadelphia: Open University Press.

Torrance, H. (1995b). Teacher involvement in new approaches to assessment. In H. Torrance (Ed.), *Evaluating authentic assessment* (pp. 44–56). Philadelphia: Open University Press.

Traub, R. E. (1997). Classical test theory in historical perspective. *Educational Measurement: Issues and Practice, 16*, 8–13.

Tucker, M. (1991). Why assessment is now issue number one. In G. Kulm & S. Malcom (Eds.), *Science assessment in the service of reform* (pp. 3–15). Washington, DC: American Association for the Advancement of Science.

van der Linden, W. J., & Hambleton, R. K. (1996). *Handbook of modern item response theory*. New York: Springer.

Ware, J. E., & Gandek, B. (1998). Overview of the SF-36 Health Survey and the International Quality of Life Assessment (IQOLA) Project. *Journal of Clinical Epidemiology, 51*, 903–912.

Warkentin, R., Bol, L., & Wilson, M. (1997). Using the partial credit model to verify a theoretical model of academic studying. In M. Wilson, G. Engelhard, & K. Draney (Eds.), *Objective measurement IV: Theory into practice* (pp. 71–96). Norwood, NJ: Ablex.

Webber, C. (1989). The mandarin mentality: Civil service and university admissions testing in Europe and Asia. In B. R. Gifford (Ed.), *Test policy and the politics of opportunity allocation: The workplace and the law* (pp. 33–60). Boston: Kluwer.

Wertsch, J. V. (1998). *Mind as action*. New York: Oxford University Press.

White, B. Y., & Frederiksen, J. R. (1998). Inquiry, modeling, and metacognition: Making science accessible to all students. *Cognition and Instruction, 16*, 3–118.

Wiggins, G. (1989b). Teaching to the (authentic) test. *Educational Leadership, 46*(7), 41–47.

Willet, J., & Sayer, A. (1994). Using covariance structure analysis to detect correlates and predictors of individual change over time. *Psychological Bulletin, 116*, 363–380.

Wilson, M. (1989). Saltus: A psychometric model of discontinuity in cognitive development. *Psychological Bulletin, 105*(2), 276–289.

Wilson, M. (Ed.). (1992a). *Objective measurement: Theory into practice*. Norwood, NJ: Ablex.

Wilson, M. (1992b). The ordered partition model: An extension of the partial credit model. *Applied Psychological Measurement, 16*(3), 309–325.

Wilson, M. (Ed.). (1994a). *Objective measurement II: Theory into practice*. Norwood, NJ: Ablex.

Wilson, M. (1994b). Measurement of developmental levels. In T. Husen & T. N. Postlethwaite (Eds.), *International encyclopedia of education: Research and studies* (2nd ed., pp. 1508–1514). Oxford: Pergamon.

Wilson, M. (2003). Cognitive psychology and assessment practices. In R. Fernandez-Ballesteros (Ed.), *Encyclopedia of psychological assessment* (pp. 244–248) Newberry Park, CA: Sage.

Wilson, M. (2004). On choosing a model for measuring. *Methods of Psychological Research—Online*.

Wilson, M. (in press). Assessment tools: Psychometric and statistical. In J. W. Guthrie (Ed.), *Encyclopedia of education* (2nd ed.). New York: Macmillan Reference USA.

Wilson, M., & Adams, R. J. (1995). Rasch models for item bundles. *Psychometrika, 60*, 181–198.

Wilson, M., & Case, H. (2000). An examination of variation in rater severity over time: A study of rater drift. In M. Wilson & G. Engelhard (Eds.), *Objective measurement: Theory into practice* (Vol. 5, pp. 113–134). Stamford, CT: Ablex.

Wilson, M., & Draney, K. (1997). Partial credit in a developmental context: The case for adopting a mixture model approach. In M. Wilson, G. Engelhard, & K. Draney (Eds.), *Objective measurement IV: Theory into practice*. Norwood, NJ: Ablex.

Wilson, M., & Draney, K. (2000, June). *Developmental assessment strategies in a statewide testing program: Scale interpretation, standard setting, and task-scoring for the Golden State Examinations*. Paper presented at the Council of Chief State School Officers National Conference on Large Scale Assessment, Snowbird, UT.

Wilson, M., & Engelhard, G. (Eds.). (2000). *Objective measurement V: Theory into practice*. Stamford, CT: Ablex.

Wilson, M., Engelhard, G., & Draney, K. (Eds.). (1997). *Objective measurement IV: Theory into practice*. Norwood, NJ: Ablex.

Wilson M., & Hoskens, M. (2001). The rater bundle model. *Journal of Educational and Behavioral Statistics, 26*, 283–306.

Wilson, M., Kennedy, C., & Draney, K. (2004). *GradeMap 3.1* (computer program). Berkeley, CA: BEAR Center, University of California.

Wilson, M., Roberts, L., Draney, K., Samson, S., & Sloane, K. (2000). *SEPUP Assessment Resources Handbook*. Berkeley, CA: BEAR Center Research Reports, University of California.

Wilson, M., & Sloane, K. (2000). From principles to practice: An embedded assessment system. *Applied Measurement in Education, 13*, 181–208.

Wolf, D., Bixby, J., Glenn, J., III, & Gardner, H. (1991). To use their minds well: Investigating new forms of student assessment. *Review of Research in Education, 17*, 31–74.

Wright, B. D. (1968). Sample-free test calibration and person measurement. *Proceedings of the 1967 Invitational Conference on Testing* (pp. 85–101). Princeton, NJ: Educational Testing Service.

Wright, B. D. (1977). Solving measurement problems with the Rasch model. *Journal of Educational Measurement, 14*, 97–116.

Wright, B. D. (1997). A history of social science measurement. *Educational Measurement: Issues and Practice, 16*, 33–45.

Wright, B. D., & Masters, G. N. (1981). *Rating scale analysis*. Chicago: MESA Press.

Wright, B. D., & Stone, M. (1979). *Best test design*. Chicago: MESA Press.

Wu, M. L. (1997). *The development and application of a fit test for use with Marginal Maximum Likelihood estimation and generalized item response models*. Unpublished master's thesis, University of Melbourne.

Wu, M. L., Adams, R. J., & Wilson, M. (1998). ACER*ConQuest* [computer program]. Hawthorn, Australia: ACER.

Yamamoto, K., & Gitomer, D. H. (1993). Application of a HYBRID model to a test of cognitive skill representation. In N. Frederiksen & R. J. Mislevy (Eds.), *Test theory for a new generation of tests* (pp. 275–295). Hillsdale, NJ: Lawrence Erlbaum Associates.

Yen, W. M. (1985). Increasing item complexity: A possible cause of scale shrinkage for unidimensional Item Response Theory. *Psychometrika, 50*, 399–410.

Zessoules, R., & Gardner, H. (1991). Authentic assessment: Beyond the buzzword and into the classroom. In V. Perrone (Ed.), *Expanding student assessment* (pp. 47–71). Alexandria, VA: Association for Supervision and Curriculum Development.

Author Index

Subject Index